Every
CHRISTIAN'S
Book on
JUDAISM

Every
CHRISTIAN'S
Book on
JUDAISM

Exploring Jewish Faith and Law for a
Richer Understanding of Christianity

IRA L. SHAFIROFF

Noga Press™
Torrance, California

For Cindy

Noga Press™
P.O. Box 11129
Torrance, California 90510-1129

Manufactured in the United States of America
10 9 8 7 6 5 4 3 2 1

Cover design by Lightbourne Images, Copyright © 1997
Interior design by The Roberts Group

Publisher's Cataloging-in-Publication
(Provided by Quality Books, Inc.)

Shafiroff, Ira L.
     Every Christian's book on Judaism : exploring Jewish faith and
law for a richer understanding of Christianity / Ira L. Shafiroff.
-- 1st ed.
     p. cm.
     Includes bibliographical references and index.
     Preassigned LCCN: 97-75514
     ISBN: 0-9661229-3-3

     1. Judaism.   2. Judaism--Relations--Christianity.   I. Title.

BM535.S43 1998   296'.396
                                QBI97-41307

Contents

*How very good and pleasant it is
when kindred live together in unity!*

Psalm 133:1

Preface

Although this book has taken me some two years to write, it has been in the making for almost three decades, beginning with my inquiry into Christianity when I was seventeen years of age. Ordinarily there would be nothing unusual about a young man exploring Christianity—except for the fact that I am Jewish, and Jewish boys growing up in Brooklyn in 1969 did not read about Christianity. Period.

Given that the Holocaust had ended only twenty-four years earlier, it is understandable that my interest in Christianity would be cause for concern in my family. Would another Jew be lost? Still, the familial fears were not altogether shared by my father. Maybe he knew that my journey was nothing to dread. He was right. I was and remain a Jew.

And herein lies a great moral. If a Jew can learn about Christianity and remain a faithful Jew, a Christian can learn about Judaism and remain a faithful Christian. This is my hope and prayer.

Passages quoted from Scripture are taken from the *New Revised Standard Version*. My preference for this translation was based upon familiarity, readability, and availability. Traditional Jewish sources, not well known to most Christians, are fully referenced in the accompanying notes and are explained in the glossary. Passages quoted from these Hebrew sources are my own renderings.

The reader should note that the *New Revised Standard Version* does not capitalize pronouns that refer to God ("he," "him," and "his"). For the sake of consistency, I have followed this convention in the text of this book, as well as in the quotations.

It is appropriate that I thank those who have given me assistance in writing this book.

I am indebted to Dr. Eugene Fisher, Secretariat for Relations with the Jews, National Conference of Catholic Bishops, for reading the manuscript and making numerous suggestions, many of which I adopted. While I am honored to acknowledge Dr. Fisher's assistance, any errors in this book (I pray there are none) are my own, and any criticism must be directed to me alone.

I must also thank my wife Cindy for her unwavering support in this undertaking. As Scripture states: "The heart of her husband trusts in her, and he will have no lack of gain. She does him good, and not harm, all the days of her life" (Prov. 31:11-12).

Finally, I am grateful to God for granting me good health and allowing me to complete this book.

Introduction

lthough anyone seeking to learn about Judaism will learn much from this book, I have tailored this work especially for Christians. But what's this? Christians learning about Judaism? Should not Christians confine themselves to learning about Christianity? Why do Christians need to learn about Judaism? There are four important reasons.

1. *Christians need to learn about Judaism to understand their own heritage.* Christianity arose from Judaism. Indeed, most of the major personalities in the New Testament were Jews. This includes not only Jesus, his family, and his disciples, but the masses who listened to him, as well as those who opposed him. In fact, with the possible exception of Luke, each and every one of the authors of the New Testament was Jewish. Christianity is, therefore, inextricably bound up with and related to Judaism. And while most Christians know that there is this relationship to Judaism, questions still abound. For example:

- What exactly is Judaism?
- What are the traditional Jewish beliefs?
- What are the traditional Jewish practices?

Understandably, few Christians can answer these essential questions. Indeed, while there are many fine books available for Jews who want to practice Judaism and for Christians who want to lead a life based on the

Gospel teachings of Jesus, there is a conspicuous absence of material available to Christians who want to learn about Judaism and their Jewish heritage.[1] This book, written particularly for Christians, offers readers the opportunity to obtain answers to these and many other critically important questions.

2. *Christians need to learn about Judaism to better understand the New Testament.* Because the New Testament is a collection of Jewish writings concerning the Jewish people living in or around the Land of Israel, it naturally contains Jewish concepts, terms, and philosophies. But the vast majority of Christians who read the Gospels do not fully grasp the significance of these Jewish ideas. Chief among these concepts is "the law," as when Jesus said in the Sermon on the Mount, "Do not think that I have come to abolish the law . . . I have not come to abolish but to fulfill."[2] Many Christians believe that the law is the Ten Commandments. While the law certainly includes the Ten Commandments, there is more to the law—much more. We, therefore, need to ask:

- ◆ What is the law?
- ◆ Who is bound by the law?
- ◆ Who wrote the law?
- ◆ What was Jesus' view of the law?
- ◆ What was Paul's view of the law?

Without some knowledge of Judaism, Christians who read the foregoing passage from the Sermon on the Mount (and other passages in the New Testament) will quite understandably not fully discern the significance of Jesus' teaching. Similarly, the Gospels portray the Pharisees and Sadducees as the opponents of Jesus.[3] But who were the Pharisees and Sadducees? What were their beliefs and practices? What happened to them in history? What legacy did they leave? Christians who do not have some knowledge of Judaism will not be able to answer these and other questions and, consequently, will not fully appreciate the Gospel. This book will provide answers to these and many other questions, enabling the Christian reader to appreciate and understand the New Testament as never before.

3. *Christians need to learn about Judaism to obtain a deeper understanding of Jesus.* Every Christian wants to be able to envision Jesus the man: who he was and what he did, especially in everyday life. Perhaps one of the best-kept secrets (among Jews and Christians alike) is that Jesus of Nazareth was a Jew and, as acknowledged by the Gospel writers,[4] a pious one at that. Yet to look at the many paintings that were made of him through the ages, one would think that with his sharp features, fair skin, blue eyes, and blonde goatee, Jesus was a Swede. Too few people picture Jesus as he really was: a Galilean Jew, with rich black hair, dark skin, brown eyes, and a full untrimmed beard.[5] And because Jesus was a Jew, he lived a life unique to the descendants of Abraham, Isaac, and Jacob: When he was eight days old, he was circumcised.[6] As he grew older, he studied Judaism's sacred texts with the rabbis.[7] And like any Jew, he attended synagogue prayer services and celebrated all of the Jewish holidays.[8] Knowing these facts, we are again faced with significant questions:

- ◆ Why is circumcision so important in Judaism?
- ◆ What are Judaism's sacred texts?
- ◆ Why do Jews devote much time to the study of these texts?
- ◆ What is a rabbi?
- ◆ What is a synagogue?
- ◆ What is the significance of the major Jewish holidays?

In short, a Christian who cannot answer these questions cannot fully know the Jewish Jesus. This book will be invaluable to those who wish to understand Jesus the person.

4. *Christians need to learn about Judaism to participate in dialogue with their Jewish brothers and sisters.* Until recent times, Jewish-Christian relations were unquestionably quite poor. Today, however, animosity has given way to mutual respect and, in many cases, outright friendship. As a result, many denominations within Christianity now expressly advocate dialogue with the Jewish people. But dialogue without foundation is impossible. For example, before engaging in dialogue, a Christian would want to know:

- Who is considered a Jew?
- Do all Jews share the same beliefs?
- Do Jews believe in the coming of the Messiah?
- If they do, why do they not believe that Jesus was the Messiah?

This book will provide the necessary foundation for Christians to engage in dialogue with their Jewish brothers and sisters and will pave the way for greater respect and understanding, all of which is simply not possible without knowledge.

By reading and studying *Every Christian's Book on Judaism: Exploring Jewish Faith and Law for a Richer Understanding of Christianity*, Christians will not only gain great insight and understanding regarding Judaism and the Jewish people, but also learn of the large area of common ground that they share with their Jewish cousins. But while there is much common ground between Judaism and Christianity, there are also significant differences, and I have not hesitated to point out and explain these differences. In so doing, however, I have made no attempt to "prove" one religion or the other right or wrong in any given instance. In this age of mutual understanding and respect, dialogue will help to bring the people of our two great religions closer. But history establishes that when disputation replaces dialogue, no one is well served. Thus, although I respectfully point out the differences between Judaism and Christianity, and the reasons for those differences, I go no further.

I have written this book solely to help Christians better understand Christianity and to strengthen Jewish-Christian relations. Although I think that the material will speak for itself, I wish to make the following point unequivocally clear so that there is no misunderstanding: It is not my intention to convert my Christian readers to Judaism. As a matter of fact, as is more fully explained later,[9] Judaism has traditionally not sought out converts.[10] Indeed, a fundamental Jewish teaching is, "The righteous of all nations have a share in the World to Come."[11] Thus, no Christian need be concerned that his or her faith will in any way be compromised by reading and learning from this book.

⟨⟩

One final point is in order: As stated in the preface, I am a Jew. I do not share with my Christian brothers and sisters their belief that Jesus is the Messiah and Son of God. Some may therefore think it unusual that a Jew would want to teach non-Jews. But I do not think that it is at all unusual. As Scripture teaches, "Have we not all one father? Has not one God created us?"[12]

Shalom!

⟨⟩

Overview

In this volume, the reader is presented with a summary and analysis of some of Judaism's most basic and fundamental beliefs and concepts. Chapter 1 looks at Judaism as a religion and explores its origins and major tenets. Particular attention is given to the Thirteen Principles of Faith. Chapter 2 establishes that Judaism is not just a religion, but also a legal system (in fact, the world's oldest continuously functioning legal system).

The next five chapters examine the sources of the laws which comprise this unique religious-legal system. Chapter 3 deals with an in-depth analysis of the Ten Commandments. Chapter 4 provides a summary and analysis of some of the many other commandments (in addition to the Ten Commandments) which are found throughout the Pentateuch, the first five books of the Bible. Chapter 5 addresses the authorship of the Pentateuch and the commandments. Chapter 6 examines still additional sources of Jewish law, sources that most Christians are not typically familiar with: the *Mishnah* and the *Gemara*. Chapter 7 discusses the Seven Laws of Noah, the laws which Judaism teaches bind the Gentile nations.

Chapter 8 examines Judaism's view of the importance of the other two sections of the Hebrew Bible: the Prophets and the Writings. Chapter 9 explores Jesus' view of the law and the prophets. Chapter 10 addresses a matter which has been pondered by many and which was addressed by Jesus: the greatest of the commandments. Chapter 11 explores

Judaism's view on the relative importance of faith and deeds. Chapter 12 addresses who is deemed to be a Jew under Jewish law.

We conclude with chapter 13, which establishes that Judaism, in addition to being a religion and a legal system, is also a way of life.

CHAPTER 1

Judaism as a Religion

I n this initial chapter, we learn the origins of Judaism and its traditional beliefs. We also learn that not all Jews subscribe to these fundamental teachings.

The Birth of Judaism

To fully appreciate the origins of Judaism, we need to examine humankind's religious practices through the ages, before Judaism existed. We start with Adam and Eve.

Adam and Eve Were Monotheists

The Bible tells us that after God created the first humans, Adam and Eve, he did not take a passive role in their existence. To the contrary, the Creator was actively involved in their lives, warning them to not eat from the tree of knowledge,[1] punishing them when they violated his instruction,[2] and clothing them[3] before exiling them from the Garden of Eden.[4] Because of his direct and overt involvement in their lives, Adam and Eve quite understandably knew and worshipped the One and only true God.[5]

Idolatry Begins

But with the passing of Adam and Eve and their children, people eventually ceased worshipping God and turned instead to worshipping the things that God had created: the sun, the moon, and the stars.[6] Later still, people came to believe that carvings of stone and wood had godlike powers, which controlled the events in the universe.[7] Humankind thus fell into the deep abyss of idolatry and all the evils that went along with it: human sacrifice,[8] ritual rape,[9] temple prostitution,[10] as well as other immoralities, such as bestiality.[11]

Why did people engage in such hideous practices? Because the high priests and leaders of the land taught the populace that the murder of children and the rape of virgins were essential rites in order for the gods to be appeased.[12] Consequently, many young children had their throats slashed and many young girls suffered sexual torture, all so that the people could obtain the blessings of the gods.[13] And there were many gods, each of which had to be assuaged in some way or another.[14] There was a god to ensure that the rain would fall at the proper time of year.[15] There was another god to make certain that the land would be safe from invading armies.[16] Then there was a god to protect individual households from sickness.[17] There was also a god to assure fertility.[18] For each concern and every fear, there was a god. Many innocent people were subjected to unspeakable cruelties in the names of the gods. In fact, the world had become such a horrible place that "the LORD saw that the wickedness of humankind was great in the earth, and that every inclination of the thoughts of their hearts was only evil continuously. And the LORD was sorry that he had made humankind on the earth, and it grieved him to his heart."[19]

"Noah Found Favor in the Sight of the LORD"

In this world of evil, however, there lived a good man, Noah, who "found favor in the sight of the LORD."[20] Thus, when God decided to destroy the world, he spared Noah, telling him to make an ark to save himself, his family, and some of the animal kingdom.[21] Noah obeyed God,[22] and after the flood waters receded, "Noah built an altar to the LORD" and worshipped him.[23] As a consequence of their close relationship with God,

Noah and his family, the sole inhabitants of the earth, worshipped only God, as had Adam and Eve. But as time passed and the earth became repopulated, God was once again forgotten. Idolatry and evil returned to the earth.[24]

Abraham Reasons There Is Only One God

But there was one young man during that time who did not believe that these gods were anything more than the inanimate objects they appeared to be. This man's name was Abram (who would one day be renamed *Abraham*, as we shall see). By using only his own reasoning abilities, Abram came to understand that it was God, the One and only God, who created the universe and who alone continued to sustain it.[25] Abram also reasoned that this God did not want children sacrificed to him. Rather, God wanted people to act humanely toward each other. Armed only with his conviction in the existence of the merciful God, Abram went into his father's home and destroyed each and every idol that he could lay his hands on.[26]

Soon thereafter, however, King Nimrod of Mesopotamia, the ruler of the land, found out what Abram had done and had him thrown into a burning furnace.[27] But nothing happened to Abram. He walked out of the fire totally unharmed.[28] In the years that followed, Abram, along with his wife, Sarai (who would become *Sarah*), began teaching others about the existence of the One and only God, who alone is to be worshipped and who demands kindness and justice from people.[29] Thus, Abram and Sarai brought light to a dark time. The age of ethical monotheism had appeared.

Abraham Was Greater Than Adam and Noah

But had not Adam and Noah also practiced ethical monotheism? To be sure, they had. But these individuals, as great as they were, paled in comparison to Abram. Adam and Noah had accepted the sovereignty of God because God had spoken to them and interacted with them overtly.[30] But Abram came to know and understand God and practice and teach others ethical monotheism solely as a result of his own reasoning abilities[31]— and not because God had first spoken to him. Indeed, it was only after many years following Abram's destruction of his father's idols and the subsequent miracle in King Nimrod's furnace that God finally revealed himself overtly to Abram, who was by this time getting on in age:

> Now the LORD said to Abram, "Go from your country and your kindred and your father's house to the land that I will show you. I will make of you a great nation, and I will bless you, and make your name great, so that you will be a blessing. I will bless those who bless you, and the one who curses you I will curse; and in you all the families of the earth shall be blessed."
>
> So Abram went, as the LORD had told him; and Lot went with him. Abram was seventy-five years old when he departed from Haran. Abram took his wife Sarai and his brother's son Lot, and all the possessions they had gathered, and the persons whom they had acquired in Haran:[32] and they set forth to go to the land of Canaan.[33]

Abraham Was the First Jew

When Abram was ninety-nine years old, God changed his name to *Abraham*, meaning "father of many nations."[34] God also changed Sarai's name to *Sarah*,[35] meaning "princess of many nations." It was at that time that God also entered into a sacred and everlasting covenant with Abraham and his progeny through the rite of circumcision[36] (and which has been a notable part of the Jewish people's faith ever since). As part of this covenant, God promised Sarah, who was old and well past child-bearing years, that she would give birth to a son, who was to be called Isaac.[37] Through Isaac and his issue, God would ensure that his everlasting covenant with Abraham would endure.[38] Thus was Judaism born.

Judaism's Thirteen Principles of Faith

But what exactly is Judaism and what are its primary beliefs? To answer these questions we turn to one of Judaism's great teachers, Rabbi Moses ben Maimon, also known as Maimonides or Rambam (an acronym for Rabbi Moses ben Maimon). Rambam was born in Spain in the year 1135.

In 1159 or 1160, his family moved to North Africa to escape religious persecution at the hands of the Almohads, a zealous Muslim movement.[39] When he grew up, Rambam became a highly regarded physician. In fact, he was the personal physician of Saladin, the great Muslim leader. But Rambam was not just a man of science. He was also a rabbi, and a great one at that. Consequently, in addition to writing a large number of medical texts, Rambam also wrote many dissertations on Judaism.[40] One of these works included a fourteen-volume treatise, the *Mishneh Torah* ("Relearning the Law"). The *Mishneh Torah* is a classic text on Jewish law and remains necessary reading for all who study Judaism in depth. One of the Rambam's other great works was his *Thirteen Principles of Faith*.

The Essence of Orthodox Belief

The Thirteen Principles of Faith summarize the essence of traditional or Orthodox Jewish belief. Before proceeding, however, we need to point out that there are presently four major movements or branches within Judaism: Orthodox, Conservative, Reform, and Reconstructionist. Orthodox Judaism is the most "conservative" and the oldest branch of Judaism, tracing its heritage back to well before the time of Jesus.[41] Orthodox Judaism is often referred to as traditional Judaism. Jews within the Orthodox movement are commonly referred to as either Orthodox Jews or observant Jews.

Conservative, Reform, and Reconstructionist Movements Compared

In comparison to the Orthodox movement, the other branches of Judaism represent more recent developments and are more liberal in their interpretation of Scripture and law. The most liberal are the Reform and Reconstructionist movements, which arose in the 1850s and 1930s, respectively. In between Orthodoxy, which may be envisioned as the right, and Reform/Reconstructionism, which may be envisioned as the left, is the Conservative movement, which arose shortly after the Reform movement. These branches are not in any way similar to the various denominations within Christianity. Though there are significant differences among the branches of Judaism, it is more accurate to consider these branches as schools or movements rather than as denominations because a Jew who identifies with the Reform movement can nevertheless fully participate in an Orthodox prayer service, and vice versa, whereas a Baptist cannot receive communion in the Roman Catholic Church. In the material which follows, I indicate where the beliefs of the Conservative, Reform, and Reconstructionist movements differ from the beliefs of the Orthodox movement, as epitomized in the Thirteen Principles of Faith.

I stress Orthodoxy in this book for two reasons. First, Orthodox Judaism is traditional Judaism whereas the other movements are recent innovations. Second, Jesus himself was familiar with much of Orthodoxy's teachings. Indeed, although Rambam reduced the Thirteen Principles to writing in the twelfth century, these principles were well known to all Jews long before Jesus' time.

Introduction

The Thirteen Principles of Faith are typically sung in Orthodox prayer services as a popular hymn during the morning prayer service,[42] and recited as supplemental reading after the weekday morning prayer service. The Thirteen Principles of Faith also must be accepted by one who is undergoing conversion to Judaism under the auspices of an Orthodox rabbi.[43] When recited, each principle is introduced by the words, "I firmly believe with complete faith that . . ."; the principle then follows. We now examine each of the Thirteen Principles.

Principle 1: God Exists and Is the Creator

The first principle is, *"I firmly believe with complete faith that God exists and that he alone created, creates and will create all things."*

It is a given that God exists.[44] No proof of this fact is necessary. Indeed, the Bible begins with the assertion "In the beginning . . . God created the heavens and the earth,"[45] not with a proof of God's existence. Moreover, not only does God exist, but he alone has created everything that has ever existed or will exist.[46] In this regard, the Talmud,[47] a massive compendium of Jewish law and analysis,[48] addresses the reason that God created only Adam on the sixth day of creation, and not both Adam and Eve: so that no one could later say that although God created Adam, perhaps another god created Eve.[49]

But it is not enough to say that God exists and that he alone created the universe.[50] We must also recognize that God is not a passive God.[51] It is only through God's continued involvement in the universe that it endures.[52] Many people search for miracles to add meaning to an otherwise mundane life. To the Jew (be that person Orthodox, Conservative, Reform, or Reconstructionist)—or Christian—who recognizes God's sovereignty, however, the sun rising like a bright fireball on a hot summer morning and the harshness of a long winter receding with the spring thaw are themselves manifestations of God's continuing majesty. Should God will it, the universe would shrivel to nothingness,[53] as it existed before the so-called big-bang. And if that ever happens, if all the solar systems in the universe come to an end, God will nevertheless continue to exist.[54] He will endure even if all else ceases.[55] Thus, God existed before anything was created, and he will exist after everything else ends.[56] Put another way, time is utterly meaningless as applied to the Creator.[57]

All branches of Judaism accept this first principle of faith (that God exists and is the Creator), although the Reformers and Reconstructionists believe that God, after having created the universe and set it in motion, has ceased to be an active God. The belief of the Conservatives, and certainly of the Orthodox, is that God remains active in all worldly events.[58] As the Psalmist wrote, "Blessed be the Lord, who daily bears us up; God is our salvation."[59]

Principle 2: God Is Unique and Is One

The second principle is, *"I firmly believe with complete faith that God is unique and is One."*

Judaism was the first monotheistic religion. While other civilizations worshipped many gods, Jews worshipped the One God. This principle is encapsulated by, "Hear O Israel: the LORD is our God, the LORD is One."[60] Traditional Christianity too recognizes the One God, in Three Persons: Father, Son, and Holy Spirit.[61] How God is perceived is one of the major differences between Judaism and Christianity. While Jews do not agree on all matters, there is one belief which unites them all, be they Orthodox or Reform, Conservative or Reconstructionist: the Holy Trinity is incompatible with the Jewish view of the One God. For Christians, of course, the Holy Trinity does not in any way violate the Unity of God's Oneness, and is no less Divine Revelation than the giving of the law on Mount Sinai was for the Jewish people.

A new phenomenon, which has unfolded in this century, is that of Jews who convert to Christianity by choice and, consequently, subscribe to the Trinitarian concept of God.[62] Although these individuals are still Jews[63]—a Jew cannot relinquish his or her Jewish heritage notwithstanding the adoption of any other religion[64]—they are not practicing Judaism. Rather, they are practicing Christianity. A Jew can no more practice Judaism while believing in Jesus than a Christian can practice Christianity without believing in him.

Principle 3: God Is Not Physical

The third principle is, *"I firmly believe with complete faith that God is not physical and has no physical characteristics whatsoever."*

Judaism believes that God is formless and incorporeal.[65] He never has had and never will have any bodily form.[66] The basis for this belief is the Bible's account of the Revelation on Mount Sinai, when God spoke the words of the Ten Commandments (the Decalogue) to the Israelites, who heard but did not see the Almighty:

> *Then the* LORD *spoke to you out of the fire. You heard the sound of words but saw no form; there was only a voice. He declared to you his covenant, which he charged you to observe, that is, the ten commandments; and he wrote them on two stone tablets. And the* LORD *charged me at that time to teach you statutes and ordinances for you to observe in the land that you are about to occupy. Since you saw no form when the* LORD *spoke to you at Horeb out of the fire, take care and watch yourselves closely, so that you do not act corruptly by making an idol for yourselves, in the form of any figure. . . .*[67]

The ancient rabbis taught that to believe that God has a bodily form would pave the way for idolatry ("so that you do not act corruptly by making an idol for yourselves").[68]

But do not the Hebrew Scriptures themselves bestow human attributes on God? For example, the Bible refers to the "eyes of the LORD"[69] and the "hand of the LORD."[70] While the Bible regularly resorts to the use of anthropomorphisms, this is done only because we need assistance in conceiving of the One who is formless, incorporeal, and inconceivable.[71]

From the Jewish perspective, this fundamental tenet of Judaism, that God is formless and incorporeal, is inconsistent with the basic belief of Christianity, that God took on a human nature: "In the beginning was the Word"[72] and "the Word became flesh."[73] But from the Christian standpoint, the mystery of the Incarnation is itself Divine Revelation and does not in any way diminish God's absolute limitlessness.

Turning from theology to history, when Judaism and Christianity were competing with each other during the first and second centuries, vast numbers of pagans went over to Christianity and not to Judaism. Why did they choose Christianity over Judaism? One reason is that Christianity enabled its followers to more easily envision the personal God of Creation. One can easily imagine Jesus walking on water,[74] touching a sick person,[75] or being nailed to a cross.[76] Judaism, with its definition of the formless and unseen God, could not offer the benefits of a visualized Creator.

All branches of Judaism are united and firm in their support of this principle of faith.

Principle 4: God Is the First and the Last

The fourth principle is, *"I firmly believe with complete faith that God is the first and the last."*

As stated earlier, time is totally meaningless as applied to God.[77] He is eternal and will continue to exist after everything else ceases.[78] The Bible makes this point exceedingly clear when it declares of God, "I am the first, and I am the last."[79] All of Judaism's movements accept this principle of faith.

9

Principle 5: It Is Proper to Pray to God Only

The fifth principle is, *"I firmly believe with complete faith that it is proper to pray to God and only God and that no one else is to be the recipient of our prayers."*

Jews are prohibited from directing prayers to anyone but God.[80] Prayer devoted to idols,[81] ancestors,[82] or even angels[83] is absolutely and totally forbidden.[84] Moreover, no intermediary is needed in praying to God since Jews are to pray to God directly.[85] The first of the Ten Commandments states, "I am the LORD *your* God,"[86] meaning that God is personal to all who believe in him.[87] Consequently, when we pray to God, we can have a relationship with him which is both direct and intimate.[88]

All of Judaism's movements accept this principle of faith.

Principle 6: The Words of the Prophets Are True

The sixth principle is, *"I firmly believe with complete faith that the words of the prophets are true."*

Throughout history, God has communicated with humankind through the prophets,[89] and all of the prophecy stated in Scripture is absolutely true.[90] But who are the prophets in the Hebrew Scriptures? There are many. Abraham was a prophet.[91] Moses was too,[92] as were his siblings, Aaron[93] and Miriam.[94] Other prophets included Elijah,[95] Elisha,[96] Ezra, Nehemiah, Isaiah, Jeremiah, Ezekiel, Daniel, Hosea, Joel, Amos, Obadiah, Jonah, Micah, Nahum, Habakkuk, Zephaniah, Haggai, Zechariah, and Malachi.[97] All of their teachings and writings are absolutely correct.[98] While modern Biblical scholarship (which would include the Reform and Reconstructionist movements and, to a lesser extent, the Conservative movement) will often take issue with this last point, to the Orthodox Jew, faith in the authenticity of the words of the prophets is fundamental to being Jewish.[99] It should be noted, however, that irrespective of their views on authenticity, all movements within Judaism hold the prophets in high regard for their ethical teachings.

Of course, Christians too believe in the words of the prophets.[100] Jews and Christians interpret the words of the prophets differently, however, with Christians finding Christological meaning in the words.[101]

Principle 7: Moses Was the Greatest of the Prophets

The seventh principle is, *"I firmly believe with complete faith that the prophecy of Moses was true and that Moses was the greatest of the prophets, of those who preceded him and those who followed him."*

Moses was the greatest prophet[102] because he had a special relationship with God: He (Moses) was able to communicate with God whenever *he* (Moses) chose to.[103] This was quite unusual because God spoke to all of the other prophets only when *he* (God) chose to.[104] To emphasize this special relationship that Moses had with God, the Bible tells us that God spoke to Moses "face to face, as one speaks to a friend."[105] But there was one additional reason why Moses was the greatest of all the prophets: Moses was the only one to whom God gave his *Torah*;[106] none received a Torah before Moses and none will receive a Torah in the future.

The Conservative and Reform movements, like their Orthodox brothers and sisters, acknowledge Moses as Judaism's greatest prophet and teacher. The Reconstructionist movement, which emphasizes Judaism as a civilization, does not have the same regard for Moses as a prophet. Nevertheless, even those in the Reconstructionist movement would acknowledge Moses as a great man in history.

Principle 8: God Himself Gave Moses the Torah

The eighth principle is, *"I firmly believe with complete faith that God himself revealed the Torah to Moses and the Torah that was revealed to Moses is identical to the one we now possess."*

The first five books of the Bible (Genesis, Exodus, Leviticus, Numbers, and Deuteronomy) are often called the Pentateuch, which is Greek for "five books." In Hebrew, these five books are called the *Chumash* (from the Hebrew root meaning "five") or the *Torah*. Torah is often interpreted to mean "law," but it actually means "instruction." The Torah, according to traditional belief, was authored by God himself, who dictated it to Moses.[107] As we shall learn in a subsequent chapter, the Torah is the cornerstone of Judaism because it is in the Torah where we find God's commandments, which are more than ten.[108]

By tradition, the authentic Biblical text that was given to Moses from God was preserved from one generation to another.[109] Thus, the Torah that Moses received at Sinai is identical to the one that exists now. In this respect, Orthodox Judaism and traditional Christianity have much in common: Both believe that the Torah is the preserved work of God. Note that the traditional Jewish view is not that the Torah was written by men inspired by God, as was the case with other books of the Bible, such as the Book of Psalms, but that it was authored by God himself, with Moses as the scrivener. The more modern movements within Judaism take an approach that is different from the Orthodox. The Reform movement and a substantial part of the Conservative movement believe that the Torah is God's will but that it was written down by humans, thus accounting for perceived errors. The Reconstructionist movement does not believe that the Torah was divinely written or even inspired, but that it was created solely by humans in search of God.

If God did indeed author the Torah, as Jews and Christians have traditionally believed, then the Torah takes on a significance that is nothing if not stupendous: it is the Divine Revelation itself. As such, the Revelation is not just a historic occurrence. Rather, it becomes the greatest event in the history of the world because it is literally God's own words to humankind. And the Torah's injunction, "You must follow exactly the path that the LORD your God has commanded you, so that you may live, and that it may go well with you, and that you may live long in the land that you are to possess,"[110] takes on a beauty and majesty that words cannot even come close to describing.

Admittedly, there are modern Biblical scholars, not from the school of Orthodox Judaism or traditional Christianity, who contend that the Torah was not written by God. From such a perspective, the Torah becomes no more authoritative than the Code of Hammurabi or any other ancient text. The consequences of such a belief are dramatic. The Ten Commandments then become mere suggestions, and utilitarianism or nihilism can readily supplant ethical monotheism. This is not to suggest that all ethical monotheists are ethical and all non-monotheists are evil. Indeed, throughout the ages, men have committed terrible crimes in the name of the One God. For example, tens of thousands of innocent people were killed when Catholics and Protestants fought each other in the Thirty Years War (1618-1648). Nevertheless, it is also indisputable that only ethical religions have produced enduring systems of morality. In fact, more people were killed by the atheistic Nazi and Communist regimes in the twentieth century than in all the religious wars in history combined.

Principle 9: The Torah Is Immutable

The ninth principle is, *"I firmly believe with complete faith that God will never change the Torah nor will he ever give another Torah."*

Judaism, like Christianity, believes that God is perfect.[111] As such, God could only give a perfect Torah. In fact, it would be nothing less than a sad and frightening ecclesiastical joke if God, who is perfect, tricked the Jewish people by giving them something that was flawed. Of course, God did no such thing. And for that reason it is written, "The law of the LORD is perfect."[112] Just as God is supreme and perfect in every sense, so it must be said of his Torah. A perfect God gave a perfect Torah, and it is impossible to improve upon that which is perfect. Consequently, Orthodox Judaism teaches that the Torah is absolutely immutable. As the Torah itself says, "You must neither add anything to what I command you nor take away anything from it, but keep the commandments of the LORD your God with which I am charging you."[113]

While the immutability of the Torah is an integral part of Orthodox belief, such is not the case with the other movements within Judaism. Within the Conservative movement, some take a position close to Orthodoxy by holding that the Torah is immutable except for clear errors in transmission. Others within the Conservative movement hold that the Torah can change to adapt to new situations because the Revelation is a continuing Revelation and one which did not end at Sinai (as the Orthodox believe). The Reform movement's position is that only the Torah's moral laws are binding; the ritual laws (such as Jewish dietary laws)[114] are not and each individual determines whether to abide by such laws. The Reconstructionist movement, which emphasizes Judaism as a civilization, teaches that each generation "reconstructs" Judaism to ensure its continuation, but that individuals determine what rituals they wish to perpetuate.

But irrespective of differences, all of Judaism's movements agree that the Torah was not and never will be superseded by a new testament. This leads us to our next point: Christianity's view on the subject. More specifically, do Christians believe that the Torah (Old Testament) was replaced by the Gospel (New Testament)? As a starting point, we look to what the author of Hebrews[115] wrote:

> But when Christ came as a high priest of the good things that have come, then through the greater and perfect tent (not made with hands, that is, not of this creation), he entered once for all into the Holy Place, not with the blood of goats and calves, but with his own blood, thus obtaining eternal redemption. For if the blood of goats and bulls, with the sprinkling of the ashes of a heifer, sanctifies those who have been defiled so that their flesh is purified, how much more will the blood of Christ, who through the eternal Spirit offered himself without blemish to God, purify our conscience from dead works to worship the living God! For this reason he is the mediator of a new covenant, so that those who are called may receive the promised eternal inheritance, because a death has occurred that redeems them from the transgressions under the first covenant.[116]

Through the centuries, as a consequence of this and other New Testament passages,[117] many Christians have taken the position that Jesus' death and resurrection have rendered Judaism a historical phenomenon; it has ceased being a vibrant and continuing religion. Indeed, in their study of the Old Testament (the Hebrew Scriptures), most Christians typically emphasize not the Pentateuch (the Torah),[118] but the balance of the Old Testament (the Writings and the Prophets). This emphasis is largely due to the Messianic prophecies in these books,[119] which Christians believe were fulfilled in Jesus.[120] Jews, on the other hand, emphasize the Torah in their study of the Bible because all branches of Judaism teach that the Torah was, remains, and always will be a living doctrine to enable people to live a proper and righteous life.[121]

But must the "new covenant" of Christianity necessarily supersede the "old covenant" of Judaism? I believe that it is possible for one to be a Christian and believe fully in the Virgin Birth, the Holy Trinity, and the Resurrection, all of which represent the foundations of Christianity, and yet not look at Judaism as merely a historical phenomenon. One can take the position that the teachings of Jesus and the New Testament brought a form of ethical monotheism to the Gentiles,[122] which in no way impacts on the viability of Judaism. In this regard, it may be helpful to compare the Noachide Covenant, which God entered into with all humanity after the Great Flood,[123] to the Sinaitic Covenant, which God subsequently entered into with the Jewish people on Mount Sinai. Just as the latter covenant did not revoke the former, so too may a Christian believe that the New Testament did not in any way supersede or revoke the Old Testament. Rather, the New Testament exists as a branch from the Old Testament, intertwined with Judaism, as a form of ethical monotheism for non-Jews. To hold otherwise presents a grave theological problem, as we shall now discuss.

If one truly believes that God revoked his Torah (the Old Testament) and everlasting covenant with his chosen people (Jews) for another covenant (the New Testament) and a new people (Christians), then God broke his promise to Abraham: "So shall my covenant be in your flesh for an everlasting covenant."[124] And if it is true that God broke his promise, what would stop God from abrogating the New Testament with the Christian people and establishing yet another "everlasting" covenant (now the third) with yet another group of people? After all, if God went back on his word once, why can he not do it again?

For any Christian, the very thought that God would revoke the New Testament is unsettling at best and frightening at worst, in addition to being heretical. Indeed, the teaching of the Roman Catholic Church (as well as other churches) is that God does not repent of the promises he makes and, as such, the covenant he entered into with the Jewish people continues, and will endure through the ages.[125] As the Torah itself states, "Because the LORD your God is a merciful God; he will not forget the covenant with your ancestors that he swore to them."[126]

Nevertheless, it also must be acknowledged that there are denominations within Christianity which do believe that the New Testament has, in fact, supplanted the Abrahamic and Sinaitic Covenants of the Torah. In fact, this "replacement theology" is the very reason that the Southern Baptist Convention adopted a resolution in the summer of 1996 to commission a ministry specifically for the purpose of converting Jews to Christianity. Many within the Jewish community responded to the Baptist resolution with great disappointment, and it remains to be seen whether relations between Jews and Christians within the Southern Baptist Convention will consequently suffer.

Principle 10: God Is Omniscient

The tenth principle is, *"I firmly believe with complete faith that God is omniscient."*

God knows all.[127] He knows not only all of our deeds, but all of our needs too. As Jesus himself taught, "Your Father knows what you need before you ask him."[128] Nothing can be hidden from the Creator, who knows us so intimately that he knows even our private thoughts.[129] Many people look at God's omniscience as something terrifying because they feel that every impure thought they have is being recorded by God for use by him at some later time, as a basis for punishment. With such a perspective of God, it is quite understandable why many individuals feel burdened by religion, not uplifted by it. Judaism, however, does not look at God's omniscience in this manner. Rather, God's omniscience ensures us of a personal God. True, the Almighty knows all of our thoughts. But he also knows all of our good deeds, as well as the many obstacles we encounter every day as we strive to rise above our bad thoughts to do good. As the first commandment of the Decalogue states, "I am the LORD *your* God, who brought you out of the land of Egypt, out of the house of slavery."[130] God is the God of each of us. Yes, he knows our most intimate thoughts, but not for the purpose of punishing us. Rather, it is for the purpose of being our God.

On a related matter, it should be pointed out that Judaism teaches that God does not punish us for our thoughts;[131] we are punished only for our actions. We address this subject in much greater depth in the next principle of faith and later again in our discussion of the Ten Commandments.[132]

All branches of Judaism recognize God's omniscience, but only the Orthodox places great emphasis upon it because of its relationship to reward and punishment, which we discuss next.

Principle 11: God Rewards and Punishes

The eleventh principle is, *"I firmly believe with complete faith that God rewards those who keep his commandments and punishes those who transgress his commandments."*

God is not only merciful[133] but just, too.[134] As such, evildoers must necessarily be punished,[135] since if they were not, the distinction between good and evil would be inconsequential and meaningless.[136] As an ancient rabbinical dictum teaches, "He who is kind to the cruel is cruel to the kind."[137] God, of course, is not cruel to anyone, let alone the kind. Thus, there must necessarily be reward and punishment,[138] if not now,[139] then in the "World to Come," that is, the hereafter.[140]

Judaism has traditionally taught that our reward or punishment is determined by whether we keep God's commandments,[141] as the Torah makes clear:

> *See, I have set before you today life and prosperity, death and adversity. If you obey the commandments of the LORD your God that I am commanding you today, by loving the LORD your God, walking in his ways, and observing his commandments, decrees, and ordinances, then you shall live and become numerous, and the LORD your God will bless you in the land that you are entering to possess. But if your heart turns away and you do not hear, but are led astray to bow down to other gods and serve them, I declare to you today that you shall perish: you shall not live long in the land that you are crossing the Jordan to enter and possess. I call heaven and earth to witness against you today that I have set before you life and death, blessings and curses. Choose life so that you and your descendants may live. . . .[142]*

The laws that are referred to here ("commandments, decrees, and ordinances") are not just the Ten Commandments. As we shall see, there are 613 commandments that bind the Jewish people, and seven broad categories of commandments that bind Gentiles.[143] Reward and punishment are thus based on whether we keep these commandments. That said, it is nevertheless sad to come across an individual who believes that God is going to mete out harsh punishment for each and every omission.[144] God is also a merciful God. As it is written, "for his steadfast love endures forever."[145] But mercy as well as justice requires that evildoers be punished: "[To him] who struck down great kings, for his steadfast love endures forever."[146] Indeed, what kind of God would he be if Mother Teresa and Adolf Hitler were given the same reward? Thus, even when punishing, God is acting in a merciful manner.

Moreover, the traditional Jewish view is that God does not punish mere thoughts. The Tenth Commandment, "You shalt not covet,"[147] applies only when we take action in furtherance of those thoughts. Thus, a Jew who desires to eat a prohibited food, such as pork,[148] but abstains, has committed no sin. Indeed, because God is omniscient, he is aware of the person's desires, but because the person has not acted on them, no punishment is warranted. To the contrary, God will actually reward this person for having complied with the commandment to not eat pork. As the Torah states: "If you follow my statutes and keep my commandments and *observe them* faithfully, I will give you your rains in their season, and the land shall yield its produce, and the trees of the field shall yield their fruit. Your threshing shall overtake the vintage, and the vintage shall overtake the sowing; you shall eat your bread to the full, and live securely in your land."[149]

For Christians, the idea that deeds are important but thoughts are not is understandably difficult to accept. This is because the essence of Christianity is faith.[150] On the other hand, as we have just seen[151] and as we shall explore in much greater depth later in this book,[152] the essence of Judaism is behavior: performing God's commandments.

Of course, just as one should not observe God's commandments out of irrational fear of him, one should also not observe his commandments out of a desire to obtain a reward.[153] Rather, one should obey God and observe his commandments out of love for him. As the Mishnah[154] teaches,

"Do not be like servants who serve the Master expecting to receive a reward, but be like the servants who serve the Master without expecting to receive a reward. And let the awe of Heaven be upon you."[155]

The concept of reward and punishment is not significant in the Reform and Reconstructionist movements. It is significant only within some parts of the Conservative movement. For the Orthodox movement, the concept of reward and punishment (often referred to as the "measure for measure" principle[156]) is fundamental to Judaism.

One final note on this subject is appropriate here. As indicated earlier, humanlike physical qualities are imputed to God so that we may obtain a small glimpse, such as it is, of the One who is beyond comprehension. For example, we speak of the "eyes of the LORD."[157] Similarly, humanlike emotions are also imputed to God. He is described as "merciful,"[158] "righteous,"[159] and "loving."[160] Yet, just as God does not have humanlike physical qualities, neither does he have humanlike emotional qualities. We apply these qualities to God only to better conceive and understand he who is quite simply not conceivable and not fully understandable. Thus, although the Torah itself uses humanlike terms to describe God, it is only because, as the Talmud states, "the Torah speaks in the language of men."[161] Nevertheless, it is important to realize that God does not get "angry" any more than he stretches out his "arm."

Principle 12: Messiah Will Come

The twelfth principle is, *"I firmly believe with complete faith that the Messiah will come, and though he may tarry, daily is his coming awaited."*

Contrary to what many people believe, the concept of a Messiah is Jewish in origin, and the observant Jew daily awaits his coming with eagerness. Of course, for Christians, the Messiah has already come in the person of Jesus.

A common question which Christians have is: If Jews believe in the Messiah, why do they not believe that Jesus is the Messiah? This is an important question, and one which must be answered for Christians to have a good grasp of Judaism. Before we answer this question, however, we first need to recall that there are four major branches of Judaism today: Orthodox, Conservative, Reform, and Reconstructionist. It is only the Orthodox movement that believes in the coming of the Messiah. The modern Reform and Reconstructionist movements do not share in this belief, while the Conservative movement believes in the eventual coming of a Messianic-like Age, but without an individual who will be the Messiah. That said, let us now address why Orthodox Jews do not believe that Jesus was the Messiah.

The Messiah is the person who will lead humankind into a Golden Age, a time when war, famine, disease, and pestilence will no longer exist.[162] After Jesus' death, the world continued to suffer from these ills.[163] Consequently, Orthodox Jews believe that whoever Jesus was, he could not have been the Messiah. It is, of course, true that Christians believe that war, famine, disease, and pestilence will no longer exist when Jesus returns to earth again.[164] But the idea of a Second Coming is fully a Christian concept and has no basis whatsoever in Judaism.

There is a second reason why Jews, Orthodox or otherwise, do not believe that Jesus was the Messiah. Traditional Christianity teaches that Jesus is the Second Person of the Holy Trinity: Father, Son, and Holy Spirit.[165] This view of God represents a position that is irreconcilable with the Jewish view of God.[166] Thus, as stated earlier, no Jew can believe in Jesus and remain true to Judaism any more than a Christian cannot believe in him and remain true to Christianity.

Principle 13: Resurrection of the Dead

The thirteenth principle is, *"I firmly believe with complete faith that there will be a physical resurrection of the dead at a time when it pleases the Creator."*

Judaism, like Christianity, subscribes to the belief in an afterlife of the soul.[167] But in addition to the belief that the soul endures after the body ends, there is also a fundamental belief among Orthodox Jews, but not among adherents of the other movements within Judaism, that there will also be a bodily resurrection of the dead when the Messianic Age unfolds.[168] Thus, those who are not deemed unworthy will be allowed to live a bodily existence again in the Age of the Messiah. This last point is similar to the Christian belief of a resurrection of the dead, which is part of both the Apostles' Creed and the Nicene Creed.[169]

The foregoing Thirteen Principles of Faith are the basic beliefs of Judaism. But Judaism is more than a religion, as we shall now explore.

CHAPTER 2

Judaism as a Legal System

In addition to being a religion, Judaism is simultaneously a legal system. In fact, it is the world's oldest continuously functioning legal system, dating back to the giving of the law on Mount Sinai, around 1312 B.C.E.[1] In this chapter, we first examine why we need to understand Judaism as a legal system. Next, we explore secular legal systems and the common threads which bind them together: criminal laws, civil laws, and a judiciary. Thereafter, we introduce Judaism's legal system, which also has criminal and civil laws—as well as religious laws—and a judiciary. This chapter concludes with a brief discussion of the rabbi's role as judge (and teacher). In chapters three and four we discuss Judaism's legal system in greater depth: the Ten Commandments as an integral part of this legal system, and 603 other commandments, lesser known perhaps, but no less important.

The Need to Understand Judaism as a Legal System

Why should a Christian be interested in learning about Judaism's legal system? There are several reasons. First, one cannot understand Judaism unless one understands its legal system, since Judaism's legal system is as much a part of its identity as the Exodus from Egypt, the Revelation on Mount Sinai, and the coming of the Messiah. All are part of Judaism's essence. Second, Judaism's legal system is no less a part of the Divine Revelation than the prohibition against idolatry in the Ten Commandments.[2] Just as God required the Jewish people to worship only him, so too did he command them to set up courts of justice.[3] Third, as the Gospel indicates, Jesus may have been brought before a Jewish legal tribunal.[4] Consequently, a full understanding of the New Testament is impossible without understanding Judaism's legal system.

Secular Legal Systems

Initially, before we study Judaism's legal system, it may be helpful to recognize that all nations, past and present, have legal systems to govern their people. Throughout history, some nations have had fair and just legal systems. Others have not. The legal systems of the United States and England fall into the former category, while those of Nazi Germany and the Soviet Union fall into the latter. But the common denominator of all legal systems—good or bad—is that they have criminal and civil laws, as well as a judiciary to interpret and decide questions regarding the laws of the land.

Criminal Laws

Laws which govern a person's relationship with society as a whole are often referred to as penal or criminal laws. By way of illustration, the American legal system has many rules that govern a person's relationship with society as a whole. For example, murder, rape, robbery, burglary, theft, and kidnapping are all forbidden activities. Anyone who commits any of these acts is subject to prosecution, not by the individual victim but by society itself, that is to say, the government: the state, the people, or the United States (e.g., *People v. Smith*). Upon conviction, the defendant can be imprisoned or, in the case of murder, be put to death.

Civil Laws

Another category of rules found in any legal system is one that regulates relationships with fellow citizens. These rules may be referred to as civil laws. For example, in our system of jurisprudence, a person who injures another while carelessly driving an automobile must pay monetary damages to the person injured. Similarly, an employer who wrongfully withholds an employee's salary can be sued by the employee to recover the wages.

In short, as a consequence of a significant body of penal and civil laws, our system of jurisprudence regulates a large part of our lives.

The Judiciary

To interpret and enforce the criminal and civil laws of the land, every nation has a judiciary, a system of courts. For example, in the United States, most states have three levels of courts. At the lowest level is the trial court, typically called the Superior Court. This is where a defendant stands trial for murder (criminal case) or where a person injured in an accident sues the person responsible for the injuries (civil case). Above the Superior Court is an intermediate Court of Appeal.[5] This court can hear only certain cases, typically, appeals from the Superior Court. At the highest level is the state Supreme Court. It too can hear only certain cases, most often appeals from the intermediate Court of Appeal.

Of course, to become a judge, whether at the Superior Court level or at the Supreme Court level, one must first become a lawyer. This is accomplished by studying at a law school and passing the bar exam.[6]

With this background now laid, we are prepared to examine Judaism's legal system.

Judaism's Legal System

Just as all nations have legal systems, so too does the Jewish nation (and even when the Jewish nation did not exist from 135 C.E. until its reestablishment in 1948, its legal system endured, as we shall discuss later in this chapter). And just as all legal systems have criminal and civil laws, and a judiciary to interpret these laws, so too does Judaism's legal system. But unlike the legal systems of most nations, the Jewish legal system also has religious laws. We now proceed to examine this fascinating system.

Criminal and Civil Laws

Judaism also regulates the lives of its adherents. As with American law, Judaism correspondingly has laws that regulate a Jew's relationship with society as a whole (criminal or penal laws) and with fellow citizens (civil laws). Thus, Jewish law too makes murder a crime,[7] and allows an employee to sue an employer for back wages.[8] But while American law regulates only certain areas of a citizen's life, Jewish law regulates virtually every aspect of a person's life. For example, Jewish law requires its citizens to give to charity,[9] while American law has no counterpart (although one may certainly argue that tax money used for social welfare programs is not too far removed from the Jewish requirement of tithing).

Religious Laws

Moreover, in addition to regulating a Jew's relationship with society and with fellow citizens, Judaism also has a third category of laws which many other legal systems lack: laws that directly govern a person's relationship with God (and, of course, as a consequence of the First Amendment to the Constitution, there is no American counterpart to this). Thus, Jewish law mandates that a Jew is forbidden to work on the Sabbath[10] or worship other gods,[11] and is required to fast on the Day of Atonement[12] and circumcise one's son on the eighth day of his life.[13] We explore the basis for these rules in greater detail in a later chapter.[14]

The Judiciary: Introduction

To interpret and enforce its criminal, civil, and religious laws, Judaism also has a well-defined judiciary.[15]

The Beth Din

Ancient Israel had three levels of courts to hear disputes.[16] First, at the lowest level, was the local *beth din* ("house of judgment").[17] These local courts, as was true for all Jewish tribunals, were presided over by men who were learned in the law.[18] Typically the judge was a *rabbi* ("my master," meaning a teacher), a person who was trained and knowledgeable in all aspects of Jewish law.[19] The beth din, the equivalent of the local superior court in the United States today, heard the typical civil cases (negligence, divorce, etc.) as well as most criminal cases, except those that carried the death penalty.[20] In ancient times, every Jewish town and community had a beth din, which was composed of three judges.[21]

As we shall discuss later in this chapter, the beth din has endured through the ages and can be found today in Israel and in every Jewish community worldwide.

The Lesser Sanhedrin

The next level in the court structure was the *Lesser Sanhedrin*. The term *Sanhedrin* comes from the Greek word *synedrion*, which means "sitting in council." The Lesser Sanhedrin was composed of twenty-three men[22] and could be convened in any town with more than 120 adult males.[23] To be a member of the Lesser Sanhedrin, one had to be exceptionally learned in the law since members of this body had much responsibility, presiding over any criminal case where the defendant could suffer the death penalty.[24]

The Lesser Sanhedrin did not hear appeals from the beth din because judges on the beth din were themselves to reverse an opinion they subsequently determined was erroneous.[25] A judge whose error caused a litigant harm could be held personally liable for monetary damages.[26]

The Great Sanhedrin

The highest court in ancient Israel was the *Great Sanhedrin*. The Great Sanhedrin was the equivalent of the United States Supreme Court in stature. It consisted of seventy-one judges[27] and sat in Jerusalem, in the Holy Temple itself.[28] By any standard, the Great Sanhedrin had immense responsibility. It approved the appointment of Israel's kings,[29] selected the judges to the Lesser Sanhedrin,[30] and resolved ambiguous areas of law.[31] The Great Sanhedrin also presided over the trial of a false prophet,[32] the trial of an entire city or tribe that committed idolatry,[33] the trial of a high priest in a capital case,[34] and the trial of a rebellious elder.[35] Moreover, certain types of wars could not be fought unless prior approval was given by this illustrious body.[36] All this was in accordance with the Scriptural decree, "Let them bring every important case to you."[37] It was because of its enormous responsibility that the judges who were members of the Great Sanhedrin were without doubt the most learned men in the Land of Israel.

The Sanhedrin in the New Testament

The Gospels (New Revised Standard Version) report that Jesus appeared before the "council,"[38] by which the Gospel writers probably meant the Sanhedrin. Did Jesus appear before the Great or Lesser Sanhedrin? The Gospel of John reports that some sort of hearing took place in the palace or house of the high priest.[39] Because the Great Sanhedrin could meet only in the Temple itself,[40] it would seem that the body that Jesus appeared before could not have been the Great Sanhedrin. Moreover, because the Gospels indicate that Jesus was tried for blasphemy,[41] a crime that only the Lesser Sanhedrin had jurisdiction over, it is a virtual certainty that Jesus could not have appeared before the Great Sanhedrin. One may thus infer that when the Gospel writers used the term "council," they had in mind some tribunal other than the Great Sanhedrin. Perhaps it was the Lesser Sanhedrin, or even an informally convened body.[42] Nevertheless, based on all available sources, the possibility that Jesus appeared before the Great Sanhedrin cannot be totally ruled out.[43]

The Book of Acts also provides several accounts of the Sanhedrin,[44] including a moving speech by Rabbi Gamaliel, one of Judaism's great teachers, who prevailed upon his colleagues on the Great Sanhedrin to acquit the Apostles of any charges of wrongdoing.[45]

The Sanhedrin Ends

Following the destruction of the Temple by the Romans in 70 C.E., the Great Sanhedrin moved to the town of Yavneh in Judea (what is Israel today). Its powers were greatly reduced, however, especially in light of the destruction of the Jewish nation in the year 135 C.E. in the unsuccessful war with Rome. By the beginning of the fifth century C.E., in light of Roman persecution, both the Great and Lesser Sanhedrins had come to an end.

The Beth Din Endures

But though the Sanhedrin ceased to exist, Jewish law miraculously endured. Rabbis continued to convene local three-judge courts (*bahtim din*)[46] in Palestine as well as in the Diaspora to resolve business disputes among Jewish merchants and to make certain that Jewish couples obtained divorces in compliance with Jewish law.[47] And when they were not acting as judges, the rabbis were codifying the laws of Judaism[48] and providing written opinions on all types of legal matters as guidance for Jews throughout the world. As a matter of fact, no other legal system in history has survived when the nation and its highest court ceased to exist. But Judaism's legal system did survive—and then some. Indeed, as we prepare to enter the next millennium of the Common Era, increasing numbers of Jews (and Gentiles!) are agreeing to submit their claims to local rabbinical courts, where the cases are adjudicated in a short period of time and the costs are a fraction of what is normally spent in secular American courts.

The Future of the Sanhedrin

But what of the future of the Great and Lesser Sanhedrins? Will those grand bodies ever be reconstituted in the modern State of Israel? Although that matter was considered shortly before and after independence was achieved in 1948, it was decided that for a variety of political and practical reasons, the Sanhedrin could not yet be reinstated. (The Orthodox movement believes that the Sanhedrin will be reinstated when the Third and final Temple is built, which will happen when the Messiah comes.) In addition, it was also decided at that time that Jewish law would not be the sole law of Israel. Instead, a compromise was reached by which English law (Britain governed Palestine under mandate from the League of Nations and the United Nations until 1948) would govern except in two areas: (1) where English law did not address a particular matter, in which case Jewish law would be adopted; and (2) in all matters of family law, such as marriage and divorce, where Jewish law would be the law of the land.

Rabbi as Judge (and Teacher)

As indicated earlier, judges in the Jewish judiciary have traditionally been rabbis. *Rabbi* literally means "my master" and refers to an individual who is learned in Jewish law. The title appears to have been used for the first time in the first century C.E. (probably during Jesus' lifetime). In ancient times, there were no lawyers *per se*, just rabbis, individuals who were experts in the law.[49] How did a man (only men could become rabbis until recent times)[50] become a rabbi? In ancient times, much as it is today, the student would study in a *yeshiva* ("sitting," meaning that the student sits to learn), a school of higher Jewish education, under the auspices of a rabbi. After years of study and a demonstration of competence, the rabbi would ordain his student. During the first century C.E., however, it appears that one could secure the title of rabbi in a less formal manner. Indeed, some were called rabbi as an honorary title, out of respect.

It is important to note, however, that although a judge is typically a rabbi, a rabbi is first and foremost a teacher (as the word *rabbi* implies) and advisor on Jewish law and practice to the members of his or her synagogue (a house of prayer and learning, and which came into being as a substitute for the First Temple that was destroyed by the Babylonians in 586 B.C.E.[51]). Such a person is consequently given appropriate respect in the community. But one should not think that a rabbi is virtually identical to a Christian priest or minister. For example, in the Roman Catholic Church, a priest is necessary for the Eucharist (Mass) and the Sacrament of Reconciliation (known also as Penance or Confession), neither of which has a rabbinical counterpart. In fact, a rabbi is not even needed to preside over the three daily communal prayer services. To reiterate, some rabbis are judges but all rabbis are teachers.

Jesus as Rabbi

According to the Gospels, Jesus was referred to as "rabbi,"[52] but more than this is not known. Thus, we do not know if Jesus was in fact ordained, or if the title given him in the Gospel was intended as an honorary title to show respect. As noted above, during the first century C.E., one could become known as a rabbi through community recognition.

Rabbinate Traditionally Limited to Men

By traditional law, only men could become rabbis. This legal position is based on the principle that a Jew must act modestly at all times;[53] and the educational, judicial, and pastoral duties of a rabbi could conflict with a woman's duty of propriety. Nevertheless, the Reconstructionist movement has accepted women in its rabbinical seminary since the opening of its rabbinical program in 1967. In 1972, the Reform movement ordained the first American woman rabbi. And in 1983, the Conservative movement decided to admit women to its rabbinical program. Thus, in the Conservative, Reform, and Reconstructionist movements, women rabbis may serve as judges on Jewish courts. The Orthodox movement, however, remains steadfast in its position to ordain only men.[54] Consequently, to date, only men serve as judges on Orthodox courts.

Within Christianity, there is a similar range of responses to the ordination of women. While women are now ordained as ministers in many denominations, the Roman Catholic Church and the Eastern Orthodox Church remain firm on the matter of not ordaining women.

And so we see that Judaism is simultaneously a religion and a legal system. It is a religion because God is the focal point of everything that an observant Jew believes and does. At the same time, Judaism is also a legal system because there are rules of law that govern all aspects of a Jewish person's life.

Having established that as a legal system Judaism has three categories of laws—criminal, civil, and religious—we are now prepared to examine the laws within these categories in still greater depth. To do so, we present five questions for discussion: (1) What is the significance of the Ten Commandments, and what does each of them mean? (2) What other kinds of laws exist in Judaism, and where are all of these laws found? (3) Who is the author of all of these laws? (4) What is the oral law? (5) Are both Jews and Gentiles bound by these laws? In the next five chapters, we explore these questions.

CHAPTER 3

The Ten Commandments

A lthough everyone is quite familiar with the Ten Commandments, few Christians learn them from a Jewish perspective, which provides an interpretation that is decidedly unique, and one which Jesus certainly knew.

The Significance of the Ten Commandments

From a historical perspective, the Ten Commandments is without doubt the greatest legal document ever given. Not only did the Decalogue (a term often used as a synonym for the Ten Commandments, derived from the Greek word *deka*, meaning "ten") become the foundation for Jewish law, but it became the infrastructure for all of Western civilization as well. Indeed, until relatively recent United States Supreme Court decisions in the 1960s and 1970s, representations of the two tablets of the Decalogue were commonly displayed in courthouses, schools, and other public buildings throughout the United States. Ironically, notwithstanding these and other court decisions, the Decalogue is still displayed inside the United States Supreme Court Building.

From a religious perspective, however, the Decalogue is nothing if not astounding. In presenting it to Israel, God spoke to an entire nation, and we can barely imagine what it must have been like:

> *On the morning of the third day there was thunder and lightning, as well as a thick cloud on the mountain, and a blast of a trumpet so loud that all the people who were in the camp trembled. Moses brought the people out of the camp to meet God. They took their stand at the foot of the mountain. Now Mount Sinai was wrapped in smoke, because the LORD had descended upon it in fire; the smoke went up like the smoke of a kiln, while the whole mountain shook violently.[1]*

"Then God Spoke All These Words"

And then came the Revelation itself: "Then God spoke all these words."[2] For the Jew or Christian who believes that the Torah is truly the work of God,[3] it nevertheless strains the imagination to even begin to comprehend what it means that "God spoke." Not through a prophet, nor through an angel did God speak, but by himself. He revealed himself directly and not symbolically, to literally millions of Israelites.[4] Let us now analyze this remarkable document.

First Commandment: Believe in God

"I am the LORD your God, who brought you out of the land of Egypt, out of the house of slavery."[5] This, in Jewish tradition, is the first of the Ten Commandments (although some denominations within Christianity look at this as the prologue, and not a commandment). The ancient rabbis interpreted this commandment to mean that one is to believe in God.[6] And because God stated that he is "the LORD *your* God" (emphasis added), he is the God of every person: rich or poor, schooled or unschooled, healthy or sick. Moreover, because God is the God of everyone,[7] it is possible for a person to commune with him directly,[8] to praise him,[9] and to petition him for one's needs,[10] as well as for the needs of family members or others.[11] One may also confess sin to him directly.[12]

No rabbi is needed (which is to be contrasted with Roman Catholicism, for example, where a priest is necessary for the Sacrament of Penance).

Second Commandment: Have No Other Gods

The second commandment states, "You shall have no other gods before me. You shall not make for yourself an idol, whether in the form of anything that is in heaven above, or that is on the earth beneath, or that is in the water under the earth. You shall not bow down to them or worship them; for I the LORD your God am a jealous God, punishing children for the iniquity of parents, to the third and the fourth generation of those who reject me, but showing steadfast love to the thousandth generation of those who love me and keep my commandments."[13]

This commandment forbids Jews from worshipping anyone or anything else but God.[14] So strong is this commandment that a Jew is prohibited from merely making an idol, even if not for the purpose of worshipping it ("you shall not make").[15] That God is "a jealous God" means that he will not share his kingship with any idol or false god.[16] Of course, as stated earlier,[17] jealousy is a human emotion and not actually applicable to God.[18] Nevertheless, the term assists us in understanding he who is inconceivable.[19]

Innocents Not Punished

That God punishes idolaters is made clear ("punishing . . . the iniquity of parents"). But is it fair that God should punish another whose wrong is simply to be born to an evildoer ("punishing . . . to the third and the fourth generation of those who reject me")? In short, does the second commandment mean that God will indeed punish the children and grandchildren of evildoers?

This is one of the most misunderstood passages in the Torah, and it does not mean what most people think it means. Consequently, we need to state in the most unequivocal manner that God does not inflict punishment upon innocent people.[20] Indeed, the Torah elsewhere expressly teaches, "Parents shall not be put to death for their children, nor shall children be put to death for their parents; only for their own crimes may persons be put to death."[21] Because the Torah is the work of God and is perfect,[22] it obviously cannot have any inconsistencies. How then do we reconcile "only for their own crimes may persons be put to death" with the second commandment of the Decalogue?

The ancient rabbis interpreted the second commandment as meaning that God punishes the children, grandchildren, and great-grandchildren, but only if they too purposefully and knowingly follow in the evil footsteps of their ancestor.[23] But even then God's jealousy is limited to four generations. Why four generations? Because four is the maximum number of generations that can live together in one household,[24] where the children, grandchildren, and great-grandchildren can learn and freely accept the evil ways of the head of the household. But while God remembers the deeds of evildoers for only three or four generations, he remembers a person's good deeds ("those who love me and keep my commandments") without limitation ("showing steadfast love to the thousandth generation of those who love me and keep my commandments").[25] Consequently, a person's good deeds can benefit not only that one individual, but that person's progeny for all time and throughout the ages, that is, for thousands of generations.

Third Commandment: Do Not Take God's Name in Vain

The third commandment teaches, "You shall not make wrongful use of the name of the LORD your God, for the LORD will not acquit anyone who misuses his name."[26] God actually has a personal name, composed of the Hebrew letters *yud, hay, vav, hay*. In English it is transliterated into *YHWH*. This name of God is absolutely sacred and is never pronounced as written (the Germanic version, with vowels added, is *Jehovah*). In everyday speech or writing, the name of God that is most commonly used is *Hashem*, meaning literally "the name." In formal prayer, it is pronounced *Adonoy*. Because God's name is holy, to use God's name for no purpose is disrespectful of God and is a desecration of his name. Thus, this commandment prohibits speaking God's name for no purpose, or making an oath for which there is no purpose.[27]

Change in Person

One last point on the third commandment is in order at this juncture. The first two commandments refer to God in the first person: "*I* am the LORD your God" and "You shall have no other gods before *me*" (emphasis added). Beginning with the third commandment, however, the commandments refer to God in the third person: "the LORD will not acquit anyone who misuses *his* name" (emphasis added). Some modern Biblical scholars use this fact to attempt to prove that the Decalogue was written not by God, but by people. Needless to say, to the believing Jew or Christian, such a statement is heretical. Nevertheless, there is a traditional Jewish explanation for the change in form: After God spoke the first two commandments, the people were so overcome with emotion at hearing God speak that they could not comprehend him any further.[28] Consequently, according to this view, the remaining commandments were understood only by Moses,[29] who then taught them to the Jewish people, thus accounting for the change in person.

Fourth Commandment: Remember the Sabbath

The fourth commandment deals with the Sabbath: "Remember the sabbath day, and keep it holy. Six days you shall labor and do all your work. But the seventh day is a sabbath to the LORD your god; you shall not do any work—you, your son or your daughter, your male or female slave, your livestock, or the alien resident in your towns. For in six days the LORD made heaven and earth, the sea, and all that is in them, but rested the seventh day; therefore the LORD blessed the sabbath day and consecrated it."[30] All acts of creation ("work") are to cease on the holy sabbath because God himself ceased creating the universe on the seventh day. Thus, the sabbath is a weekly reminder of God's omnipotence.[31] Irrespective of how high a Jew's workbench is, he or she is to cease working on the sabbath, just as God did, in a manner of speaking (just as God does not have physical characteristics or human emotions, so too does he not "work").[32]

When the Sabbath Begins

The seventh day of the week in the Jewish calendar is Saturday in the secular calendar. But the sabbath does not begin on Saturday; it begins on Friday. This is because in the account of the Creation, the Torah states, "And there was evening and there was morning, the first day."[33] Thus, first came evening, then came morning. But what constitutes "evening"? Is it when the sun sinks below the horizon (sunset), or some later time such as nightfall (when the stars are visible)? Jewish law teaches that the twilight period, the time between sunset and nightfall, is actually the overlapping of two days.[34] The sabbath, therefore, begins at sunset on the seventh day (Friday), and ends at nightfall on the following day (Saturday). To make certain, however, that the sabbath is not accidentally desecrated by engaging in prohibited activities, the sabbath legally begins a short time before sunset, typically eighteen minutes.[35]

The Sabbath as a Joy

Throughout the centuries, the sabbath has been an island of tranquility for the Jew. It is a time when the family eats several sabbath meals together, goes to synagogue to pray, and spends time together and with friends. To the sabbath-observing Jew, the seventh day is a weekly joy. Indeed, when the sabbath ends at nightfall on Saturday, the observant Jew looks forward to the next sabbath with anticipation and delight.

Sign of the Covenant

But the sabbath has not just been a great benefit to the Jew; it has also been a great benefit to Judaism. More specifically, the sabbath has helped keep Judaism and the Jewish people alive, even in their darkest hours, at times of persecution and even genocide.[36] Josephus, the ancient historian, wrote that when the Syrians invaded Judea in 167 B.C.E. and outlawed the sabbath, Jews met secretly in caves to observe it. During the Holocaust, even while awaiting their end at the hands of the murderous Nazis, there are remarkable stories of Jews who did their best to secretly celebrate the sabbath in the death camps. Why have Jews risked their lives to celebrate the sabbath? Because, as the Torah states, "It is a sign forever between me [God] and the people of Israel. . . ."[37]

The sabbath has thus served to elevate each Jew to a higher spiritual level, one which allows Jews to recognize that regardless of their wealth, status, or education, each shares in the legacy of the Revelation which took place at Mount Sinai many centuries ago.[38] One Jewish writer of the nineteenth century put it well when he said, "More than the Jews have kept the sabbath, the sabbath has kept the Jews."[39]

The Sabbath a Burden?

Many people nevertheless have the idea that the sabbath is a burden. Going to the movies at the local mall is prohibited (one cannot drive or carry money on the sabbath). Gardening in the backyard is proscribed (cutting and planting are not allowed). Catching up on the bills is forbidden (writing too is prohibited). But to the observant Jew, the spiritual and physical pleasures received from observing the sabbath far outweigh the minor gratifications gained from participating in these common activities.

Many Christians believe that the Jewish sabbath is a burden because Jesus said, "The sabbath was made for humankind, and not humankind for the sabbath."[40] But this is virtually identical to a rabbinical teaching, "The sabbath was given to you, not you to the sabbath,"[41] meaning that rather than being a burden, the sabbath is an island of peace and tranquility, which Jews (including Jesus) have well understood for many centuries.

I once heard a Christian clergyman speak to his congregation about the Jews and the sabbath. The minister pointed out a number of interesting statistics: that crime is not significant among Jewish people; that the number of Jews in this country who are in law, medicine, and higher education is way out of proportion and far higher than one would expect based solely on the group's population (there are only six million Jews in the United States and eighteen million in the world today); and each year an inordinate number of Jews win various awards such as the Nobel and Pulitzer prizes. "What can be the reason for this?" the minister asked rhetorically. Answering his own question, he declared, "It is the sabbath." The minister then went on to observe that while many American families sincerely desire to spend more time together, Jews who observe the sabbath actually do so every week. On Friday, as the sun is about to set, the Jewish father goes to synagogue with his children, and when they come home together, he blesses them. To his sons he says, "May God make you like Ephraim and Manasseh."[42] To his daughters he says, "May God make you like Sarah, Rebecca, Rachel and Leah." The father then continues, "May the LORD bless you, and keep you. May the LORD make his face shine upon you, and be gracious to you. May the LORD lift up his countenance upon you, and give you peace."[43] To his wife, he sings in Hebrew the words to "A Woman of Valor."[44] The father then recites various blessings, after which the family eats a sumptuous meal together, during which they discuss God and the Torah. The sabbath as a burden? Not hardly.

A Taste of the World to Come

The Talmud[45] tells us that one day, the Jewish people asked God what the "World to Come," the Messianic Age, will be like. To this question God replied, "I have already given you a small taste of the World to Come. I have given you the sabbath."[46]

Fifth Commandment: Honor Parents

The fifth commandment requires that we give proper consideration to our parents. "Honor your father and your mother, so that your days may be long in the land that the LORD your God is giving you."[47] Just as Jews must honor God and not do anything for him out of selfishness, so too must they behave toward their parents. Children are to honor their parents by doing things for them without having any selfish motive in mind,[48] such as receiving an inheritance.

Honoring God by Honoring One's Parents

The first four commandments relate to God. The fifth commandment relates to one's parents. Yet all five commandments are on the first tablet of the Decalogue. The ancient rabbis did not think this a coincidence. "When one honors his parents, one honors God," they taught.[49]

Sixth Commandment: Do Not Murder

The sixth commandment proclaims, "You shall not murder."[50] Although some translations, such as the King James Version, render this verse as "You shall not kill," the translation provided in the New Revised Standard Version is more accurate since Judaism does not prohibit killing another in self-defense.[51]

Murder Includes Suicide and Euthanasia

The sixth commandment includes not just murder in a narrow sense of the word; suicide[52] and euthanasia[53] are also prohibited. As the Torah states, "For your own lifeblood I [God] will surely require a reckoning . . . and from human beings, each one for the blood of another, I will require a reckoning for human life."[54] Anyone who takes a life, be it his own or another's, will be called to account.[55]

Murder Includes Humiliating Another

By rabbinical interpretation, the sixth commandment includes not just the literal taking of life. According to the rabbinical sages, publicly humiliating someone is figuratively akin to murder.[56] How is this so? When one commits murder, the blood of the victim flows. Similarly, when one humiliates another, the blood of the one humiliated flows (as it rushes to the face to cause blushing). Consistent with the view that humiliating another is analogous to murder, the rabbis taught, "He who humiliates his fellow in public has no share in the World to Come."[57]

Jesus' View on Humiliating Another

Jesus too taught that it is a great sin to publicly humiliate another, and that to do so is figuratively akin to murder: "You have heard that it was said to those of ancient times, 'You shall not murder'; and 'whoever murders shall be liable to judgment.' But I say to you that if you are angry with a brother or sister without a cause you will be liable to judgment; and if you insult a brother or sister, you will be liable to the council [the Sanhedrin]; and if you say, 'You fool,' you will be liable to the hell of fire."[58]

Is Abortion Murder?

For many Christians, the prohibition against murder also includes abortion. Although it is too complex a subject to address here in any great depth, suffice it to say that, contrary to what many people believe, Orthodox Judaism too does not allow abortion on demand (the other branches of Judaism are more liberal in this regard). Abortion is allowed, however, when the mother's life is in danger.[59] In fact, in such circumstance—and here Orthodox Judaism parts with a number of Christian denominations—Jewish law provides that abortion is actually required.[60] The reasoning behind this position is that although the fetus has the potential to be a human being and must, therefore, be treated with great respect, it is not deemed to be a human being until born.[61] Consequently, the life of the mother, who is a human being, must take precedence over the life of the fetus. This is to be contrasted with the position of the Roman Catholic Church, as well as a number of other Christian denominations, which holds that human life begins at the moment of conception.[62] Such a view makes abortion unacceptable under any circumstance.

Seventh Commandment: Do Not Commit Adultery

The seventh commandment declares, "You shall not commit adultery."[63] It is interesting that this commandment follows the prohibition against murder. The reason that it does is to impress upon us the importance of fidelity in marriage. Just as murder takes away the life of a person, adultery takes away the life of a marriage. Moreover, adultery not only demeans the holy state of marriage, but it creates the possibility that a person can be born as a consequence of the adulterous and illegal relationship.

The Child Born of an Adulterous Union

In Jewish law, a person born of an adulterous relationship is called a *mamzer*.[64] A mamzer is often interpreted as "bastard" in English.[65] But the Hebrew meaning of the term is much more limited.[66] It applies only to children born of an adulterous or incestuous relationship.[67] It does not apply to a situation where a woman has relations before marriage.[68] In Jewish law, a mamzer can only marry another mamzer, or a convert to Judaism.[69] It may now be seen why adultery is looked upon as something quite horrendous in the Jewish community. One irresponsible act can adversely affect not just one's marriage, but one's progeny as well.[70]

Many ask whether it is fair to punish the child for the sinful actions of the parents.[71] To this difficult question the ancient rabbis could only declare that God himself cries over the plight of the mamzer, who will receive God's comfort in the hereafter.[72]

The reader should note that although a mamzer is limited with respect to whom he or she can marry, the status of being a mamzer has no other consequences. For example, the Talmud teaches that a mamzer inherits as does any other child,[73] and can even be the king of Israel.[74]

It is only the Orthodox movement which now enforces the law of the mamzer. The Conservative movement accepts the law's validity, but believes that it is not possible to enforce it at this time because we simply do not know what one's ancestors did nine or ten generations ago. The Reform and Reconstructionist movements do not accept the validity of the law of the mamzer.

Jesus' View of the Seventh Commandment

Jesus not only upheld the seventh commandment,[75] but also advised against even looking at a woman in a lusting manner: "You have heard that it was said, 'You shall not commit adultery.' But I say to you that everyone who looks at a woman with lust has already committed adultery with her in his heart."[76] Why did Jesus counsel against even looking? Because with the act of looking may come conversation, from which may come seclusion, followed by the actual act of adultery itself.[77] For this reason, Judaism has traditionally prohibited a man from being alone with any woman that is not his wife, mother, or daughter.[78] In short, both Judaism and Christianity believe that it is better for all concerned to not put temptation in the path of a man or woman.[79]

Eighth Commandment:
Do Not Steal

The eighth commandment is, "You shall not steal."[80] But what is it that one is prohibited from stealing? Many Jewish commentators[81] hold that the prohibition refers to the stealing of human beings, that is, kidnapping. How do we know this? The penalty for kidnapping is death,[82] as it is also for murder[83] and adultery,[84] which are prohibited by the sixth[85] and seventh[86] commandments of the Decalogue. But for mere theft, the Torah provides that the thief pay back several times what he stole.[87] Because it would have been odd for the sixth and seventh commandments, which both prohibit capital crimes, to be followed by a commandment prohibiting a crime that did not also carry the death penalty, most Jewish commentators take the position that the eighth commandment is limited to kidnapping. Nevertheless, some rabbinical commentators[88] hold that the eighth commandment prohibits any and all sorts of fraud, misrepresentation, and dishonesty.

It is noteworthy that unlike many other legal systems, past and present, Judaism does not inflict the death penalty or any type of corporal punishment on ordinary, nonviolent thieves. In such cases, restitution or compensation to the victim is the goal.[89]

Ninth Commandment:
Do Not Bear False Witness

The ninth commandment teaches us, "You shall not bear false witness against your neighbor."[90] There is an old adage, "Sticks and stones can break my bones, but words can never harm me." Judaism, however, does not subscribe to this expression. We have previously seen that using words to humiliate someone is deemed murder in a figurative sense.[91] With the ninth commandment, we again see how words can be harmful. If witnesses lie, a person may wrongfully be deprived of his property or life.[92] It is, therefore, understandable why truth in testimony is one of the Ten Commandments. Indeed, truth in testimony is deemed so important that a witness who lies could even be subject to the death penalty.[93]

Ninth Commandment Includes All Types of Lies

The ninth commandment is not limited to fraudulent testimony in court. The sages held that the ninth commandment would also prohibit a litigant from trying to bluff a legal adversary into thinking that there are witnesses against him.[94] By rabbinical interpretation, the ninth commandment also prohibits gossip and slander generally.[95] Why is malicious talk also prohibited? The Torah is aware that it takes a lifetime to build a reputation, but only a moment to have it come crashing down. "I heard that he beats his wife and children" will destroy anyone's reputation, notwithstanding actual innocence.[96] In brief, the ninth commandment requires people to act truthfully all the time.[97]

Tenth Commandment: Do Not Covet

The last commandment prohibits coveting of any type: "You shall not covet your neighbor's house; you shall not covet your neighbor's wife, or male or female slave, or ox, or donkey, or anything that belongs to your neighbor."[98]

It is interesting that although the first commandment of the Decalogue deals with faith, to believe in God,[99] the other commandments all deal with action: to not make or bow down to idols;[100] to not utter God's name in vain;[101] to keep the sabbath holy;[102] to honor one's parents;[103] and to not murder, philander, steal, or lie.[104] But coveting seems to deal strictly with emotions and thoughts. Does God punish someone for having emotions and thoughts?

God Does Not Punish Mere Thought

The traditional Jewish view of the tenth commandment is that a person does not incur sin merely by having a thought or an emotion.[105] As the prophet Micah wrote, "They covet fields, *and seize them*."[106] Sin is incurred only when the person *acts* on the thought or emotion. Thus, if a married man has impure sexual thoughts when seeing a woman other than his wife, but does not act on those thoughts, he does not incur sin.

But why does Judaism teach that God does not punish mere thought? The answer is that while faith is important in Jewish life,[107] and one should perform God's will with proper intention,[108] Judaism is essentially a religion of action and deeds.[109] Consequently, action is what is most important, not thought and not emotion.

None of which is to say that Judaism encourages a person to have impure thoughts.[110] To the contrary, a person should strive to have only pure thoughts.[111]

Jesus' View of the Tenth Commandment

As discussed earlier, with regard to the seventh commandment, Jesus taught, "You have heard that it was said, 'You shall not commit adultery.' But I say to you that everyone who looks at a woman with lust has already committed adultery with her in his heart."[112] Did Jesus teach that mere thought incurs sin? Many Christians do indeed take that position.[113] But is it also possible to interpret Jesus' teaching in a manner consistent with the traditional Jewish view that one does not incur sin as a result of mere thought?

It may be argued that a man who "looks at a woman with lust" has gone beyond mere thought; he *looks* to lust after her, meaning that flirtation of some sort has begun. Consistent with the view that Judaism deems looking to be a type of action, and beyond mere thought, is the rabbinical teaching that a man who walks behind a woman crossing a stream has committed sin: If she were to lift up her dress to avoid getting wet, he would see her in an immodest light.[114] Note that the man has committed sin merely by walking behind the woman; she may not actually lift up her dress. Thus, the man is punished not for looking and seeing, but for looking in order that he might see. In this regard, the traditional Jewish view that thought does not incur sin but looking does can be readily reconciled with Jesus' teaching that looking to lust is sinful. Of course, those Christians who interpret Jesus' words to mean that mere thought is sinful would hold a view different from that found in Judaism.[115]

The Two Versions of the Ten Commandments

One final matter needs to be addressed at this point: the two versions of the Ten Commandments. The version of the Ten Commandments that is stated in Exodus[116] is slightly different from the one found in Deuteronomy.[117] For example, in Exodus, the commandment is to "remember the sabbath,"[118] but in Deuteronomy, it is to "observe the sabbath."[119] How can we account for the difference? The traditional answer is that God miraculously spoke both versions at the same time.[120] For this reason, a sabbath-observing Jew will both remember the sabbath,[121] by sanctifying it as a holy day, and observe the sabbath,[122] by not desecrating it.

In the next chapter, we discuss the second of the five questions which we have previously set out:[123] What other kinds of laws exist in Judaism, and where are all of these laws found?

CHAPTER 4

Other Commandments

We have earlier seen that Judaism is both a religion and a legal system comprising three categories of laws: criminal, civil, and religious. In this chapter, we shall learn that the laws of Judaism are more numerous than those found in the Decalogue.

The Need for Laws in the New Nation of Israel

With the Exodus from Egypt[1] and the subsequent Revelation on Mount Sinai,[2] the Jewish people were poised to take possession of the land which God had given them when he entered into his covenant with Abraham.[3] The Jewish people had thus become a nation. But what were to be the laws for this new nation? Certainly the Ten Commandments[4] were to form an integral part of the jurisprudence of the Jewish people. But as with any nation, to regulate the many aspects of life, numerous laws would be necessary, and not just the ten provided in the Decalogue.

Many Laws Needed

There would have to be a wide range of laws to deal with societal problems, as well as interpersonal relationships. Thus, the Israelites would need laws to deal with criminal behavior and tortious conduct, as well as laws to determine the manner in which criminal and civil trials would be conducted. Legislation would also be necessary to regulate the conduct of property owners and businessmen. Furthermore, recognizing that every society has a segment that is poor, ordinances would be required to deal with those who were least able to fend for themselves. And what about marriage and divorce? Laws would be needed to handle this, too. In addition, because the Israelites were allowed to own property, laws providing for the distribution of a decedent's estate would also be indispensable. Moreover, since Israel had an army, laws would be essential to regulate its military. Consequently, there would have to be commandments in a wide variety of fields: criminal law, tort law, judicial law, business law, social welfare law, family law, inheritance law, and even military law, to name just a few categories. What's more, since Israel was founded as a theocracy, there would have to be religious laws.

The reader is undoubtedly interested in knowing the author of these laws. Briefly, the traditional Jewish view is that because God is the author of the Torah,[5] he is necessarily also the author of all of the Torah's laws. We discuss this point in greater depth in the next chapter.

We will now consider some of the commandments in these various areas of law. It must be emphasized that this analysis is not in any way even close to being a complete examination of Jewish law. To reduce Jewish law to a few pages would be no more possible than similarly reducing the whole of American jurisprudence. As such, I have merely attempted to expose the reader to a small sample of Jewish law, and to reveal some of its more interesting aspects.

Criminal Laws

Every society needs to protect its citizens by punishing those who have committed criminal acts against fellow citizens, and Israel was no different.

Murder and Capital Punishment

We have previously seen that the sixth commandment of the Decalogue prohibits murder,[6] the taking of human life with malice aforethought.[7]

The Bible also provides that the punishment for murder shall be death.[8] Capital punishment is thus Biblically sanctioned. Nevertheless, the defendant was given many procedural protections. For example, two witnesses were necessary; a defendant could not be convicted on the basis of one witness alone.[9]

Manslaughter

But what if someone kills another not intentionally but accidentally? For example, someone is chopping wood and the hatchet negligently slips out of his hand, killing a passerby.[10] This crime is modernly called involuntary manslaughter. The Torah says about such a crime: "Whoever strikes a person mortally shall be put to death. If it was not premeditated, but came about by an act of God, then I will appoint for you a place to which the killer may flee."[11] Although a murderer is to be put to death,[12] someone who negligently causes the death of another ("came about by an act of God") does not suffer the death penalty. Rather, such a person flees to one of a number of cities which God has provided ("a place to which the killer may flee"), a city of refuge.

Cities of Refuge

What was the purpose of these so-called cities of refuge? It was to give the wrongdoer a place to go to flee from the "avenger,"[13] that is, a relative of the decedent. In ancient times, if a person killed another, whether accidentally or on purpose, the clan of the decedent would exact vengeance. But Jewish law prescribed otherwise. Because Judaism is an ethical legal system, individuals and their families were not to mete out vigilante justice. Only the courts could punish, and only when there was due process. As the Torah states, "Justice, and only justice, you shall pursue."[14] Thus, in the case of a killing, the alleged killer could flee to a city of refuge and be safe from the avenger. Trial would then be held at the place where the killing took place, during which time the alleged killer would be under the protection of the judiciary. If the trial established that the defendant was not guilty, he would then be set free, and the avenger was forever prohibited from exacting vengeance. On the other hand, if the trial established that the defendant was guilty of murder, he would be executed in accordance with the law. If the trial established that he was guilty of involuntary manslaughter, the defendant would be exiled to a city of refuge as punishment.[15] Thus, the city of refuge served as a temporary haven for one accused of murder, as well as a place of exile in the event that the defendant was convicted of involuntary manslaughter.

Incest

Another crime was incest, and the Torah sets out all of the prohibited relationships.[16] These prohibited relationships are with one's parents; mother-in-law; stepmother; sister and half-sister; granddaughter; father's and mother's sister; wife of father's brother; daughter-in-law; brother's wife; stepdaughter and step-granddaughter; and the wife's sister during the wife's lifetime.[17] For some of these illicit relationships, capital punishment was prescribed.[18] Thus, "the man who lies with his father's wife has uncovered his father's nakedness; both of them shall be put to death; their blood is upon them."[19] In other ancient societies, incestuous relationships were often the norm. But because Israel was a holy nation, its people were not to engage in such behavior: "So keep my charge not to commit any of these abominations that were done before you, and not to defile yourselves by them: I am the LORD your God."[20]

Homosexual Intercourse

Similarly, other societies allowed or even encouraged homosexual intercourse. To this day, ancient Greece remains the most notorious in this regard. But the Jewish people are absolutely prohibited from engaging in this kind of conduct: "You shall not lie with a male as with a woman; it is an abomination."[21] The penalty for homosexual sodomy is death.[22] Bestiality is also prohibited and, like homosexual sodomy, is punishable by death.[23] Penile-vaginal intercourse between a man and his wife, for love and procreation, is the only appropriate type of intercourse.[24]

Theft

We now turn to another crime, theft, which is dealt with in the Book of

Exodus: "When someone steals an ox or a sheep, and slaughters it or sells it, the thief shall pay five oxen for an ox, and four sheep for a sheep."[25] The Torah further provides that in all other cases of theft, the thief "shall pay double."[26] It is interesting to note that the Torah does not inflict any sort of corporal punishment on an ordinary thief. Rather, by making the wrongdoer pay back several times what was taken, the victim is compensated for the loss and the thief learns that crime truly does not pay.

Punishment for Criminals

One may wonder why the thief does not go to prison. The reason is that Jewish law does not use incarceration as a method of punishment for any criminal, thief or otherwise. The only time that a defendant is constrained is for the short period of time while being bound over for trial.[27] During that time, the defendant is placed in a holding cell, what the county jail is used for in our own system of criminal jurisprudence. Other than that, the traditional punishments for a convicted criminal are execution, as in the case of a murder or other capital crime;[28] exile to a city of refuge in the case of an accidental killing;[29] money damages in the case of theft;[30] or lashes.[31]

Lashes Limited in Number

Where lashes were in order, they could not exceed forty.[32] This is to be contrasted with other societies where wrongdoers were often whipped to death. Indeed, as late as the nineteenth century, the British Royal Navy often administered literally hundreds of lashes to seamen who had violated various rules of conduct, typically killing the offenders in the process. But Israel was to be different from the other nations of the world.

To make certain that the number of lashes would not exceed forty by mistake, the ancient rabbis decreed that thirty-nine was the maximum number that could be administered. Moreover, the physical condition of the wrongdoer was a significant factor in the determination of his sentence. A defendant who was not strong received fewer lashes than one who was robust. If the defendant was not able to tolerate the sentence during its administration, the sentence could be commuted then and there. If the defendant died during the administration of the lashes, the one charged with carrying out the sentence could be tried for involuntary manslaughter.[33]

The Scourging and Crucifixion of Jesus

The scourging of Jesus was ordered by Pontius Pilate, a Roman official, and carried out by a Roman military detachment under Roman law.[34] Jesus' subsequent crucifixion was also governed solely by Roman law, as Jewish law absolutely prohibited this slow and ghastly torturous means of death.[35] Indeed, the victims of crucifixion often languished in agony for several days before death mercifully overtook them. Jewish law, on the other hand, provided that the execution of the defendant had to be virtually instantaneous. The basis for this law is founded on the Torah's injunction, "you shall love your neighbor."[36] Even while requiring justice, the Torah mandates compassion.

In this regard, a "hanging" in Jewish law stands in contrast to the horror of crucifixion: "When someone is convicted of a crime punishable by death and is executed, and you hang him on a tree, his corpse must not remain all night upon the tree; you shall bury him that same day, for anyone hung on a tree is under God's curse."[37] This law requires one who has been convicted of idolatry or blasphemy and already executed ("and is executed") to be hung upon a tree ("and you hang him on a tree") for a brief period of time ("his corpse must not remain all night upon the tree"). The hanging of a corpse from a tree for a few moments is obviously different from the hanging of a living person from a cross for several days.[38] The purpose of briefly hanging the corpse was to impress upon the people that the defendant committed the terrible crime of idolatry or blasphemy ("for anyone hung on a tree is under God's curse").[39]

Jewish Criminal Law Today

As mentioned earlier,[40] Jewish criminal law is not presently operative in the modern State of Israel. Nevertheless, its importance should not in any way be minimized since Jewish criminal law has had a tremendous impact on Western jurisprudence in general, and American jurisprudence in particular. For example, in the famous United States Supreme Court case of *Miranda v. Arizona*[41] (where it was held that police must advise a defendant in custody of the right to remain silent), the court discussed at some length how Jewish law precludes a person from self-incrimination.

Tort Laws

A tort is defined as a civil wrong not involving contract. Thus, when someone negligently injures another, such action comes under the umbrella of tort law. If found liable, the wrongdoer must pay monetary damages. In ancient societies, if a person accidentally took out the eye of another, the family of the injured person would often do the same to the wrongdoer, or worse, such as taking out both eyes of the wrongdoer or even killing him. Ancient Israel could not engage in this kind of bestial retaliation, however. With a well-defined body of tort law, the remedy given to the victim was for the wrongdoer to pay money damages. For example, "When individuals quarrel and one strikes the other with a stone or fist so that the injured party, though not dead, is confined to bed, but recovers and walks around the outside with the help of a staff, then the assailant shall be free of liability, except to pay for the loss of time, and to arrange for full recovery."[42] Thus, the person who assaults another must pay for the damages suffered by the victim, which include the cost of medical care. Similarly, if one's animal injures another's, one must pay damages to the owner of the injured animal.[43] If one sets a fire on his own property, and the fire spreads to another's property, "the one who started the fire shall make full restitution."[44]

Many people think that the "eye for an eye" doctrine sanctioned physical retaliation.[45] This is not a correct interpretation of Jewish law, however, as we shall see when we discuss the oral law.[46]

Judicial Laws

No society can be civilized and decent without an independent and honest judiciary. The many millions of innocent victims who died in Hitler's Germany and Stalin's Russia are testimony to this fact. Thus, ancient Israel had many laws directed to the judiciary to ensure that it would remain of the highest integrity. For example, judges were instructed, "You shall not pervert the justice due to your poor in their lawsuits,"[47] meaning that a judge must not prevent a poor person from having his or her case heard. Judges were further exhorted, "Keep far from a false charge, and do not kill the innocent and those in the right, for I [God] will not acquit the guilty. You shall take no bribe, for a bribe blinds the officials, and subverts the cause of those who are in the right. You shall not oppress a resident alien; you know the heart of an alien, for you were aliens in the land of Egypt."[48] In short, nothing less than the highest degree of integrity was demanded of Israel's judiciary.

As discussed earlier,[49] while the Sanhedrin does not presently exist, the three-judge court (*beth din*) has endured in Israel (formerly Palestine) and in all Jewish communities worldwide, where it is instrumental in allowing Jewish couples to obtain a religious divorce. The three-judge court is also helpful in resolving disputes among Jewish businesspeople, who may seek to avoid the secular court system (and its costs and delays) by submitting their case to the local beth din.

Business Laws

Just as honesty is required of the judiciary, so too is it required of merchants. "You shall not have in your bag two kinds of weights, large and small. You shall not have in your house two kinds of measures, large and small. You shall have only a full and honest weight; you shall have only a full and honest measure, so that your days may be long in the land that the LORD your God is giving you."[50]

Not only is honesty required, but fairness is, too. Thus, many laws existed to make certain that one would not take unfair advantage of another. For example, creditors were to give their debtors a release after seven years.[51] Consequently, if a person in dire circumstances encumbered himself with too much debt, he could be assured of a fresh start after seven years (the precursor to modern bankruptcy protection). With respect to real estate, additional rules made certain that a desperate person would not permanently dispossess himself of the family home. This was done by providing that real estate could not be sold to another in perpetuity; a landowner could "sell" his property for a maximum term of fifty years only.[52] After that time, the land automatically reverted to the original owner or his heirs. Thus, few if any Israelites would ever permanently suffer from homelessness. Every Jew would have a place to call home.

In the realm of employment law, employers are prohibited from taking advantage of employees: "You shall not withhold the wages of poor and needy laborers, whether other Israelites or aliens who reside in your land in one of your towns. You must pay them their wages daily before sunset, because they are poor and their livelihood depends on them; otherwise they might cry to the LORD against you, and you would incur guilt."[53]

And in any transaction, the Torah declares, "you shall not cheat one another."[54]

Social Welfare Laws

Legislation existed to make certain that those who may have difficulty in taking care of themselves would nevertheless be assured of a life of dignity. For example, "You shall not wrong or oppress a resident alien, for you were aliens in the land of Egypt."[55] The oppression in slavery and Exodus from Egypt are recalled daily in Jewish prayers. Here the Exodus serves to remind the Jew to be compassionate to one who is not native born. Racism and xenophobia have no place in Judaism.

"You shall not abuse any widow or orphan."[56] The widow and the orphan are traditionally the most powerless and helpless members of society. The Torah here makes it clear that they are to be treated compassionately, and not taken advantage of in any way. To make it clear that these individuals are to be treated properly, the Jewish people are warned by God, "If you do abuse them, when they cry out to me, I will surely heed their cry; my wrath will burn, and I will kill you with the sword, and your wives shall become widows and your children orphans."[57] Elsewhere farmers are instructed, "When you reap your harvest in your field and forget a sheaf in the field, you shall not go back to get it; it shall be left for the alien, the orphan, and the widow, so that the LORD your God may bless you in all your undertakings."[58]

The poor have always been a segment of every society. Jewish law specifically makes provision for them in many respects. For example, "If you lend money to my people, to the poor among you, you shall not deal with them as a creditor; you shall not exact interest from them."⁵⁹ Thus, a Jew who makes a loan to another Jew cannot charge interest. As a consequence, since ancient times, Jewish Free Loan Societies have been an integral part of Jewish communities, wherever they may arise. In fact, to this day, there are Free Loan Societies in Israel, as well as in Jewish communities throughout the Diaspora. For those who need outright assistance, and not mere loans, such assistance must be given without any equivocation: "Every third year you shall bring out the full tithe of your produce for that year, and store it within your towns; the Levites, because they have no allotment or inheritance with you, as well as the resident aliens, the orphans, and the widows in your towns, may come and eat their fill so that the LORD your God may bless you in all the work that you undertake."⁶⁰ It is because of these and other social welfare laws that giving to charity has always been a significant part of Jewish law and life.

Other segments of society which need special attention are people who are blind or otherwise disabled, whether physically or spiritually. Jewish law mandates special treatment for them too: "You shall not revile the deaf or put a stumbling block before the blind; you shall fear your God: I am the LORD."⁶¹

Perhaps the best known of all the social welfare laws is to love one's neighbor: "You shall love your neighbor as yourself: I am the LORD."⁶² This, one rabbinical sage declared, is a basic precept of Jewish law.⁶³

Family Laws

There is a holiness associated with marriage and the marital relationship.⁶⁴ In fact, so important is marriage that the Bible states: "When a man is newly married, he shall not go out with the army or be charged with any related duty. He shall be free at home one year, to be happy with the wife whom he has married."⁶⁵

Nevertheless, Judaism recognizes that a bad marriage is not good for anyone concerned. Therefore, Jewish law, while recognizing the beauty and holiness of marriage, also provides for divorce: "Suppose a man enters into marriage with a woman, but she does not please him because he finds something objectionable about her, and so he writes her a certificate of divorce, puts it in her hand, and sends her out of his house; she then leaves his house and goes off to become another man's wife."[66]

Still, even though divorce is available, limitations are imposed. One significant limitation is the *kettubah*, the significant marriage settlement that the husband must pay his wife to obtain a divorce.[67] The requirement of the kettubah makes certain that no husband treats divorce lightly. The kettubah also ensures that no Jewish wife is left destitute following a divorce. Unlike her counterparts in other societies, past and present, a Jewish woman is not to be left financially abandoned following a marital dissolution.

Jewish family law remains fully operative today, not only in Israel, but in the Diaspora as well. Thus, in the United States, an observant Jew who obtains a civil divorce decree must also secure a religious divorce from a rabbinical court.

Inheritance Laws

Most societies have laws dealing with the distribution of a decedent's estate. Ancient Israel, as a nation that recognized the right to own property, also had inheritance laws to provide for the distribution of a person's estate at death. "If a man dies, and has no son, then you shall pass his inheritance on to his daughter. If he has no daughter, then you shall give his inheritance to his brothers. If he has no brothers, then you shall give his inheritance to his father's brothers. And if his father has no brothers, then you shall give his inheritance to the nearest kinsman of his clan, and he shall possess it."[68] While the son was to have priority over daughters, the daughters were nevertheless to be provided for by the income from the estate, and if that was not sufficient, then from the principal itself.[69] Thus, unlike many other societies where the sons inherited the estate and the unwed daughters were cast out penniless, leaving them to choose between a life of slavery or prostitution for survival, the laws of ancient Israel were different, ensuring that Jewish girls did not end up in brothels.[70]

The succession laws of the modern State of Israel comport with traditional Jewish law in a number of aspects. Thus, we see yet again how Jewish law is very much a vibrant doctrine.

Military Laws

Unfortunate though it may be, a strong military is necessary for any nation, especially one that is surrounded by hostile or potentially hostile nations (as was the case with ancient Israel, and still is the case with the modern State of Israel). Ancient Israel therefore needed a set of laws dealing with its citizen army. The following laws are illustrative.

Soldiers Must Be Adults

First, no one fought who was under the age of twenty: "From twenty years old and upward, everyone in Israel [must be] able to go to war."[71] This is to be contrasted with the armies of many other societies, past and present, who have used children to fight. During World War II, for example, as the Allies were closing in on a depleted German Army, the Nazis drafted boys as young as thirteen years of age to fight. During the Iranian-Iraqi war in the 1980s, Iran used schoolchildren to walk across minefields to clear the way for its infantry. In Africa today, warring factions regularly use children to fill up the ranks, and it is not unusual to see a ten-year-old toting an AK-47 assault rifle (which is often not much smaller than the "soldier" carrying it). In fact, according to a recent United Nations report ("The Impact of Armed Conflict on Children"), several hundred thousand children were under arms at any given time in 1996. The report also stated that two million of these "soldiers" had died in combat during the previous ten years. Many of those killed were as young as ten years of age. But Israel was to be different from other nations.

Countryside Cannot Be Wasted

In preparing to lay siege to a city, it was common for ancient armies to destroy all trees within miles of the city to make battering rams, catapults, siege towers, etc. As a consequence, fruit-bearing trees were destroyed, which deprived the local inhabitants, often innocent noncombatants, of an important source of food. But Israel could not wage unrestricted warfare: "If you besiege a town for a long time, making war against it in order to take it, you must not destroy its trees by wielding an ax against them. Although you may take food from them, you must not cut them down. Are trees in the field human beings that they should come under siege from you? You may destroy only the trees that you know do not produce food; you may cut them down for use in building siege works against the town that makes war with you, until it falls."[72]

Enemy to Be Offered Peace

Before storming a city, the Israelites had to offer its inhabitants peace, thus making certain that all diplomatic efforts failed before blood was shed: "When you draw near to a town to fight against it, offer it terms of peace. If it accepts your terms of peace and surrenders to you, then all the people in it shall serve you at forced labor."[73] Only if the idolatrous nation refused to accept peace could the Israelites attack it.[74] Among the terms of peace that the city had to agree to was the renunciation of idolatry,[75] which typically involved the practices of human sacrifice and ritual rape.[76]

Modest Treatment of Women

In contrast to other nations, Jewish soldiers had to treat the women of the conquered city in a proper manner. When ancient armies subdued a foreign nation, the women were brutally raped on the battlefield.[77] Indeed, this behavior has continued even into modern times. For example, when Imperial Japanese Army soldiers captured the city of Nanking in 1937, the victors brutally raped not just thousands, but scores of thousands, of Chinese women. Many others were taken prisoner and forced to serve in brothels, as sex slaves for Japanese troops. The soldiers of Nazi Germany did likewise to many young Jewish women, sparing them from death in the gas chamber for death in a brothel.

But the armies of ancient Israel could not participate in such a grotesque behavior:

> *When you go out to war against your enemies, and the*
> *Lord your God hands them over to you and you take them*
> *captive, suppose you see among the captives a beautiful woman*
> *whom you desire and want to marry, and so you bring her*

home to your house: she shall shave her head, pare her nails,
discard her captive's garb, and shall remain in your house a
full month, mourning for her father and mother; after that
you may go in to her and be her husband, and she shall be your
wife. But if you are not satisfied with her, you shall let her go
free and not sell her for money. You must not treat her as a
slave, since you have dishonored her.[78]

Thus, when a Jewish warrior saw a woman whom he wanted, he could not rape her on the battlefield. He had to first take her home ("bring her home to your house"). Then she had to make herself unattractive to him ("she shall shave her head, pare her nails"). She then mourned for her parents, who probably had died in the fighting. The mourning lasted for a full month. Only then could the soldier have her ("go in to her"), but, and this is significant, she then became his wife ("she shall be your wife"). The importance of this cannot be underestimated. A Jewish wife is to be provided for in various ways. As the Torah states, "he shall not diminish the food, clothing, or marital rights of the . . . wife,"[79] meaning that by Biblical law, a husband owes his wife food, clothing, and sexual relations (in which the *wife* must be sexually satisfied). In essence, an Israelite soldier could take a woman, but he could not be intimate with her for at least a month. When he did become intimate with her, she became his wife, and he secured for himself all the responsibilities that went with it. Truly, these were great disincentives for a soldier to want a captive woman. We can thus see how the Torah sought to bring humanity even to the battlefield. As the Book of Proverbs says of the Torah, "Her ways are ways of pleasantness, and all her paths are peace."[80]

"Purity of Arms" Doctrine

We have previously discussed how Judaism is not a mere historical phenomenon, but a vibrant religious-legal system. With its many rules of conduct, Judaism allows a person to lead a life that is virtuous and, by so doing, to reach a new and higher level of holiness. This is well illustrated in the way that the armed forces of modern-day Israel, the Israel Defense Forces (IDF), conduct warfare.

An integral part of IDF policy is its "Purity of Arms" doctrine, which is founded on the ethical principles of warfare we have just discussed. Purity of Arms requires Israeli forces to accomplish their military objectives while minimizing civilian (Arab as well as Jewish) casualties as much as possible, even while increasing the risk to their own soldiers. Moreover, Purity of Arms is not just theory, but a regularly applied principle. For example, when the IDF captured east Jerusalem from the Jordanian Army in the 1967 Six-Day War, it did so without the benefit of air support in an effort to minimize Arab civilian casualties. In 1982, when the Israeli Air Force bombed the Iraqi nuclear plant under construction, a Sunday was purposely selected as the day of the attack because workers would not be on the job site. (A scientist who had gone in to catch up on some paperwork was the only casualty in the raid.) In 1996, when the IDF launched a land, sea, and air attack against Iranian-backed Hezbollah guerrillas in Lebanon, Israel gave targeted villages six hours notice before beginning the attack so that civilians could safely leave the area before the shooting began. Would that others conduct warfare in the manner of the IDF! But until that happens, Israel again stands apart from the other nations of the world.

Religious Laws

Many of the laws of the Torah are religious in nature. Of course, all of the laws of Judaism are religious in a sense because, as we shall see, each and every one was promulgated by God.[81] We now give a few examples of the religious laws that govern the life of the Jew.

Passover

Many religious laws deal with the celebration of various festivals. One of the most popular is Passover, which commemorates the Exodus of the Jewish people from hundreds of years of slavery in Egypt. An extremely important part of this festival is to eat unleavened bread (*matzah*), as did the Israelites, who did not have time to bake their bread with leaven: They had to bake it quickly and eat it in haste because Egypt had just been struck with the last of the ten plagues, the slaying of the firstborn, and the Redemption was about to begin. The Torah beautifully explains this joyous holiday:

The LORD said to Moses and Aaron in the land of Egypt: This month shall mark for you the beginning of months; it shall be the first month of the year for you. Tell the whole congregation of Israel that on the tenth of this month, they are to take a lamb for each family, a lamb for each household. If a household is too small for a whole lamb, it shall join its closest neighbor in obtaining one; the lamb shall be divided in proportion to the number of people who eat of it. Your lamb shall be without blemish, a year-old male; you may take it from the sheep or from the goats. You shall keep it until the fourteenth day of this month; then the whole assembled congregation of Israel shall slaughter it at twilight. They shall take some of the blood and put it on the two doorposts and the lintel of the houses in which they eat it. They shall eat the lamb that same night; they shall eat it roasted over the fire with unleavened bread and bitter herbs. Do not eat any of it raw or boiled in water, but roasted over the fire, with its head, legs, and inner organs. You shall let none of it remain until the morning; anything that remains until the morning you shall burn. This is how you shall eat it: your loins girded, your sandals on your feet, and your staff in your hand; and you shall eat it hurriedly. It is the passover of the LORD. For I will pass through the land of Egypt that night, and I will strike down every first born in the land of Egypt, both human beings and animals; on all the gods of Egypt I will execute judgment: I am the LORD. The blood shall be a sign for you on the houses where you live: when I see the blood, I will pass over you, and no plague shall destroy you when I strike the land of Egypt.

This day shall be a day of remembrance for you. You shall celebrate it as a festival to the LORD; throughout your generations you shall observe it as a perpetual ordinance.

Seven days you shall eat unleavened bread; on the first day you shall remove leaven from your houses, for whoever eats leavened bread from the first day until the seventh day shall be cut off from Israel. . . . For seven days no leaven shall be found in your houses; for whoever eats what is leavened shall be cut off from the congregation of Israel, whether an alien or a native of the land. You shall eat nothing unleavened; in all your settlements you shall eat unleavened bread.[82]

As many Christians are aware, Jesus' Last Supper was the celebration of Passover.[83]

Feast of Weeks

Another religious law requires the Jewish people to observe the Feast of Weeks:

You shall count seven weeks; begin to count the seven weeks from the time the sickle is first put to the standing grain. Then you shall keep the festival of weeks to the LORD your God, contributing a freewill offering in proportion to the blessing that you have received from the LORD your God. Rejoice before the LORD your God—you and your sons and your daughters, your male and female slaves, the Levites resident in your towns, as well as the strangers, the orphans, and the widows who are among you—at the place that the LORD your God will choose as a dwelling for his name.[84]

The "seven weeks" to be counted corresponds to the seven weeks from the Exodus to the giving of the Ten Commandments on Mount Sinai. Thus, not only was this holiday to correspond to harvest time ("from the time the sickle is first put to the standing grain"), but also, and more importantly, it was to correspond to the Revelation. This holiday, called *Shavuot* in Hebrew ("weeks"), is known in the Christian religion as Pentecost.[85] Note also that the holiday is a happy one ("rejoice before the LORD"), in which even non-Jewish servants ("your male and

female slaves") are free to participate. Jewish servants are, of course, required to participate because they are Jewish.

Feast of Tabernacles

The Feast of Tabernacles, called *Sukkot* in Hebrew ("booths" or "tabernacles"), is yet another holiday that Jews must celebrate:

> *You shall keep the festival of booths for seven days, when
> you have gathered in the produce from your threshing floor
> and your wine press. Rejoice during your festival, you and your
> sons and your daughters, your male and female slaves, as well
> as the Levites, the strangers, the orphans, and the widows resi-
> dent in your towns. Seven days you shall keep the festival to
> the* LORD *your God at the place that the* LORD *will choose; for
> the* LORD *your God will bless you in all your produce and in all
> your undertakings, and you shall surely celebrate.*[86]

As with Shavuot, although the Feast of Tabernacles is tied to an agricultural event ("when you have gathered in the produce from your
threshing floor and your wine press"), the holiday is also tied to the Exodus. During the forty years that the Jewish people wandered in the desert,
their shelters were temporary or movable booths (tabernacles). As the
Torah states: "You shall live in booths for seven days; all that are citizens
in Israel shall live in booths, so that your generations may know that I
made the people of Israel live in booths when I brought them out of the
land of Egypt: I am the LORD your God."[87]

Jewish New Year

The celebration of *Rosh Hashanah* (literally, "head of the year") is the
Jewish New Year, and is another Biblical holiday. An important part of
the holiday is to hear in synagogue the blowing of a ram's horn (*shofar* in
Hebrew), what the New Revised Standard Version renders as "trumpet":
"In the seventh month, on the first day of the month, you shall observe a
day of complete rest, a holy convocation commemorated with trumpet
blasts."[88] The blowing of the ram's horn was first heard by the Israelites
just prior to the Revelation on Mount Sinai.[89] At that moment, the Jewish

people were at such a high state of spirituality that "all the people saw the thunderings."[90] Incredibly, they did not just hear thunder; they actually saw it. As the ram's horn heard at Mount Sinai was the precursor to the Revelation and the high state of spirituality of the Jewish people, the blowing of the ram's horn on each Rosh Hashanah is a call for the Jewish people to raise their level of spirituality by engaging in repentance.

Day of Atonement

Ten days after Rosh Hashanah is *Yom Kippur* ("day of atonement"), a solemn day in which Jews ask God to forgive them for sins they committed against him. Yom Kippur is a day of prayer and introspection, all for the purpose of changing wayward behavior. Part of the holiday includes a twenty-five-hour fast. "Now, the tenth day of this seventh month is the day of atonement; it shall be a holy convocation for you: you shall deny yourselves and present the LORD's offering by fire; and you shall do no work during that entire day; for it is a day of atonement on your behalf before the LORD your God."[91]

Contrary to what many erroneously believe, fasting and prayer on Yom Kippur can atone only for sins committed against God, but not for sins committed against one's neighbor. To obtain atonement for sins committed against one's neighbor, one must either right the wrong or, if that is not possible, beg the person's forgiveness. This view of atonement is, of course, decidedly different from the view of atonement held by many— but not all—Christians: "For we hold that a person is justified by faith apart from works prescribed by the law."[92]

Prayer Attire

The religious laws prescribing the celebration of various holidays serve to praise God for his wonders and triumphs, and to raise the level of spirituality and observance of the Jewish people. But the celebration of these yearly holidays is not the only way that Jews are reminded of God's omnipotence and their own need to attain greater spirituality. There are other ways. One way is to observe the weekly sabbath.[93] Another is to abide by laws prescribing appropriate prayer attire.

For morning prayers excluding the sabbath, a Jewish man must wear *tefillin* (phylacteries): two leather straps, one worn on the head and the other bound around his arm. The basis for this is found in the Torah: "Bind them as a sign on your hand, fix them as a frontlet on your forehead. . . ."[94] In addition to wearing phylacteries, a Jewish man also must wear a prayer shawl, called a *tallit*. Unlike phylacteries, the tallit is worn every day during morning prayers. The basis for the tallit is also found in the Torah: "Speak to the Israelites, and tell them to make fringes on the corners of their garments throughout their generations and to put a blue cord on the fringe at each corner."[95] Furthermore, Jewish men wear hats or *yarmulkes* (skullcaps) whenever they participate in prayer services. Orthodox men cover their heads all their waking hours. The covering over the head serves as a reminder of the Almighty, who is over us all. In ancient times, the head was covered typically by draping the tallit over the head. Married Orthodox Jewish women cover their heads with a scarf or wig when they are in public because a married woman's hair is said to be her "crowning glory" and is to be viewed only by her husband.[96] Among the Conservative, Reform, and Reconstructionist movements—but not the Orthodox movement—a woman may also wear phylacteries, a tallit, and a yarmulke in the same manner as men.

Although most Christians and Jews do not envision Jesus wearing tefillin and a tallit, it is without doubt that he did.

Diet

Other religious laws deal with diet. One such law prohibits Jewish people from consuming blood, a custom practiced by many pagan societies. "If anyone of the house of Israel or of the aliens who reside among them eats any blood, I will set my face against that person who eats blood, and will cut that person off from the people."[97] Nor may a Jew eat any animal, but only that which "has divided hoofs and is cleft-footed and chews the cud—such you may eat."[98] Thus, a Jew may not eat "the camel, for even though it chews the cud, it does not have divided hoofs. . . . [nor the] hare, for even though it chews the cud, it does not have divided hoofs. . . . [nor the] pig, for even though it has divided hoofs and is cleft-footed, it does not chew the cud. . . ."[99]

Many people, Jews and Christians alike, believe that Jewish dietary

law is based on reasons of health since undercooked pork can cause illness. While undercooked pork can certainly cause illness, undercooked
chicken can, too. But chicken is not prohibited to the Jewish people while
pork is. Thus, there must be some other reason to explain why Jews can
eat chicken, but not pork. What is this reason? It is to make the Jewish
people holy.[100]

Spiritualism and Witchcraft Prohibited

Another religious law proscribes spiritualism and witchcraft: "No one
shall be found among you who makes a son or daughter pass through
fire [a pagan practice], or who practices divination, or is a soothsayer, or
an augur, or a sorcerer, or one who casts spells, or who consults ghosts or
spirits, or who seeks oracles from the dead."[101] Why were such paganlike
practices prohibited and dealt with so harshly? Because, as we have previously seen,[102] idolatry and its offshoots not only deny the One God,
but also cause people to engage in hideous practices, including child
sacrifice ("makes a son or daughter pass through fire").

We have examined only a small sampling of the many laws of Judaism. In fact, a total of 613 laws or commandments (*mitzvot* in Hebrew)
apply to the Jewish people (including the Ten Commandments); 248 in
the positive ("you shall") and 365 in the negative ("you shall not").[103]
Thus, there are many more commandments than those recited in the
Decalogue, that is, the Ten Commandments. And all of these 613 laws
or mitzvahs are found in the first five books of the Bible: Genesis, Exodus, Leviticus, Numbers, and Deuteronomy. As stated earlier,[104] these
books are commonly referred to as the Pentateuch, which is Greek for
"five books." In Hebrew, these five books are referred to as the *Torah*.
Although Torah is often interpreted as "law," it in fact means "instruction" or "understanding." The significance of this meaning will become
more apparent as we discuss our next question: Who is the author of
these laws?

CHAPTER 5

God the Author

Who is the author of the Torah and, therefore, of the laws of Judaism? To answer this question fully, we need to recall that there are currently four major movements within Judaism: Orthodox, Conservative, Reform, and Reconstructionist.[1] Orthodox Judaism is identified with the Judaism that has been practiced through the centuries, whereas the other movements are relatively recent developments. The Reform movement began in the mid-nineteenth century and was soon followed by the Conservative movement, whose members believed that traditional Judaism (which came to be known as Orthodox Judaism) was too rigid and Reform Judaism too liberal. In the 1930s, the Reconstructionist movement arose, believing that Judaism must "reconstruct" itself every generation to adapt to changing times and needs of the Jewish people. Let us now examine their views on the origins of the Torah. Then, we will discuss the laws of the Torah that seem "irrational." We conclude this chapter with a discussion of whether the Torah is "incomplete."

The Orthodox View of the Torah

As stated in the Thirteen Principles of Faith,[2] the traditional or Orthodox Jewish view is that the Torah is the literal word of God. Each and

71

every word was spoken by God to Moses, who dutifully wrote it down.[3] That work, originally in the Hebrew language, and copies of it were subsequently passed down from generation to generation. Of course, the original, like the tablets of the Ten Commandments, is either no longer in existence or remains hidden (many will recall the Harrison Ford movie, *Raiders of the Lost Ark*). But the traditional Jewish view is that the Hebrew-language text that is available now is the exact same text that was given to Moses some 3,600 years ago at Sinai.[4]

"The Law of the LORD"

Because God himself is the author of the entire Torah, he is also necessarily the author of all of the 613 commandments found therein.[5] Indeed, throughout the Torah, the *mitzvot* ("commandments") are typically prefaced with God telling Moses, "Thus you shall say to the Israelites,"[6] or "Speak to the people of Israel and say to them."[7] Moreover, there are numerous references in Scripture to the term "law of the LORD."[8] The Gospel of Luke also refers to the Torah as the "law of the LORD" when it states that Mary and Joseph complied with all aspects of the law.[9] The Bible sometimes refers to the Pentateuch as the "law of Moses"[10] only because Moses received the law directly from God and then wrote it down as directed by him for posterity.[11] It must always be remembered, however, that while Moses was the scrivener, the traditional Jewish view is that God and God alone is the author of each and every word of the Torah. This traditional view, one which existed through the centuries— and during Jesus' time—is espoused today by the Orthodox movement. The other movements within Judaism, however, do not share this perspective.

The Conservative View of the Torah

While the Orthodox view is easy to state, such cannot be said with respect to the Conservative movement. This is because there are three competing views regarding the origin and binding effect of the Torah within the Conservative movement:

1. One view holds that although God dictated his will at Sinai, humans

wrote it down, and this accounts for errors in the Torah.[12] Generally speaking, except for these errors, the laws of the Torah—both moral and ritual—must be obeyed by the Jewish people.

2. Another perspective is that humans wrote the Torah, but that they were Divinely inspired. This position, which recognizes the historical role of humans in the redaction of the Torah, gives the rabbinical community authority to distinguish the Divine from the human aspects of the Torah and to make changes in the laws to keep Judaism relevant for the times.

3. Still another Conservative perspective is that God did reveal himself to the Jewish people at Sinai, but that historical event was recorded in the Torah by humans. This position too allows for change in the laws. Although this view seems similar to the preceding one, the difference is that the proponents of this position emphasize the encounter individuals have had with God while simultaneously recognizing the need for tradition in the Jewish community.

All three positions hold that the Divine Revelation did take place at Sinai, but that humans also played a significant role in the Torah's redaction, thus necessitating scholarship that is both Biblical and historical in nature.

The Reform View of the Torah

The Reform movement takes the position that the Torah is God's will as written down by humans, and that as time progresses, we are better able to understand his will. As part of this "progressive revelation," the Reform movement holds that only God's moral laws have continuing authority; individuals may adhere to the ritual laws (such as the dietary laws), but they are not required to comply with them.

The Reconstructionist View of the Torah

The Reconstructionist movement, which emphasizes Judaism as a civilization, contends that the Torah was written by humans in search of God. As such, there is no Divine aspect to the Torah. Consequently, the

Reconstructionist movement teaches that each generation is free to "reconstruct" Judaism to make it more meaningful for its times. As with the Reform movement, each individual decides whether he or she is going to obey the ritual laws of the Torah.

All Movements Revere the Torah

In light of the traditional or Orthodox view that the Torah is the work of God, the Torah may be seen to be God's teaching or instruction to the Jewish people to enable them to lead a righteous life.[13] With its 613 commandments, the Torah is thus a complete text for virtuosity.[14] Orthodox Judaism believes that because a perfect God could give only a perfect Torah,[15] his Torah and the commandments therein are necessarily forever and for all time.[16] This is not, however, the traditional Christian view, as we have pointed out earlier. The Christian view is that the Torah, while good, finds perfection only in Jesus.[17] This belief represents a significant and fundamental difference between Orthodox Judaism and Christianity.

But what of the modern movements within Judaism? For the Conservatives and Reformers, the Torah is still the Divine Revelation and the bequest of the generation of the Exodus. As such, the Torah is more than just the embodiment of great teachings: It is the essence of Judaism because it represents the Jewish understanding of the Divine, as manifested through the commandments. Indeed, even the Reconstructionist movement holds the Torah dearly because it is the great pillar of Jewish civilization. And while all of these recent movements may allow change in varying degrees (such as driving to synagogue on the sabbath, something absolutely prohibited by the Orthodox movement), all believe that the Torah as a whole is a unique doctrine and, as such, cannot be supplanted or significantly changed by another testament.

The Torah as "Irrational" (or Superrational)

As indicated above, the traditional view is that the Torah is the work of God. In this regard, however, there appear to be two problems with the Torah. One problem is that not all of the laws seem to make sense. Certainly it makes sense for the Torah to prohibit murder, theft, and adultery. No civilization could long endure with its population engaged in these actions.[18] But there are other laws that do not appear to be supported by a rational reason. For example, the Torah prohibits Jews from wearing any garment made of linen and wool,[19] as well as from eating pork.[20]

But why cannot a Jew wear a garment of linen and wool? Maimonides, the great codifier of Jewish law,[21] opined that pagan priests often wore garments of linen and wool, and God did not want Israel to mirror such societies.[22] Another rabbi reasoned that the prohibition against mixing linen and wool has its roots in the struggle between Cain and Abel, which led to mankind's first murder.[23] Still, no civilization has ever foundered because of the clothing content of its people.

And why cannot a Jew eat pork? Although undercooked pork can cause disease, so can undercooked chicken. Yet chicken may be eaten, but pork is prohibited. What then is the reason for these and other seemingly irrational rules?[24]

Mortals Do Not Understand, but God Does

Initially, let it be conceded that these laws do not make sense to us. But they do make sense to God. That is to say, because the Torah is the work of God (according to the Orthodox and, to a lesser extent, among the Conservatives and Reformers)[25]—and God is perfect[26]—the Torah does not always make sense to our limited intelligence. We can try to understand why Jews cannot wear garments of linen and wool but can wear garments of cotton and linen.[27] But in the final analysis, we simply do not know the reason for this commandment. We also do not know why pork cannot be eaten, but chicken can be. But God knows. Similarly, we also do not know how certain diseases arise, nor do we understand the effect of language on thinking, or what ninety percent of the brain does. But again, God knows. As human knowledge grows, science may one day answer these questions. In the meantime, no one denies that cancer kills, language skills are important, and the brain's power dwarfs even the most powerful computer. So it is with the laws of the Torah. Not all of the Torah's laws make sense to us mortals, but an observant Jew (one who obeys the commandments) would no more deny their validity than the awesomeness of the brain. Thus, an observant Jew does not eat pork[28] and does not commit murder.[29] Both are prohibited by God. And just as science will one day determine how disease begins, humanity will one day learn the reason for the so-called irrational—or superrational—laws of the Torah.

Purpose of the Superrational Laws

According to the Orthodox, the day of understanding the reasons for the Torah's superrational laws will come when the Messiah arrives,[30] at which time he will teach us the purpose for all these laws. Nevertheless, until that day comes, this much can be said for these superrational statutes: In some way, in some manner, they imbue a holiness to those who comply with the desire of the Creator. For example, with respect to dietary laws, the Torah states: "For I am the LORD who brought you up from the land of Egypt, to be your God; you shall be holy, for I am holy."[31]

Do the Reformers and Reconstructionists comply with the superrational laws of the Torah? Many do because they find a rich heritage in these laws. The idea that they are doing the same thing that their grandparents and great-grandparents did, which helped keep Judaism alive and unique through the centuries, even in the face of persecution and death, is itself reason to comply with dietary and other superrational laws. Remember the song from *Fiddler on the Roof*? "Tradition!"

The Torah as "Incomplete"

But there is still a second problem with the Torah: It is seemingly incomplete. A few examples will illustrate the difficulty. The Torah teaches that the Jew must cease work on the sabbath.[32] But what exactly constitutes "work"? Is it work to milk a cow? To cook food? What about going to a pharmacy to get life-saving medicine for a sick person? The Torah itself is silent on this point. Another example of the Torah's apparent incompleteness is with regard to the law of slaughter. The Torah states that when the Jewish people wish to eat meat, they may, provided that they slaughter the animal as God "commanded" them.[33] But how exactly did God command his people to slaughter the animal? The Torah is absolutely silent in this regard. Yet another example is the Torah's requirement that a murderer is to be put to death.[34] But exactly how is the trial of the defendant to be conducted? What kind of evidence can be used against him? Is his confession to the crime admissible? Once more we must conclude that the Torah is totally silent on these and other vital matters. One final example of the Torah's seeming incompleteness: The Torah states that when one person negligently injures another, the punishment is "eye for [an] eye, tooth for [a] tooth."[35] But what if the wrongdoer who negligently takes out the eye of another is already blind? How would "eye for an eye" work in such a case? Thus, we see yet one more instance where the Torah is seemingly unclear or incomplete.

But how can that be? How can the Torah be incomplete or unclear? We certainly can accept the Torah's lack of completion and unclarity if it was the creation of man (which is the Reconstructionist view). But the traditional Jewish (and Christian) view is that the Torah was the creation of God.[36] As such, how could God, who is perfect,[37] all powerful,[38] and all knowing,[39] give Moses an incomplete or unclear Torah?

The answer is that God did not give Moses an incomplete or unclear Torah. Rather, God gave Moses two Torahs, as we shall next explain.

CHAPTER 6

The Oral Law

As we have discussed, a fundamental Jewish teaching is that God gave Moses the written Torah.[1] But to clarify and elucidate the many finer points of the written Torah, God also gave Moses the oral Torah (see discussion below). In Hebrew, this oral Torah is commonly called the *Mishnah*.[2] In this chapter, we will discuss the Mishnah and the subsequent rabbinical debates on it, called the *Gemara*.[3] Together, the Mishnah and Gemara are referred to as the *Talmud*.[4]

Why should a Christian want to know about the Mishnah and the rabbinical debates on it? Because the Gospels discuss the oral law (the "tradition of the elders").[5] Consequently, a full understanding of the Gospels is not possible without a basic understanding of this important aspect of Judaism.

The Mishnah

The term *Mishnah* is derived from the Hebrew root *shanah*, meaning "to repeat," and implies that which is learned by repetition or oral teaching. As the Mishnah itself states: "Moses received the law [written and oral] from God at Sinai and transmitted it to Joshua. Joshua transmitted it to the elders. The elders transmitted it to the prophets. The prophets transmitted it to the men of the Great Assembly,"[6] an august body of 120 men

79

who helped govern Israel during the Age of the Prophets and who were the predecessors of the Pharisees.[7] The Revelation, therefore, included not just the written Torah, but the Mishnah as well. As such, the Mishnah is as important and authoritative as the Torah itself.

While the preceding analysis (that the Mishnah is part of the Revelation at Sinai) is the Orthodox approach, the Mishnah is nevertheless also recognized as a critical part of Judaism's foundation by the modern Conservative, Reform, and Reconstructionist movements. For the Conservatives and Reformers, the oral law is part of a "continuous" or "progressive" Revelation, meaning that although the oral law was not part of the Revelation at Sinai, it was promulgated by Divinely inspired rabbis through the centuries. For the Reconstructionists, the Mishnah is an integral part of the civilization of the Jewish people in their attempt to know God.

The Mishnah Is Reduced to Writing

Although the Mishnah was orally transmitted for many centuries, Rabbi Judah, one of Judaism's great sages, reduced it to writing around the year 200 C.E. Why did Rabbi Judah break with tradition and put the Mishnah to writing? Because of necessity. By the year 200 C.E., the Land of Israel had ceased to exist as an independent nation (it was destroyed by the Romans in the year 135 C.E.), and the Jewish people were largely in exile. Rabbi Judah, concerned that the structure necessary to ensure the proper transmission of the Mishnah might one day cease to exist, penned and edited the Mishnah to preserve it for the Jewish people for all time.

The Organization of the Mishnah

The Mishnah is divided into six major divisions or "orders," which cover the following topics:

1. Agricultural laws.

2. Laws of the sabbath and festivals.

3. Laws of women.

4. Criminal and civil laws.

5. Laws of the Temple.

6. Laws of purity.

Within each order are a number of texts or "tractates," each dealing with a particular subject. For example, within the order of criminal and civil laws is the tractate "Sanhedrin," which deals with the court system. In total, there are sixty-three tractates in the Mishnah.[8]

The Mishnah Clarifies the Torah

The Mishnah provides many rules that are not found in the Torah.[9] For example, it provides us with thirty-nine major categories of activities that are prohibited on the sabbath.[10] The Mishnah also makes clear that for the purpose of saving someone's life, virtually all of the commandments are suspended, as is the case where one transacts business on the sabbath to purchase life-saving medicine for a sick person.[11] The Mishnah also details the manner in which an animal fit for consumption is to be slaughtered,[12] and the procedures to be followed in the trial of a criminal defendant.[13] And, as mentioned in the previous chapter, it also teaches that "eye for an eye" does not mean physical retaliation.[14]

But while the Mishnah answered many questions about the Torah, the rabbis of old would often raise questions about the Mishnah itself! This led to still another source of Jewish law, which has come to be known as the *Gemara*. We now explore this monumental work.

The Gemara Clarifies the Mishnah

From the time of the second century B.C.E. until the fifth century C.E., the rabbis of Babylon and Jerusalem, the two great centers of Jewish learning during that period, engaged in the study and debate of the Mishnah. These debates were themselves put to writing as a commentary on the Mishnah. In Hebrew this commentary is called the *Gemara*, which means "completion," since the Gemara completes the Mishnah (although many rabbinical commentaries on the Gemara itself have been published through the centuries!). Because the Jerusalem and Babylonian academies carried on their research and studies independently, there are two separate Gemaras: the Jerusalem and the Babylonian. Nevertheless, since many of the great scholars resided in Babylon after the fall of the Second Temple in 70 C.E., and because the Babylonian Gemara is eight times the size of the Jerusalem Gemara, the Babylonian Gemara (thousands of pages and two and one-half million words) is deemed more authoritative than its Jerusalem counterpart. From the rabbinical debates that are recorded in the Gemara, there subsequently evolved additional rulings of law. Thus, the Gemara provides us with still another source of law.

The Talmud

The Mishnah and the corresponding Gemara together are referred to as the *Talmud*, which means "study." Because the Babylonian Talmud is more authoritative than the Jerusalem Talmud, when Jews speak of "the Talmud," they invariably mean the Babylonian Talmud. While the Mishnah has been published as a separate text, the Gemara is never published alone. It is always published along with the Mishnah, as the Talmud.[15]

The Talmud Is Not a Legal Code

Considering the organization of the Talmud—six orders and sixty-three tractates—there is a tendency among many to look at the Talmud as a code of Jewish law. While it is true that there is a basic organization to the Talmud, it is not fully correct to view the Talmud as a legal code, at least not in a strict sense. First, the organization of the Mishnah (one part of the Talmud) is not as rigid as a contemporary legal code. For example, in the tractate on the Sanhedrin, there is considerable material that deals with the Messianic Age.[16] Second, the rabbinical debates of the Gemara (the other part of the Talmud) are not limited to a discussion of law, or what in Hebrew is called *halacha* (meaning literally "to walk" or "the path"). In fact, a significant part of the Gemara, perhaps even the majority of it, is not halacha at all, but *aggadah* ("narrative"). Aggadah comprises the nonlegal aspects of the Talmud: history, ethics, theology, and even folklore.

Maimonides, the author of the *Thirteen Principles of Faith*,[17] was one of the first to organize the corpus of Jewish law into a true code in his

Mishneh Torah ("Relearning the Law"). Another great codifier of Jewish law was Rabbi Joseph Caro, who lived in the sixteenth century and authored the *Shulchan Arukh* (literally, "the set table"). Both texts are widely studied in academies of Jewish learning.

The Talmud Is Absent from Christian Teaching

Because the early Christians were Jews, it is understandable that the Hebrew Scriptures became part of the Christian canon. Not only did the Hebrew Scriptures have intrinsic value to the Jewish-Christians, but these Jewish writings were also often seen as a prophecy of the coming of Jesus and as an introduction to the Gospels. As a consequence, Christians are quite familiar with the Torah and the balance of the Jewish Bible, albeit as the "Old Testament."

But the Talmud was not seen as a passageway to the New Testament in the same manner that the Hebrew Scriptures were. The oral law was seen as a set of rules that had no significance to the coming of Jesus. Moreover, in Israel (known then as Judea and subsequently known as Palestine), by the beginning of the third century of the Common Era, virtually all of the Jewish-Christians had died in the wars with Rome, leaving the leadership of the Church in the hands of the Gentile-Christians. Because these leaders were neither Jewish nor schooled in the oral law—as Jesus apparently was[18]—they did not fully comprehend its meaning and importance. As such, the oral law is fully absent from Christian teaching. Consequently, Jews and Christians often interpret the Torah differently. Thus, for example, "eye for [an] eye"[19] is often interpreted by Christian commentators to mean that the Torah required proportionality when one physically retaliated against a wrongdoer: An eye for an eye was lawful, but not a life for an eye. In this context, Jewish law appears to be a vast improvement over the legal systems of pagan societies, which typically sought a life for an eye. But once it is recognized that "eye for an eye" did not mean physical retaliation at all, but monetary damages,[20] Jewish law is properly seen as nothing if not revolutionary for replacing the law of physical retaliation with the law of tort. It is for this reason that some Christian clergy are beginning to learn Talmud—to better understand the Hebrew Scriptures.

The Talmud on Trial

Only thirty-seven tractates of the Mishnah have a Gemara.[21] Some scholars believe that each tractate of the Mishnah had a Gemara at one time, but these manuscripts were lost through the centuries. How could these treasures become lost? They were most likely not lost in an accidental sense. Rather, they were destroyed by European governments and Church officials during the Middle Ages who considered these works to be anti-Christian. The anti-Christian charge was not true. Nevertheless, countless thousands of handwritten Talmuds (the printing press had not yet been invented) were destroyed during the Middle Ages.[22] So hated were these classical Jewish works that before these legal masterpieces were put to fire, they were sometimes actually put on trial! Of course, it is doubtful that the European censors knew what they were destroying since much of the Gemara is written in Aramaic, an ancient language derived from Hebrew and which was the popular language of the masses during the time of Jesus. But fear and ignorance are often no match for logic and sound reasoning.

The Talmud and the Spirit of Jewish Learning

One final but important point needs to be stated at this juncture. The sometimes quite heated rabbinical debates recorded in the Talmud denote the nature of Judaism: Jews are not only allowed to ask questions on sacred matters of Torah and Mishnah; they are *expected* to do so.[23] This questioning naturally leads to debate, which is both necessary and healthy for understanding. In short, memorizing without understanding is not Judaism's way.

To recapitulate the last few chapters, we have thus far seen that Jewish law comprises not only the Ten Commandments, but all of the 613 laws found in the Torah (which include the Ten Commandments). In addition to these 613 commandments, there are many hundreds of other laws provided for in the Mishnah, which serve to clarify the laws of the Torah. The traditional Jewish view (presently held by the Orthodox movement) is that all of these laws (the laws of the Torah and Mishnah) were given directly by God to Moses. But Jewish law is not limited to these laws. Jewish law also includes the many subsequently enacted rabbinical ordinances which have their roots in the Gemara. But who is bound by all of these laws? Jews only? Jews and non-Jews? We answer these questions in the next chapter.

CHAPTER 7

The Noachide Laws

According to Jewish tradition, before God offered the Torah to the Jewish people on Mount Sinai,[1] he first offered it to the other nations of the world.[2] Only after they rejected the Torah and its commandments did God offer it to Israel, which accepted it.[3] For this reason, the commandments found in the Torah and Mishnah, as well as the subsequently enacted rabbinical ordinances, apply only to Jews.[4] Thus, it is only Jews who cannot eat pork.[5] It is only Jews who must observe the sabbath.[6] It is only Jews who must circumcise their sons on the eighth day of life.[7] But do the prohibitions against murder[8] and adultery[9] also apply only to Jews? Are non-Jews allowed to murder and commit adultery? One's intuition would say no, and that would be a correct answer: Gentiles, like Jews, cannot murder or commit adultery. But if, in the Jewish view, Gentiles are not bound by the laws of the Torah, what laws forbid them from engaging in such conduct? The answer is a basic set of laws that God gave to all of humanity, which we next discuss.

The Seven Laws of Noah

Judaism teaches that after the Great Flood, God spoke to Noah and his family and gave them and their descendants seven commandments,[10] the first six in the negative and the last in the positive:

- To not engage in blasphemy.
- To not practice idolatry.
- To refrain from unlawful intercourse.
- To not murder.
- To not steal.
- To not tear a limb from a living animal.
- To establish courts of justice.

The Biblical Source for the Seven Laws of Noah

Although these laws, known as the "Seven Laws of Noah" or the "Noachide Laws," are mentioned and discussed in the Talmud,[11] there is no express Biblical source for these laws, although some Jewish scholars claim that their source is found in the Book of Genesis:

> *God blessed Noah and his sons, and said to them, "Be fruitful and multiply, and fill the earth. The fear and dread of you shall rest on every animal of the earth, and on every bird of the air, on everything that creeps on the ground, and on all the fish of the sea; into your hand they are delivered. Every moving thing that lives shall be food for you; and just as I gave you the green plants, I give you everything. Only, you shall not eat flesh with its life, that is, its blood. For your own lifeblood I will surely require a reckoning: from every animal I will require it and from human beings, each one for the blood of another, I will require a reckoning for human life. Whoever sheds the blood of a human, by a human shall that person's blood be shed; for in his own image God made humankind. And you, be fruitful and multiply, abound on the earth and multiply in it."[12]*

The commandment prohibiting murder is clearly indicated by "Whoever sheds the blood of a human, by a human shall that person's blood be shed." The injunction to establish courts of justice may also be readily inferred: In any ethical society, a fair and impartial judiciary is necessary to determine the guilt of a defendant accused of murder.[13] Regarding the prohibition against theft, it is permissible to eat "[e]very moving thing that lives . . . just as I gave you the green plants, I give you everything," but not by stealing; one is to work for food.[14] As to the prohibition against unlawful intercourse, that may be found in the commandment to "be fruitful and multiply, abound on the earth and multiply in it,"[15] which implies a heterosexual union based upon marriage.[16] The tearing of the limb from a living animal would certainly shed blood, which is inferred[17] from "you shall not eat flesh with its life, that is, its blood." The commandments to refrain from blasphemy and idol worship may be the most difficult to deduce. They may be inferred, however, from "God blessed Noah and his sons, and said to them . . . ," since by blessing them and speaking to them, God revealed himself to them, just as he did to Adam.[18] As such, only an evildoer would curse God or worship another deity.

The Noachide Laws as Seven Categories of Laws

The Seven Laws of Noah are not just seven laws, but are actually seven broad categories of laws.[19] For example, murder is the killing of a human being with malice aforethought,[20] which must certainly be punishable for a society to have order. But what of an accidental killing due to negligence (what today we call manslaughter)? Is that not punishable, too? Is there not good reason to punish one who commits a negligent homicide (albeit less severely than one who commits a murder)?[21] Just as an ordered society must punish a murderer, so too it must punish someone who commits manslaughter. Thus, manslaughter would necessarily come under the broad category of the Noachide law of "murder."

As to the specific laws that are included within each of the seven categories, the ancient rabbinical sages were not always in agreement. Some authorities hold that each Noachide (Gentile) nation is free to use its own customs in drafting a legal system that comports with the Seven Noachide Laws, so long as the laws are fair, just, and consistent with the seven Noachide categories.

On the other hand, there are other Jewish authorities who hold that the Noachide Laws must include certain specified laws of the Torah.[22] Thus, for example, in the prohibition against theft, a proper Noachide Code according to these authorities would include laws prohibiting stealing,[23] robbery,[24] moving a landmark,[25] coveting,[26] kidnapping,[27] and using false weights and measures.[28] With respect to the prohibition against sexual immorality, laws enjoining adultery,[29] incest,[30] and homosexual intercourse[31] would be required. In fact, according to these authorities, the Seven Noachide Laws include a total of sixty-six laws. As such, from this point of view, it is incorrect to state that Jews have 613 commandments to obey, but Gentiles only seven. Indeed, many of the Torah's 613 commandments are not presently operative;[32] only 271 of them are presently binding on the Jewish people. As a result, the ratio of commandments now applicable to Jews and Gentiles respectively is not 88 to 1 (613 Jewish to 7 Noachide), but a little more than 4 to 1 (271 to 66).[33]

Must Noachides Believe in God?

An interesting question is whether non-Jewish ethical monotheists—Noachides—must believe in God. Although the Seven Laws of Noah prohibit blasphemy and idolatry, they do not expressly require belief in God. Nevertheless, virtually all Jewish authorities hold that for a non-Jew to comply with the Seven Laws of Noah, he or she must believe in God. This view is derived from the prohibition against blasphemy.[34]

Abraham and the Seven Laws of Noah

Most Jews and Christians are aware that Abraham was the first Jew, the one with whom God entered into an everlasting covenant.[35] But what most Jews and Christians do not know is that Abraham was also a great scholar and teacher. As a scholar, he learned and observed all of God's laws of the Torah.[36] As the Torah itself states, "Abraham obeyed my [God's] voice and kept my charge, my commandments, my statutes, and my laws."[37] The "commandments," "statutes," and "laws" refer to all of the laws of the Torah.[38] That Abraham learned and practiced all of the laws of the Torah is testimony to his high level of spirituality and prophecy because the Revelation on Mount Sinai was still centuries away.

But Abraham was not just a great scholar; he was also a great teacher. He passed on his knowledge of Torah to his Jewish progeny to ensure that God's covenant with him would not just endure through the ages,[39] but prosper as well.

Abraham did not limit his teaching to his family, however. He also taught any strangers who would listen to him,[40] and it appears that he won over many converts from paganism.[41] What did Abraham teach his non-Jewish students? According to tradition, he taught them about the One God and the Seven Laws that he gave to Noah and his descendants.[42]

But why did Abraham not teach his disciples the laws of the Torah and have them convert to Judaism? Because Judaism teaches that it is not necessary to be Jewish to go to heaven. As the ancient rabbis taught, "The righteous of all nations have a share in the World to Come."[43] Who is included among the righteous? The righteous are Jews who obey the Torah and Gentiles who obey the Seven Laws of Noah. This view, that all righteous people go to heaven, is the main reason why throughout history Jews have seldom sought to convert others to Judaism. In Judaism, faith is not as important as deeds.[44] Indeed, to emphasize the importance of deeds over faith, Maimonides taught that a Gentile who obeys the Seven Laws of Noah, but does not believe that they were Divinely authored, is nevertheless deemed a "wise Gentile."[45]

The Purpose of the Seven Laws of Noah

What was God's general purpose in giving Noah and his descendants these seven categories of laws? It was to provide humankind with a basic set of laws so that all people, not just Jewish people, would have a code by which to lead a righteous life.

Sadly, history has shown that when any society does not adopt these basic laws, a code of conduct based on ethical monotheism, such a society will degenerate into an orgy of murder, theft, sexual immorality, and cruelty until it eventually self-destructs. For example, in ancient Rome, men fought each other to death so that others could be entertained. In ancient Greece, the sexual love between a man and a boy was deemed superior to the sexual love between a husband and his wife. Children were sacrificed to the sun god in the Aztec Empire. The sadistically corrupt government and judiciary of Hitler's Germany sanctioned mass murder and theft in the name of the fatherland, while Stalin's Russia committed the same heinous acts in the name of the proletariat. Not one of these societies has endured.

On the other hand, the laws of the United States may be said to generally comport with the Seven Laws of Noah. In America, murder is absolutely prohibited and property rights are securely protected. Even cruelty to animals (which is a prohibition derived from the law proscribing the tearing of a limb from a living animal) is a crime. But while our laws usually comply with the Noachide Laws, they do not always do so. For example, freely allowing abortion during the early stages of pregnancy and viewing homosexuality as an acceptable lifestyle are quite simply not compatible with the Seven Noachide Laws: Abortion is a derivative of murder, and homosexuality is a derivative of sexual immorality. Still, there should be no question that our society is indeed morally superior to many others, past and present. It is not a coincidence that millions try to get into the United States each year, sometimes risking their lives in the process.

The Noachide Laws ensure that everyone who is not a Jew can also live a just, humane, and civilized life by practicing ethical monotheism, in the tradition of the thousands of Gentiles who adopted the ethical monotheistic teachings of Abraham, the first Jew.

Muslims and Christians as Noachides

For a Gentile to practice the ethical monotheism embodied in the Seven Laws of Noah, such a person has to reject idolatry and recognize the One God. Judaism has always recognized Islam as a religion that comports with the Seven Noachide Laws. This is because Islam requires justice and absolutely rejects murder, sexual immorality, theft, cruelty to animals, blasphemy, and idolatry. More specifically, with respect to the last two categories of laws, Islam recognizes only the One God. Islam is, like Judaism, a monotheistic religion in the strictest sense.

A question that Christians often ask is whether Christianity is a religion that is consistent with the Seven Noachide Laws. That Christianity is an ethical religion is obvious. Like Islam, it too requires justice[46] and prohibits murder,[47] sexual immorality,[48] theft,[49] cruelty to animals,[50] blasphemy,[51] and idolatry.[52] Consequently, the ancient rabbis believed that Christianity conferred a significant benefit upon humankind. Nevertheless, many of these rabbis believed that the concept of the Holy Trinity was inconsistent with monotheism.[53] Still, there were other rabbis who believed that Christianity was, in fact, a form of monotheism acceptable for non-Jews. Indeed, the ethical differences between Trinitarian monotheism and idolatrous polytheism (especially as practiced by ancient societies) are monumental.[54] Consequently, the prevailing view today is that Christianity is a monotheistic religion that does indeed comport with the Seven Laws of Noah and is a proper religion for non-Jews.[55]

The Early Church and the Noachide Laws

In the early days of Christianity, a rift existed between Peter and Paul. Peter believed that for non-Jews to become members of the new movement, they had to first become Jews.[56] This would, of course, entail their acceptance of the Jewish dietary laws and circumcision,[57] in addition to all other laws of the Torah. On the other side was James, the brother of Jesus,[58] and Paul. They both opposed Peter.[59] Because belief in Jesus was the essence of the new movement,[60] James and Paul believed that the Gentile converts needed only to comply with some basic laws of humanity. Their position was encapsulated in a letter that was sent out to the Gentiles of Antioch and Syria:

> *Since we have heard that certain persons who have gone out from us, though with no instructions from us, have said things to disturb you and have unsettled your minds, we have decided unanimously to choose representatives and send them to you, along with our beloved Barnabas and Paul, who have risked their lives for the sake of our Lord, Jesus Christ. We have therefore sent Judas and Silas, who themselves will tell you the same things by word of mouth. For it has seemed good to the Holy Spirit and to us to impose on you no further burden than these essentials: that you abstain from what has been sacrificed to idols and from blood and from what is strangled and from fornication. If you keep yourselves from these, you will do well. Farewell.[61]*

Thus, for the Gentiles to become members of Jesus' movement, they had only to abstain from idolatry, cruelty to animals, and sexual immorality (and, we may presume, murder, theft, and blasphemy). Therefore the Noachide Code, not the Sinaitic Code (the laws of the Torah), became the moral code of the Gentile-Christians. Paul prevailed over Peter, and history was changed.

There is an anonymously written poem, slightly irreverent, which goes like this: "Roses are red, violets are bluish. If it wasn't for Paul, we'd all be Jewish." Many a truth has been said in jest.

CHAPTER 8

The Prophets and the Writings

T he Hebrew Bible (called *Tanach* in Hebrew, and well known to Christians as the "Old Testament") consists of three sections: the Torah, the Prophets, and the Writings. In this chapter, we examine these three parts, paying special attention to the Prophets and the Writings. We also examine Christianity's adoption of the Hebrew Bible.

The Torah

Up to this point, we have focused mainly on only one part of the Hebrew Bible, namely, the Torah, which comprises the first five books of the Bible: Genesis, Exodus, Leviticus, Numbers, and Deuteronomy. And there is good reason for this emphasis. As we have earlier discussed, the traditional Jewish belief is that the Torah is the work of God and, with its 613 commandments, is the foundation of Judaism.[1] But there is another reason why the Torah is important to the Jewish people: As a historical work, the Torah provides us with an account of early civilization and the Jewish people.

The Torah as a Historical Work

First, the Torah provides us with a history of early civilization. It tells us of the beginnings of the universe and the origin of humankind,[2] the first sin of humankind,[3] the murder of Abel by Cain,[4] the progeny of Adam and Eve,[5] the generation of the Flood,[6] the repopulation of the earth and the history of countries,[7] and the account of the Tower of Babel.[8]

Second, the Torah provides us with a history of the Jewish people. It tells us of the story of Abraham, the first of Judaism's Three Patriarchs, and the beginnings of the Jewish people;[9] the life and times of Abraham's child, Isaac,[10] and Isaac's child, Jacob,[11] as well as the life and times of Jacob's son, Joseph, and his brothers;[12] the enslavement of the Jewish people by the Egyptians;[13] the birth of Moses and the unfolding of God's plan for Redemption,[14] which culminates in the Exodus from Egypt[15] and the Revelation on Mount Sinai.[16]

Clearly, the Torah is an important part of the Hebrew Scriptures. But there are two other sections: the Prophets and the Writings. We next proceed to discuss these other two sections of the Hebrew Bible.

The Prophets and the Writings

The second section of the Hebrew Bible is the Prophets. The books of the Hebrew Bible that make up this division are, in the order presented: Joshua, Judges, 1 and 2 Samuel, 1 and 2 Kings, Isaiah, Jeremiah, Ezekiel, Hosea, Joel, Amos, Obadiah, Jonah, Micah, Nahum, Habakkuk, Zephaniah, Haggai, Zechariah, and Malachi.

The third and final section of the Hebrew Bible is the Writings. The books of the Hebrew Bible that make up this division are, in the order presented: Psalms, Proverbs, Job, Song of Songs, Ruth, Lamentations, Ecclesiastes, Esther, Daniel, Ezra, Nehemiah, and 1 and 2 Chronicles.

In Protestant Bibles, the sequence of books in the Old Testament is: Genesis, Exodus, Leviticus, Numbers, Deuteronomy, Joshua, Judges, Ruth, 1 and 2 Samuel, 1 and 2 Kings, 1 and 2 Chronicles, Ezra, Nehemiah, Esther, Job, Psalms, Proverbs, Ecclesiastes, Song of Solomon (titled "Song of Songs" in the Hebrew Bible), Isaiah, Jeremiah, Lamentations, Ezekiel, Daniel, Hosea, Joel, Amos, Obadiah, Jonah, Micah, Nahum, Habakkuk, Zephaniah, Haggai, Zechariah, and Malachi. Thus, the reader may see that while the books of the Hebrew Bible are identical to those in the Old Testament portion of Protestant Bibles, the organization of the Hebrew Bible is slightly different.

In Catholic Bibles, the Old Testament includes the following books which are not found in the Hebrew Bible: Tobit, Judith, 1 and 2 Maccabees, Wisdom of Solomon, Sirach, and Baruch with the Letter of Jeremiah. The Book of Esther includes six additions to Esther. The Book of Daniel includes the Prayer of Azariah and the Song of the Three Jews, Susanna, and Bel and the Dragon. The sequence of books of the Old Testament is: Genesis, Exodus, Leviticus, Numbers, Deuteronomy, Joshua, Judges, Ruth, 1 and 2 Samuel, 1 and 2 Kings, 1 and 2 Chronicles, Ezra, Nehemiah, Tobit, Judith, Esther (with additions), 1 and 2 Maccabees, Job, Psalms, Proverbs, Ecclesiastes, Song of Solomon, Wisdom of Solomon, Sirach, Isaiah, Jeremiah, Lamentations, Baruch (with Letter of Jeremiah), Ezekiel, Daniel (with Prayer of Azariah and the Song of the Three Jews, Susanna, and Bel and the Dragon), Hosea, Joel, Amos, Obadiah, Jonah, Micah, Nahum, Habakkuk, Zephaniah, Haggai, Zechariah, and Malachi.

In Orthodox Bibles, the Old Testament includes the following books not found in the Hebrew Bible: Tobit; Judith; 1, 2, and 3 Maccabees (with 4 Maccabees as an appendix); Wisdom of Solomon; Sirach; Baruch; Letter of Jeremiah; 1 Esdras; Prayer of Manasseh; and Psalm 151. The Book of Esther includes the six additions to Esther, and the book of Daniel includes the Prayer of Azariah and the Song of the Three Jews, Susanna, and Bel and the Dragon. Some editions also have 3 Esdras. The order of books varies somewhat in Orthodox Bibles, but the following is illustrative: Genesis; Exodus; Leviticus; Numbers; Deuteronomy; Joshua; Judges; Ruth; 1 and 2 Kingdoms (1 and 2 Samuel); 3 and 4 Kingdoms (1 and 2 Kings); 1 and 2 Chronicles; 1 Esdras; 2 Esdras (Ezra and Nehemiah); Esther (with additions); Judith; Tobit; 1, 2, and 3 Maccabees; Psalms (with Psalm 151); Prayer of Manasseh; Job; Proverbs; Ecclesiastes; Song of Solomon; Wisdom of Solomon; Sirach; Hosea; Amos; Micah; Joel; Obadiah; Jonah; Nahum; Habakkuk; Zephaniah; Haggai; Zechariah; Malachi; Isaiah; Jeremiah; Baruch; Lamentations; Letter of Jeremiah; Ezekiel; Daniel (including the Prayer of Azariah and the Song of the

Three Jews, Susanna, and Bel and the Dragon); and 4 Maccabees (in appendix).

The Torah Compared to the Prophets and the Writings

While Jews hold dear each of the three sections of the Bible, it is the Torah that is elevated to a much higher status than the other two sections. This is because traditional Judaism teaches that the Torah is the creation of God himself.[17] While it is true that the Prophets and the Writings were written by holy men who had a special relationship with God and were inspired by God, these books, unlike the Torah, were not written by God himself. It is also the Torah that contains the commandments. For these reasons, Jews study the Torah with a much greater intensity and devotion than the Prophets and the Writings.

But can the preeminent status of the Torah also be found in the ranks of the Conservative and Reform movements, whose schools believe that the Torah was not Divinely written but only Divinely inspired? And what of the Reconstructionist movement, which teaches that the Torah was written by humans in search of God?[18] In all these movements, the Torah is nonetheless provided a status that elevates it to a plane much higher than that of the Prophets and the Writings. Why? Because the Torah forms the basis of Jewish law, life, and civilization; and that is something that all Jews agree on. In short, irrespective of whether a Jew identifies with the Orthodox, Conservative, Reform, or Reconstructionist movement, there is a common ground: It is the belief that without the Torah there is no Judaism. For this reason, Jews of all persuasions confer a special honor to the Torah.

The Importance of the Prophets and the Writings

Although the Prophets and the Writings are secondary in importance to the Torah, one should not think that they are unimportant; they are important indeed. The Prophets and the Writings are holy works and are valuable for their accounts of history, teachings of virtue, and lessons in faith. In fact, readings from the Prophets and the Writings form an integral part of the weekly sabbath morning synagogue service.

History, Virtue, and Faith

The Prophets and the Writings trace the history of the Jewish people over a period of many centuries. For example, the First and Second Books of Samuel tell us about the rise and decline of Saul, Israel's first king; his jealousy of David, and the latter's ascendency to the throne; David's reign; and the birth of David's son, Solomon. In the First Book of Kings, we are provided with an account of the construction of the Holy Temple, the division of the kingdom upon Solomon's death, and the reigns of his successors. The Book of Esther details the deliverance of the Jews from tyranny and genocide.

But the Prophets and the Writings do not offer mere history; they also teach virtue and faith. For example, the Book of Esther details not only the deliverance of the Jews of Persia from tyranny and genocide, but also the strength of Queen Esther in being willing to sacrifice her own life to help save her people.[19] The Book of Isaiah is rich, not only in its history, but in its beautiful moral teachings: "Thus says the LORD: Maintain justice, and do what is right."[20] The Book of Psalms offers comfort: "Protect me, O God, for in you I take refuge."[21] The Book of Proverbs contains eternal wisdom: "Better the poor walking in integrity than one perverse of speech who is a fool."[22]

Thus, the Prophets and the Writings are significant works in their own right. But there is another basis for their importance in Judaism: They are a part of the morning synagogue service on the sabbath and on festivals.[23]

The Weekly Reading on the Sabbath

In the Hebrew Bible (but not in any Christian edition of the Old Testament[24]), the Torah is divided into fifty-four sections. One section is typically read and studied during each sabbath (Saturday) morning synagogue service. When a festival falls on the sabbath, there is no regular weekly Torah reading, but a special Torah reading. Consequently, a "double portion" is read on another Saturday morning in order to finish reading the entire Torah in one year.[25]

In addition to the regular weekly sabbath reading from the Torah, there is also a weekly reading from the Prophets or the Writings. These latter readings help us to better understand the moral of the weekly or holiday Torah portion.

For example, Genesis 1:1 to 6:8 is the first Torah portion.[26] Isaiah 42:5 to 43:10 is the prophetical reading that is recited after this Torah portion. The relationship between the Torah reading and the *Haftorah* (the prophetical reading) is found in the opening words of this portion of Isaiah: "Thus says God, the LORD, who created the heavens and stretched them out, who spread out the earth and what comes from it, who gives breath to the people upon it and spirit to these who walk in it. . . ."[27] In both Genesis and Isaiah, God is acknowledged as the Creator of everything. Later, just as the early world was plagued with sinfulness,[28] so too was the world of Isaiah, who declares it Israel's mission to save the world from moral decay: "Bring forth the people who are blind, yet have eyes, who are deaf, yet have ears! Let all the nations gather together, and let the peoples assemble. Who among them declared this, and foretold to us the former things? Let them bring their witnesses to justify them, and let them hear and say, 'It is true.' You are my witnesses, says the LORD, and my servant whom I have chosen, so that you may know and believe me and understand that I am he. Before me no god was formed, nor shall there be any after me."[29]

Christianity and the Hebrew Scriptures

While both Jews and Christians study the Hebrew Scriptures (as previously mentioned, Christians have adopted the Hebrew Bible as the "Old Testament"), there are significant differences in the way each religion relates to and interprets them.

Christians Emphasize the Prophets and the Writings

Whereas Jews devote significantly more time to studying the Torah than the Prophets and the Writings (because, as previously discussed, the Torah is the foundation of Judaism and, according to conventional belief, was literally dictated by God himself to Moses[30]), many Christians spend more time studying the Prophets and the Writings than the Torah.[31] One reason for this may be that Christians have traditionally seen the

Torah as having been fulfilled[32] by Jesus,[33] whose coming was anticipated in the Prophets and the Writings. Moreover, because of these Christological interpretations, the Christian rendition of the Prophets and the Writings is not always the same as the Jewish, as we shall next discuss.

Christological Interpretations of the Prophets and the Writings

Christians, for example, interpret the preceding passage from Isaiah— "my servant"[34]—as a prophecy of Jesus. Jews interpret the same passage as referring to Israel. Similarly, Jews and Christians differ on the interpretation given to one of the most famous passages in Isaiah: "For a child has been born for us, a son given to us; authority rests upon his shoulders; and he is named Wonderful Counselor, Mighty God, Everlasting Father, Prince of Peace."[35] Christians maintain that this passage portends the coming of Jesus. Jews, on the other hand, believe that it refers to King Hezekiah, one of Israel's great kings. In fact, sometimes it is not only interpretations that differ, but translations as well. Jewish translators conventionally translate the preceding passage from the original Hebrew into English as something akin to: "And his name is called: Wonderful in counsel is God the Mighty, the Everlasting Father, the Ruler of Peace." There are many passages in the Writings and the Prophets which Christians believe are Messianic prophecies that point to Jesus,[36] but which Jews believe either are not Messianic in nature or, if they are, point to the Messiah who has yet to come.[37] Thus, although Christianity uses the Hebrew Scriptures, the purposes and interpretations (and sometimes even translations) are decidedly different from those found in Judaism.

Judaism's Perspective on Christianity's Use of the Hebrew Scriptures

I once had an interesting conversation with a learned Christian, whom I shall call Ed. Ed remarked that he found it interesting that the Hebrew Bible had been compiled, analyzed, and interpreted by Jewish teachers centuries before Jesus had even been born. "Yet," Ed went on to say, "here we Christians come along and 'take' your Bible, then we interpret it differently than you do, and then we tell you that your interpretation of your Bible is wrong. How do Jews feel about that?" It was a profound question: How *do* Jews feel about Christianity's use of the Hebrew Scriptures in a manner that is not consistent with Jewish belief?

To be sure, many Jews feel a certain degree of frustration that comes from the Christological interpretations and uses of the Hebrew Bible. Yet many rabbis throughout history nevertheless believed that it is good that Christianity adopted the Hebrew Scriptures (albeit as the "Old Testament"). What was the reason for the rabbis' belief? It was the conviction that because Christianity adopted the Hebrew Bible, the words of God and his prophets have been spread throughout the four corners of the earth. As a result, billions of people who might otherwise not have been exposed to the Torah, the Prophets, and the Writings now have been.

Indeed, when the Jewish people were preparing to cross the Jordan and enter *Eretz Yisrael* ("the Land of Israel"), God instructed Moses to carve the words of the Torah on a set of stones "very clearly,"[38] by which the rabbinical commentators understood as meaning in all seventy languages known at the time.[39] Thus, while Israel was to be the trustee of the Torah, the Jewish people were not to be the only beneficiaries of it. Yet, because Christianity did not adopt into its canon the Mishnah[40] and other rabbinical sources, there are distinctive differences in the way Jews and Christians interpret the Torah, the Prophets, and the Writings.

CHAPTER 9

Jesus and the Law

H aving established that Judaism is both a religion[1] and a legal
system,[2] which is made up of many laws,[3] we are now prepared
to address a critical question, the answer to which will enable a
Christian to better understand not only the Jewish roots of Christianity,
but Jesus himself. And that critical question is this: What was Jesus' view
of the law?

The Law and the Sermon on the Mount

To determine Jesus' view of the law, we turn to a portion of the Sermon
on the Mount:

> *Do not think that I have come to abolish the law or the
> prophets; I have come not to abolish but to fulfill. For truly I
> tell you, until heaven and earth pass away, not one letter, not
> one stroke of a letter, will pass from the law until all is accom-
> plished. Therefore, whoever breaks one of the least of these
> commandments, and teaches others to do the same, will be called
> least in the kingdom of heaven; but whoever does them and
> teaches them will be called great in the kingdom of heaven.[4]*

Let us now analyze this important passage by postulating four questions: (1) What did Jesus mean by "the law"? (2) What did Jesus mean by "the prophets"? (3) What did Jesus mean when he said he did not come to "abolish" the law or the prophets? (4) What did Jesus mean when he said he had come to "fulfill" the law? We will address each of these questions in turn.

What Did Jesus Mean by "the Law"?

What did Jesus mean by "the law"?[5] As we have stated earlier,[6] the law is not limited to just the Ten Commandments; there are also 603 other commandments in the Torah.

Jesus Included the 613 Commandments of the Torah in "the Law"

With the preceding in mind, that "the law" is much more than the Ten Commandments, it is without doubt that Jesus included all of the 613 commandments of the written Torah in "the law." Why? Because virtually all Jews throughout history, including those living in Jesus' time, irrespective of any disagreements they may otherwise have had with each other, have accepted the 613 commandments as being part of the law. Thus, while the Pharisees, Sadducees, Essenes, and Zealots[7] (all movements within Judaism during Jesus' lifetime) had many disagreements with each other, all agreed that the Torah was Divinely authored, was the cornerstone of Judaism, and contained the 613 commandments that Jews were duty-bound to obey (much as the Orthodox movement subscribes to today).

Did Jesus Include the Oral Law in "the Law"?

One area of disagreement found among the Pharisees, Sadducees, Essenes, and Zealots was with regard to the oral law.[8] The Sadducees did not believe in the authority of the oral law, while the other groups, most notably the Pharisees, did. Based on some Gospel passages, there are many who believe that Jesus, like the Sadducees, did not believe in the Divine authorship of the oral law. For example, when the Pharisees took Jesus' disciples to task for not complying with the handwashing requirement of the oral law,[9] Jesus seemed to minimize the importance of this commandment: "Do you not see that whatever goes into the mouth enters the stomach, and goes out into the sewer?"[10] Moreover, Jesus labeled the Pharisees, the best-known proponents of the oral law, as "vipers."[11] Thus, at first blush, it seems that Jesus did not believe in the authenticity and authority of the oral law. But upon further analysis, as we shall now explore, it will become clear that Jesus acted in accordance with the oral law, just as he did with the written law.

Jesus Supported the Oral Law

In Matthew's and Mark's Gospels,[12] Jesus himself was never accused of having violated the oral law's handwashing requirement,[13] only his disciples were: "Why do *your disciples* break the tradition of the elders? For they do not wash their hands before they eat."[14] And though Jesus leveled harsh attacks on the Pharisees, he also had much in common with them. Both he and they believed in the coming of the Messiah, the resurrection of the dead, reward and punishment in the hereafter, and the need to perform acts of kindness and mercy. On the other hand, the Sadducees,[15] the rivals of the Pharisees, did not believe in life after death, the resurrection of the dead, or the coming of the Messiah.

Consequently, and not surprisingly, Jesus also expressly told the people in no uncertain terms that they were to obey the teachings of the Pharisees: "The scribes and Pharisees sit on Moses' seat; therefore, do whatever they teach you and follow it. . . ."[16] And since the teachings of the Pharisees included the oral law, Jesus was necessarily lending his support to this critical body of Jewish law. Thus, whatever differences Jesus had with the Pharisees, and it must be remembered that disagreement and argument over the law is itself a tradition in Judaism,[17] he acknowledged that the Pharisees were the proper successors to Moses, Judaism's greatest prophet, who transmitted both the written and oral law to the Jewish people. As the Mishnah itself states: "Moses received the law [written and oral] from God at Sinai and transmitted it to Joshua. Joshua transmitted it to the elders. The elders transmitted it to the Prophets. The Prophets transmitted it to the men of the Great Assembly,"[18] the ancestors of the Pharisees.

In short, when Jesus used the term "the law," he clearly intended to include all of the commandments found not only in the written law (Torah), but in the oral law (Mishnah) as well.

What Did Jesus Mean by "the Prophets"?

What did Jesus mean by "the prophets"?[19] The Prophets, as we have previously seen,[20] encompasses the books of the Hebrew Bible written by men who were inspired by God and who, like other teachers and Jesus, admonished the Jewish people to remain true to God's laws. As stated earlier, and in its most literal sense, *the prophets* include: Joshua, Judges, 1 and 2 Samuel, 1 and 2 Kings, Isaiah, Jeremiah, Ezekiel, and the Twelve Minor Prophets (Hosea, Joel, Amos, Obadiah, Jonah, Micah, Nahum, Habakkuk, Zephaniah, Haggai, Zechariah, and Malachi).[21] However, it is probable that when Jesus used the term "the prophets," he meant to also include the Writings: Psalms, Proverbs, Job, Song of Songs, Ruth, Lamentations, Ecclesiastes, Esther, Daniel, Ezra, Nehemiah, and 1 and 2 Chronicles. As the Gospel states, "Then beginning with Moses and all the prophets, he interpreted to them the things about himself in all the scriptures."[22]

Thus, by speaking of "the law" and "the prophets," Jesus meant the entire Hebrew Scriptures.

Jesus Did Not Come to "Abolish" the Law or the Prophets

We now come to the third and most critical question: What did Jesus mean when he said he did not come to "abolish" the law or the prophets?[23] That Jesus did not come to abolish the law or the prophets means, at its plainest and most basic level, that he did not see his mission as one that anticipated the abolition of Jewish law and Judaism. In fact, it would appear to be quite inconceivable that Jesus would have sought to destroy the law.

The reader will recall that the law includes not only the Ten Commandments, but all 613 commandments of the Torah and the many other commandments, found in the Mishnah, which explain and clarify the laws of the Torah.[24] The reader will also recall that the traditional Jewish view is that all of the laws in the Torah and the Mishnah are part of the Divine Revelation at Sinai.[25] This point is significant and cannot be minimized. If Jesus was God, as Christians believe, it would be unimaginable, even appalling, if God had suddenly changed his own laws. God is perfect,[26] and for God to change his own laws would be an acknowledgment that his earlier laws were not, in fact, perfect.[27] But that would fly in the face of the omniscient God of Judaism and Christianity.[28] On the other hand, if Jesus was a mere mortal teacher, as non-Christians believe, it is inconceivable that a Jewish teacher would want to end the religion that gave meaning and sustenance to his life, and to the life of his family and community.

Jesus Did Not Disparage or Minimize the Law

In any event, by looking at Jesus' words we know that Jesus did not seek to abolish the law. For example, if we examine the rest of the Sermon on the Mount, we see that Jesus did not in any way disparage or minimize the commandments ("the law"). In fact, if anything, he seemingly attempted to be even more exacting than the law actually required. For example, while Jesus naturally opposed murder,[29] he also opposed hurting another with mere words: "You have heard that it was said to those of ancient times, 'You shall not murder'; and 'whoever murders shall be liable to judgment.' But I say to you that if you are angry with a brother or sister without cause, you will be liable to judgment; and if you insult a brother or sister, you will be liable to the council; and if you say, 'You fool,' you will be liable to the hell of fire."[30]

Similarly, Jesus taught not only the Torah's prohibition against adultery,[31] but prohibitions against any lewd conduct, even though it did not reach the level of adultery: "You have heard that it was said, 'You shall not commit adultery.' But I say to you that everyone who looks at a woman with lust has already committed adultery with her in his heart."[32]

In like manner, Jesus did not denigrate the Torah when teaching his fellow Jews kindness. Rather, he quoted the Torah's admonishment to "love your neighbor,"[33] and only then asked people to be charitable with their enemies too.[34]

In many other respects Jesus showed his love and support of the law. For example, he celebrated Passover,[35] observed Judaism's dietary laws,[36] and attended synagogue on the holy sabbath,[37] all as any pious Jew would.[38]

Do Three Incidents Show That Jesus Sought to Relax or Change the Law?

Nevertheless, some Biblical scholars point to three incidents to try to prove that Jesus advocated relaxation or even outright abolition of the law. The first was his healing of a sick man on the sabbath.[39] The second was his defense of his disciples who had picked corn on the sabbath.[40] The third was his defense of his disciples when they did not wash their hands before eating.[41] Let us now examine each of these incidents.

First Incident: Healing the Sick Man on the Sabbath

In the first incident, Jesus came across a man with a withered hand on the sabbath.[42] The Pharisees asked Jesus, "Is it lawful to cure on the sabbath day?"[43] Under Jewish law, if the man's life was in danger, an observant Jew would do whatever is necessary to save the man's life, since saving life takes precedence over virtually all the 613 commandments.[44] But if the man's life was not in danger, an observant Jew would wait until the sabbath ended before doing something that would violate the sabbath. But what Jesus did to help the man was not in any way a violation of the sabbath, even if the man's life was not in danger, since all that Jesus did was speak to the man to heal him: "Then he said to the man, 'Stretch out your hand.' He stretched it out, and it was restored, as sound as the other."[45] And speaking is not in any way prohibited on the sabbath. Thus, even if the man's life was not in danger, Jesus did not do anything in violation of the sabbath. Consequently, this incident can in no way be used to show that Jesus sought to abolish or relax the laws of the sabbath.

Second Incident: Picking Corn on the Sabbath

In the second incident, Jesus defended his disciples who were accused of having violated the sabbath by picking corn.[46] Here it must be conceded that the actions of his disciples were a violation of the sabbath laws, but only if their lives were not in danger. If they were in danger of starving, then again, they would have been justified in picking the corn to save their lives. As the Talmud teaches, "Violate one sabbath so that you may keep many sabbaths."[47]

Were the disciples in danger of dying? Although it is initially difficult to believe that they were in such dire circumstances, Jesus' defense of them indicates that such may well have been the case. In deflecting the charge hurled at his disciples by the Pharisees, Jesus analogized their picking corn to the priest Ahimelech giving David bread which was reserved for the priests and which a commoner like David was prohibited from eating.[48] David was nonetheless permitted to eat the bread because he apparently had no provisions on him,[49] and but for the actions of Ahimelech, David may well have starved to death. Thus, once again, we see that one can—indeed, must—violate a precept of the Torah to save a life.[50]

In any case, it is important to note that Jesus himself was never accused of violating the laws of the sabbath: "Look, *your disciples* are doing what is not lawful to do on the sabbath."[51] And no man can be punished for another's misconduct. As the Torah teaches, "only for their own crimes may persons be put to death."[52]

Third Incident: Not Washing Hands Before Eating

The third incident often cited to prove Jesus' desire to abolish or relax the law is when he defended his disciples for not having washed their hands before eating.[53] "Listen and understand: it is not what goes into the mouth that defiles a person, but it is what comes out of the mouth that defiles,"[54] Jesus taught. Can these words be used to show that Jesus was not concerned about either the handwashing requirement found in the Mishnah or the dietary laws found in the Torah?[55] Because the Torah and the Mishnah are immutable,[56] as Jesus himself acknowledged,[57] Jesus was undoubtedly resorting to hyperbole to make a point, which he was wont to do. For example, on another occasion, Jesus also declared, "If your right eye causes you to sin, tear it out and throw it away; it is better for you to lose one of your members than for your whole body to be thrown into hell."[58] Yet Jesus could not have intended that his words be taken literally since Jewish law absolutely prohibits self-mutilation.[59] Similarly, in the handwashing controversy, Jesus could not have intended his words ("it is not what goes into the mouth that defiles a person") to mean that the handwashing or dietary laws were insignificant. Moreover, as was earlier indicated,[60] it was his disciples who violated the laws regarding handwashing,[61] not Jesus,[62] and notwithstanding his defense of them,[63] nothing indicates that Jesus did not wash his own hands before eating[64] or that Jesus himself was anything but scrupulous in his observance of the dietary laws of the Torah.[65]

In Luke's Gospel, however, it appears that Jesus did indeed violate the handwashing law: "While he [Jesus] was speaking, a Pharisee invited him to dine with him; so he went in and took his place at the table. The Pharisee was amazed to see that he did not first wash before dinner."[66] But on closer analysis, we will see that even here Jesus did not violate the law.

In Matthew[67] and Mark,[68] when it states that Jesus' disciples did not wash their hands before eating, the original Greek text uses the word *nipto*, meaning to cleanse or wash, especially the hands or feet.[69] But in Luke,[70] when it states that Jesus did not wash, the Greek word used is *baptizo*, which means to make fully wet or immerse,[71] as when John baptized his followers in the Jordan River.[72] Thus, although the disciples did not "wash," Jesus did not fully "immerse." This is most significant.

When Jews wash before eating, they typically do so by pouring a pitcher of water over their hands, first over the right hand, then over the left. A full immersion of the hands is not the norm.[73] Thus, the Pharisee[74] who accused Jesus of not immersing was apparently very rigorous in applying the law, but nonetheless wrong. Jesus did not immerse his hands because the law did not require him to do so. All that he had to do was wash, and we may confidently infer that he did. If he had not, the Greek text would have used the term *nipto*, as was used to describe the conduct of Jesus' disciples.

Jesus Did Not Transgress the Law in Any Manner

When the Gospels tell us that the Jewish authorities were looking to convict Jesus of some wrongdoing,[75] they did not charge him with handwashing or dietary law violations. Indeed, he was not even charged with the more substantial allegation of having violated the sabbath,[76] a charge that, if true, was a capital crime.[77] Rather, he was convicted of the crime of blasphemy.[78] To be guilty of blasphemy, a person must curse God and use God's personal name (God actually has a personal name) in the process. God's personal name is composed of the Hebrew letters *yud, hay, vav, hay*; in English, these letters are transliterated as *Y H W H*.[79] Yet nowhere does the Gospel even remotely indicate that Jesus ever pronounced God's name,[80] let alone cursed him (which, especially from a Christian perspective, is nothing less than unimaginable). Additionally, claiming to be the Messiah is not blasphemy. In fact, it is not even a crime.[81] In short, nothing that Jesus did violated the laws of the Torah or Mishnah.[82]

Admittedly, other parts of the Gospel,[83] particularly the Gospel of John, present greater difficulty from a Jewish perspective. Jesus' statements that "The Father and I are one"[84] and "I am the way, and the truth, and the life. No one comes to the Father except through me"[85] may well have been the basis for a criminal proceeding.[86] But Jesus was not convicted on the basis of having made these statements; he was not even charged with having uttered these words.[87] Why he was not charged is not clear, and one is free to speculate as to the reasons.[88]

Jesus Did Not Transgress the Teachings of the Prophets

Just as Jesus did not intend to destroy the law, so too he did not intend to destroy the teachings of the prophets. Indeed, the Gospel expressly states that Jesus read from the book of Isaiah:

> *When he came to Nazareth, where he had been brought up, he went to the synagogue on the sabbath day, as was his custom. He stood up to read, and the scroll of the prophet Isaiah was given to him. He unrolled the scroll and found the place where it was written: "The Spirit of the Lord is upon me, because he has anointed me to bring good news to the poor. He has sent me to proclaim release to the captives and recovery of sight to the blind, to let the oppressed go free, to proclaim the year of the Lord's favor."*[89]

In summary, we may confidently say that Jesus did not in any way intend to abolish or even relax the law or the teachings of the prophets. Which leads us to the last of the four questions presented earlier in this chapter: What did Jesus mean when he said he had come to "fulfill" the law?[90]

Jesus Came to "Fulfill" the Law

The dictionary states that to "fulfill" means to bring about the accomplishment of something or to execute or perform or satisfy. Certainly during his lifetime Jesus accomplished the commandments of the law by performing them and satisfying them. As we have already discussed, Jesus lived his life as an observant Jew, complying with all of God's commandments, whether that meant attending synagogue on the sabbath[91] or celebrating the Passover festival.[92] In this sense, Jesus clearly fulfilled the law. And from a traditional Christian perspective, it may be said that by fulfilling the law, Jesus brought it to perfection in a way not previously understood.[93]

But by "fulfilling" the law, could Jesus have meant to "finish" the law, that is, to have ended it in some way? To this we must answer in the negative. Jesus clearly did not intend the law to end: "For truly I tell you, until heaven and earth pass away, not one letter, not one stroke of a letter, will pass from the law until all is accomplished."[94] Earth may not pass away for billions of years, but heaven will never pass away. But what did Jesus mean when he said "until all is accomplished"? Admittedly, it is not totally clear what Jesus could have meant by this.[95] But whatever he meant, in the context of "until heaven and earth pass away," Jesus clearly did not intend the law to end. Not the smallest of the commandments shall pass; not even one letter of the commandments ("not one letter, not one stroke of a letter will pass from the law").

The Law Is Permanent

Jesus believed what all observant Jews believe, then and now: that the law is permanent and forever. As it is written, "I will keep your law continually, forever and ever."[96] Moreover, to make it clear that the law was to endure for all time, Jesus continued: "Therefore, whoever breaks one of the least of these commandments, and teaches others to do the same, will be called least in the kingdom of heaven; but whoever does them and teaches them will be called great in the kingdom of heaven."[97] Jesus thus admonished his listeners to keep even the "least" of God's commandments.[98]

Was Jesus Attacking "Pharisaic Legalism"?

Some have argued that though Jesus did not in any way advocate an end to the law, he did advocate an end to "Pharisaic legalism." But what exactly does it mean to be "Pharisaic"? And what is "legalism"?

The Gospel View of the Pharisees and Legalism

As mentioned earlier in this chapter, the Pharisees were a movement within Judaism during the time of Jesus. Many Christians have the idea that Pharisaism is a synonym for hypocrisy. Indeed, the dictionary defines "pharisee" as one who is a hypocrite. And no wonder. The general Christian understanding of the Pharisees comes only through the Gospels, which do not paint the Pharisees in a favorable light. In fact, Jesus regularly referred to the Pharisees as hypocrites, the following being a more extreme illustration: "Woe to you, scribes and Pharisees, hypocrites! For you devour widows' houses and for the sake of appearance you make long prayers; therefore you will receive the greater condemnation."[99] Strong language, to be sure. Not only are the Pharisees hypocrites who are long-winded in prayer, but they take away the houses of widows, for which they will be damned. "Legalism," which Christianity has traditionally associated with the Pharisees, implies a penchant for formalities and legalities, accompanied by an absence of true faith. We now attempt to dispel the common misconceptions about the Pharisees and so-called legalism.

The Pharisees in History

First, let us forthrightly ask: Were there hypocrites among the Pharisees? Were there those in the Pharisaic movement who looked upon the law as a web to satisfy selfish desires? Because it is undeniable that hypocrites and evildoers are found in all religions and in all eras, it is certain that there were hypocritical and evil Pharisees. Indeed, the Talmud itself actually takes such Pharisees to task.[100] But the numbers of these Pharisees were actually quite small. The vast majority of Pharisees were humane, caring, and decent people. They taught love of one's fellow man, mercy, and repentance.[101] Further, the Pharisees received the popular support of the masses. Josephus, the ancient Jewish historian, wrote that "the Sadducees are able to persuade none but the rich, and have not the populace obsequious to them, but the Pharisees have the multitude [on] their side. . . ."[102] Moreover, many of the teachings of the Pharisees were virtually the same as the teachings of Jesus. For example, Hillel, a great Pharisaic teacher who lived in the generation before Jesus, taught a pagan who wanted to convert to Judaism, "What is hateful to you do not do to others. This is the whole of the law; the rest is commentary thereto. Now go and study it."[103] Additionally, the Gospel itself notes that there were indeed good Pharisees.[104] Paul of Tarsus stated proudly that he was a Pharisee.[105] Thus, it is simply incorrect to equate Pharisaism with hypocrisy.

It is noteworthy that while the Sadducees, Essenes, and Zealots all died out, the Pharisees alone endured and became the ancestors of modern-day Judaism.

Legalism in a Positive Light

As for "legalism," it is true that the rabbis of the Talmud engaged in debates which, to the outsider, appear to be legalistic, that is to say, splitting hairs over minute points of law. But appearances can be misleading. What looks like legalism was, in fact, a heartfelt debate among pious men who tried their best to determine how God intended his law to be interpreted and applied. From this perspective, legalism becomes saintliness. The following example may help to clarify the matter.

Imagine an American soldier who is stationed somewhere on a lonely outpost in a foreign land. He has not seen his family for a long time and, due to a bureaucratic foul-up, has also not recently received any mail from them. The day finally comes, however, and he gets a long-awaited letter from his wife, whom he loves very much. We can be certain that when he reads her letter, he will not just read it once over quickly, as one reads a novel. Rather, he will read it many times over. And after he has virtually memorized the letter, he will then proceed to look at it and study it, paying careful attention to even the smallest of details. For example, the soldier may ask himself what his wife was doing when she wrote the letter. Was she preparing dinner for the children? Preparing their bath? Taking a well-deserved break? He also may be fascinated with the way she dates her letter ("1 May 1997," not "May 1, 1997") and wonder why she does this, and when she started doing this. He also will study her use of language: how she purposely disregards standard rules of grammar and syntax to make a point ("And the car, two flats it got. At the same time!").

In the same manner that our soldier will study his wife's letters, so too did the Pharisaic rabbis study the Bible and Mishnah: not out of mere technicality, but out of love.

Moreover, to criticize the Pharisees for being "legalists" fails to recognize what Judaism is: a legal system.[106] If the rabbis of the Talmud had not been legalists (here I am not using the term in a derogatory sense, but in a complimentary sense, to denote an individual who is well learned in the law), Judaism would never have survived. Let us envision what would have happened to the American legal system if it had not had its own legalists, that is, judges and lawyers who were learned and skilled in understanding and applying the law. In lieu of a well-tuned system, that has stood the test of time, we would have reverted to anarchy and the law of "might makes right" for survival.

Thus, to the extent that any Pharisees were actually being selfish and not practicing God's commandments, Jesus' criticism of them was appropriate, since such is the tradition in Judaism: to denounce wrongdoing, irrespective of who may be committing the wrong.[107] But it is one thing to criticize a few hypocrites, and something else to include in the criticism all of the righteous who were trying to understand God and his law.[108] This is something I cannot believe that Jesus ever intended or did.

To summarize, while Jesus may well have criticized the wrongdoers among the Pharisees, he could not have intended to criticize all of the Pharisees. And while Jesus may have debated the law with the Pharisees, he did not ever criticize the law, much less seek to end it.

Paul of Tarsus and the Law

Yet if Jesus did not preach an end to the law or criticize it, it must be conceded that Paul of Tarsus did both—or so it appears.

"Christ Is the End of the Law"

As to the law coming to an end, Paul stated: "For Christ is the end of the law."[109] But when Paul wrote this, did he mean it to be taken in a literal manner? Did he mean that the law of the Torah had ended and was replaced by the law of the Gospel? In short, did Paul believe that Judaism had ended as a viable religion?

Through the ages, many Christians have given a literal interpretation to Paul's writings.[110] For Jews, this teaching would have a tremendous consequence: As a result of Paul's writings, Judaism would be seen by many—but certainly not all, as we shall see—as an obsolete religion,[111] the only significant purpose of which was to portend the coming of Jesus; and when he was born and the prophecies fulfilled according to traditional Christological interpretations,[112] it ceased to be a viable religion. Indeed, the very terms accorded the two main sections of the Christian Bible are consistent with this view: the "Old Testament," implying something that is dated and worn out, and the "New Testament," implying something that is current and fresh.

But this literal interpretation of Paul is certainly not unanimously held. Another interpretation of "Christ is the end of the law"[113] is that Jesus represents the law and is the way of perfecting the law of the Torah.[114] Thus, in conjunction with the view that the law of the Torah is God's law,[115] "Christ is the end of the law" takes on a different meaning than literalists would assign to it, and one that is eschatological but not supersessionist in nature. In fact, while many theologians and clergy through the centuries presumed the demise of Judaism after Jesus, no church council ever declared this to be the case.[116] To the contrary, the Second Vatican Council (1962-1965) made it clear that Judaism has not been replaced by the new covenant of Christianity. Indeed, the teaching of the Catholic Church, as well as many Protestant churches, is that God's covenant with the Jewish people has never been revoked.[117]

"The Curse of the Law"

In addition to teaching that the law was "ended,"[118] Paul also seemingly taught that the law was not good: "Christ redeemed us from the curse of the law by becoming a curse for us. . . ."[119] It is due to a literal reading of Paul's writings[120] that many Christians, even to this day, believe that the law is something that is a curse or harsh. But as we have established earlier, to Jews, the law is not harsh at all. Indeed, from a Jewish perspective, the Torah is a most humane doctrine: Widows, orphans, and strangers, the most defenseless people in society, are required to be treated with dignity.[121] Citizens are protected from false arrest.[122] Property rights of all are secured.[123] And criminal defendants are protected against cruel and excessive punishment.[124] All this is to be contrasted with the arbitrary and unjust laws of other societies, which exist even in this day. In short, from a Jewish position, the Torah was and remains a truly just and vibrant doctrine.

But considering that Paul himself was a Jew,[125] he certainly knew that the Torah, being the work of God,[126] was something that was good. Indeed, elsewhere in the New Testament, Paul spoke highly of the Torah: "So the law is holy, and the commandment is holy and just and good."[127] So why then did Paul find it necessary to speak of the Torah as a "curse"?

Paul's letter to the Corinthians may shed some light on the problem:

> *For though I am free with respect to all, I have made myself a slave to all, so that I might win more of them. To the Jews I became as a Jew, in order to win Jews. To those under the law I became as one under the law (though I myself am not under the law) so that I might win those under the law. To those outside the law I became as one outside the law (though I am not free from God's law but am under Christ's law) so that I might win those outside the law. To the weak I became weak, so that I might win the weak. I have become all things to all people, that I might by all means save some. I do it for the sake of the gospel, so that I may share in its blessings.[128]*

Quite simply, Paul did what he had to do to preach the Gospel and obtain converts. And Paul did not think it was important how or why the Gospel was preached. What was important was that it was preached.[129]

Thus, to the extent that Paul seemingly questioned the law, it was undoubtedly for the purpose of a greater mission: to gain followers for Jesus, who Paul believed was the Christ.[130]

Moreover, we must understand Paul's actions in a historical context. During the first century C.E., many pagans looked upon Pharisaic Judaism as a meaningful religion and as a replacement for their own hideous idolatrous practices.[131] In fact, vast multitudes of pagans throughout the Mediterranean and Asia were on the verge of converting to Judaism. Paul was determined to win these converts over for Christ.[132] And to do so, he apparently believed that he had to teach them not only that they were not bound by the Torah,[133] but that the Torah was in some way, whether literally or otherwise, a "curse." Of course, history tells us that Paul was successful in his mission.

The Jewish Perspective of the Law

Needless to say, Jews do not look at the law as a curse, either literally or otherwise. As discussed above, Jews look at the Torah as just and merciful. Nevertheless, many Christians believe that the law is a curse to the Jewish people because there are so many commandments to follow, and that unless a Jew complies with all the commandments, he or she is cursed.[134] While it is true that the Book of Deuteronomy contains curses for not obeying the law,[135] the curses there relate to specific acts of wrongdoing: for example, the practice of idolatry;[136] withholding justice from a widow, orphan, or stranger;[137] engaging in bestiality[138] or incest;[139] and accepting a bribe to have an innocent person murdered.[140] Only these sinners are cursed. The common thread among these sins is that they are extreme cases of immorality and not likely to be brought before a court of law. According to one rabbi, the curse applies only to those who deny that the Torah was Divinely given.[141] But the ancient rabbis never interpreted any portion of the Torah to mean that one is cursed for not obeying all of the commandments.[142] Indeed, what kind of God would give so many commandments (613) to his people and then curse them for not obeying each and every one of them? To the Jewish mind, such a question is odd at best, because for God to have done so would place his many attributes of mercy in doubt.[143] God requires his people to be good;

but he does not require them to be perfect.

One rabbinical sage explained why God gave the Jewish people a Torah with so many commandments:[144] When God gave Adam only one commandment, that he not eat from the Tree of Knowledge,[145] he violated it.[146] When God gave the Torah and its 613 commandments to the Jewish people, God reasoned that even if they violated many of the commandments, there would still be many which they did not violate. Thus, God did not give the Torah and its many commandments with malevolence, but benevolence. This is the Jewish view of God's Torah and law.

CHAPTER 10

The Greatest Commandments

M any Christians ask, "Which of the 613 commandments of the Torah are the most important?" In this chapter, we answer this question from a traditional Jewish perspective. We also examine Jesus' view on the matter.

The Torah Gives No Hierarchy for the Commandments

The question above is significant because nowhere does the Torah itself provide a ranking for the commandments. In this regard, many think that the Ten Commandments are the most important.[1] But we cannot say that these commandments are the most important because, again, nowhere in the Torah does it say that the Ten Commandments are more important than any of the other 603 commandments.[2] Although we may reasonably surmise that murdering someone[3] is a more grievous sin than eating pork[4] (because the former carries the death penalty[5] whereas the latter only lashes[6]), observant Jews will no more eat pork than they will murder because both are prohibited by God. Indeed, as discussed earlier,[7] the reason for some commandments, such as the statute prohibiting

Jews from wearing a garment made of wool and linen,[8] cannot even be understood by humans. Nevertheless, because the Torah is the work of God, devout Jews will obey all of the commandments, even though they presently cannot fully understand the way of God and cannot be certain what the reward for observing each commandment will be. Thus, in a sense, all of the commandments are of equal importance.

An Allegory of a King and His Laborers

But why did God not provide some hierarchy for the commandments? The ancient rabbis provided an answer by way of allegory: A king told his laborers that he would pay them for tilling his garden. At the end of the day, the king determined the specific work done by each laborer. One worker tilled the garden near a palm tree and received one gold coin for his work. Another worker tilled the garden near a pepper tree and received two gold coins for his work. When the first worker found out that he had been given one coin less than the other, he protested to the king: "If I had known that working near the pepper tree would be worth two gold coins, I would not have worked near the palm tree, for which I received only one coin." To this the king responded, "But if I had told all the workers that they would receive two gold coins for tilling the ground near the pepper tree but only one gold coin for tilling the ground near the palm tree, the whole of my garden would not have been tilled."[9] Similarly, if the Torah stated that there was a reward of "two coins" for performing commandment x, but only "one coin" for performing commandment y, many might rush to perform commandment x, while paying little attention to commandment y. Thus, because God did not state which commandments are given the greater reward, observant Jews will try to perform as many commandments as they can.[10] Of course, as we have discussed earlier,[11] and which we again discuss later in this chapter, the ideal is to perform the commandments out of love for God, and not to receive a reward.[12]

Jesus and the Two Great Commandments

The Gospel relates the story of the Pharisee who asked Jesus, "Teacher, which commandment in the law is the greatest?"[13] In light of what we have already stated, the question was thoughtful and profound. In response to the Pharisee's question, Jesus replied, "You shall love the Lord your God with all your heart, and with all your soul, and with all your mind. This is the greatest and first commandment. And a second is like it: You shall love your neighbor as yourself. On these two commandments hang all the law and the prophets."[14]

The two commandments which Jesus selected as the greatest are noteworthy, as we shall now explain. The one that Jesus referred to as the "greatest and first commandment" is found in the Book of Deuteronomy: "You shall love the LORD your God with all your heart, and with all your soul, and with all your might."[15] The "second [which] is like it" is found in the Book of Leviticus: "You shall not take vengeance or bear a grudge against any of your people, but you shall love your neighbor as yourself: I am the LORD."[16] Let us now analyze these two commandments.

The Greatest Commandment: To Love God

Since long before his time, the commandment that Jesus called "the greatest and first commandment" has been part of an important prayer that Jews recite twice daily. This prayer is called the *Shema* ("hear"), and is so titled because it is the first word of the prayer and most Jewish prayers are titled by the prayer's first word. The complete Shema is a compilation of various passages from the Torah.[17]

Israel's Supreme Declaration of Faith: *Shema Yisrael*

But the Shema is not just a prayer, as Jesus well knew. It is also Judaism's most supreme declaration of faith. The opening words of the Shema, "Hear, O Israel: The LORD is our God, the LORD is One,"[18] state a fundamental precept in Judaism: that God is One.[19] Even though God has different names, which are translated from the Hebrew into "God," "LORD," "the Almighty," and "the Holy One, blessed be he," still God is One.[20] Through the centuries, it has been the desire of countless observant

Jews to die uttering the Shema, whose opening words in Hebrew are *Shema Yisrael, Hashem Elohanu, Hashem Echaud* ("Hear, O Israel: The LORD is our God, the LORD is One"). Indeed, whether they were being crucified by the Romans, burned at the stake by the Crusaders, or gassed to death by the Nazis, untold numbers of Jews have ended their lives on earth singing this great declaration of faith.

Loving the One God

The Shema not only declares the Oneness of God, but also the Jew's absolute love for him: "You shall love the LORD your God with all your heart, and with all your soul, and with all your might."[21] But how does one "love God," as the Shema commands? More specifically, how does one love the One who is absolutely formless, with no human character-istics whatsoever, and who cannot be seen, touched, or even imagined?[22] The rabbis of old answered this question by stating that one shows love of God by doing his will and performing his commandments.[23] As the Torah itself states: "So now, O Israel, what does the LORD your God require of you? Only to fear the LORD your God, to walk in all his ways, to love him, to serve the LORD your God with all your heart and with all your soul, and to keep the commandments of the LORD your God and his decrees that I am commanding you today, for your own well-being."[24] Consistent with this view, that God is loved when his commandments are performed, are the words of the Psalmist:

> *Happy are those whose way is blameless, who walk in the law of the LORD. Happy are those who keep his decrees, who seek him with their whole heart, who also do not wrong, but walk in his ways. You have commanded your precepts to be kept diligently. O that my ways may be steadfast in keeping your statutes! Then I shall not be put to shame, having my eyes fixed on all your commandments. I will raise you with an upright heart, when I learn your righteous ordinances. I will observe your statutes; do not utterly forsake me.*[25]

Jesus undoubtedly knew this Psalm,[26] and in conjunction with his love of the Torah and the commandments,[27] Jesus could not have had a view different from that of the sages as to how one manifests love for God. In short, in light of the significance that the Shema has played in the life and death of the Jewish people, it is most understandable why Jesus believed that this was the greatest of the Torah's commandments.

The Second Greatest Commandment: To Love One's Neighbor

We now turn to the "second great commandment" of which Jesus spoke, to love one's neighbor: "You shall love your neighbor as yourself."[28] But how does one love one's neighbor? Certainly no one can truly love others as much as oneself. Indeed, only saints would put another's life before their own. Moreover, since the Torah never demands that we do that which is impossible,[29] neither the Torah's nor Jesus' words can be taken literally.[30] What then does it mean to love one's neighbor as oneself? To answer this question, we explore the views of several ancient rabbis.

Manifesting Love of Others

One rabbi explained that the injunction to love one's neighbor as oneself means that we must show respect and consideration to our fellow human beings. This simple interpretation is nevertheless profound, since if the world obeyed this one commandment as interpreted by this rabbi, there would be not one murder, rape, robbery, or theft. Another rabbi interpreted the passage to mean that we should love not only righteous people, but also those who are not so easy to love. Yet another rabbi held that to love another as oneself means to love without ulterior reasons. For example, one should not love a relative in order to obtain a loan. One rabbi gave some concrete examples of how a person shows love to others. These include being truthful with them and not dishonest or hypocritical; being respectful of them; asking of their welfare; being empathetic when they are grieving or in pain; assisting them financially; and not considering oneself better than them.[31]

Why Did Jesus Reduce the 613 Commandments to Two?

The reader will recall that in answer to the Pharisee's question regarding which is the greatest of the commandments, Jesus replied: "You shall love the Lord your God with all your heart, and with all your soul, and with all your mind. This is the greatest and first commandment. And a second is like it: You shall love your neighbor as yourself. On these two commandments hang all the law and the prophets."[32] Jesus thus taught his students to love God by carrying out his commandments and to love others by respecting them or assisting them in their need. But why did Jesus even answer the Pharisee's question in the first place? Considering Jesus' love of the Torah and the law,[33] why did Jesus even attempt to reduce the 613 commandments to only two?

Jewish Sages Distilled the Essence of All the Commandments

In answering this question, we need to know that Jesus was not the first Jewish teacher who sought to summarize the commandments and teachings of the Torah. For example, Micah summarized the Torah by teaching others "to do justice, and to love kindness, and to walk humbly with your God."[34] Similarly, Isaiah instructed others to "maintain justice, and do what is right."[35] Hillel, one of Judaism's great teachers,[36] summarized the Torah in one teaching: "What is hateful to you do not do to others."[37]

A Starting Point for Repentance

But did Micah, Isaiah, Hillel, and Jesus literally mean that the essence of the Torah is but one or two sentences? Clearly they did not. Because the Torah is the work of God,[38] there is a reason for each and every commandment that is given, and no one can excise even one commandment.[39] Indeed, Jesus himself taught, "whoever breaks one of the least of these commandments, and teaches others to do the same, will be called least in the kingdom of heaven."[40] What then were Micah, Isaiah, Hillel, and Jesus trying to accomplish? Each was merely attempting to provide a direction for those who needed guidance. In short, all of these teachers gave their listeners a starting point for repentance: for sinners to peel off the veneer of wickedness that encapsulates their soul and return to God in a state of purity, the state in which every person was originally created (Judaism does not subscribe to the fundamental Christian teaching of Original Sin).[41] But why only a starting point? If all 613 commandments are important, why not just give penitents a list of all of the commandments they need to perform?

Why Only a Starting Point?

Let us suppose that a Jewish man has led a life lacking in morality: He has been unkind to his wife, fraudulent with his employer, and deceitful to his friends. Moreover, the man has not been to a synagogue in many years, never says the required blessings before and after eating meals, never honors the sabbath, and never fasts on *Yom Kippur*, the Day of Atonement. One day, however, the man realizes that his life is in total disarray: His wife wants a divorce, his boss has fired him, and his community has ostracized him. Having reached his bottom, he now wants to straighten himself out. He wants to become more observant in Jewish law, both morally and ritually. In short, the man wants to repent (*teshuva* in Hebrew); he wants to return to God and become pure, as when he was born. The man then contacts a rabbi for guidance. Will the rabbi simply give him a list of all 613 commandments and tell the man to start complying? It is doubtful.

The man in question is so far removed from a correct lifestyle that to give him a book on being an observant Jew would probably overwhelm him and defeat the purpose of helping him to repent. What then might the rabbi do? He might tell the man that he needs to start being kind to his wife and honest with his friends. He might suggest that the man write a letter of apology to his employer and make restitution for any losses caused by the deceit. Perhaps the rabbi will invite him to attend synagogue services on the sabbath. But in that first meeting, the rabbi is not going to demand that the man immediately comply with all of the Torah's commandments. Just as one cannot put up a building in one day, one cannot turn around a person in one day. Repentance is a process, and time is often crucial. When the individual performs one commandment that he previously did not perform, he infuses a holiness into the world, and he himself consequently becomes more holy.[42] And so the rabbi will undoubtedly point the individual in the proper direction. As did Micah, Isaiah, Hillel, and Jesus.

CHAPTER 11

Faith and Deeds

I n this chapter, we explore the relationship between faith and deeds and see that although faith is an important aspect of Judaism, Judaism is essentially a religion of deeds. We then contrast the Jewish view of faith and deeds with the Christian perspective.

Faith Is Integral to Judaism

It is indisputable that faith—that which cannot be proven by any human method—is quite important to any Torah-believing Jew. Indeed, the Thirteen Principles of Faith[1] make it incumbent upon a Jew to have faith that God exists[2] and that he is One,[3] incorporeal,[4] and eternal;[5] that he alone is to be worshipped;[6] that the prophets are true[7] and that God gave Moses his Torah,[8] which is the same Torah we have today[9] and which is unchangeable;[10] that God is omniscient[11] and that he will reward good and punish evil;[12] that God will send his Messiah at the proper time,[13] and at that time there will be a resurrection of the dead.[14]

The Talmud and other rabbinical literature are replete with teachings that relate to the importance of having faith in God, his Torah, and the aforementioned principles. In fact, so important are these matters of faith that one rabbi went so far as to state, "One who denies idolatry is as though he has acknowledged the entire Torah,"[15] and another declared,

"He who denies the Resurrection, the Divine origin of the Torah, and reward and punishment has no share in the World to Come."[16] From where did the ancient rabbis deduce that faith is so important? From the Hebrew Scriptures, which are brimming with references to people who had great faith in God and his Torah: from Abraham, the first of Judaism's Three Patriarchs, to Malachi, the last of Judaism's prophets.[17]

The Book of Hebrews

The New Testament Book of Hebrews provides not only a wonderful definition of faith, but also a digest of many Old Testament figures who exhibited great faith in God:

> Now faith is the assurance of things hoped for, the conviction of things not seen. Indeed, by faith our ancestors received approval. By faith we understand that the words were prepared by the word of God, so that what is seen was made from things that are not visible.
>
> By faith Abel offered to God a more acceptable sacrifice than Cain's. Through this he received approval as righteous, God himself giving approval to his gifts; he died, but through his faith he still speaks.[18] By faith Enoch was taken so that he did not experience death; and "he was not found, because God had taken him." For it was attested before he was taken away that "he had pleased God."[19] And without faith it is impossible to please God, for whoever would approach him must believe that he exists and that he rewards those who seek him. By faith Noah, warned by God about events as yet unseen, respected the warning and built an ark to save his household; by this he condemned the world and became an heir to the righteousness that is in accordance with faith.[20]
>
> By faith Abraham obeyed when he was called to set out for a place that he was to receive as an inheritance; and he set out, not knowing where he was going.[21] By faith he stayed for a time in the land he had been promised, as in a foreign land, living in tents, as did Isaac and Jacob, who were heirs with

him of the same promise. For he looked forward to the city that has foundations, whose architect and builder is God. By faith he received power of procreation, even though he was too old— and Sarah herself was barren—because he considered him faithful who had promised.²² Therefore from one person, and this one as good as dead, descendants were born, as many as the stars of heaven and as the innumerable grains of sand by the seashore.²³

All of these died in faith without having received the promises, but from a distance they saw and greeted them. They confessed that they were strangers and foreigners on the earth, for people who speak in this way make it clear that they are seeking a homeland.²⁴ If they had been thinking of the land that they had left behind, they would have had opportunity to return. But as it is, they desire a better country, that is, a heavenly one. Therefore God is not ashamed to be called their God; indeed, he has prepared a city for them.

By faith Abraham, when put to the test, offered up Isaac.²⁵ He who had received the promises was ready to offer up his only son, of whom he had been told, "It is through Isaac that descendants shall be named for you."²⁶ He considered the fact that God is able even to raise someone from the dead—and figuratively speaking, he did receive him back.²⁷ By faith Isaac invoked blessings for the future on Jacob and Esau.²⁸ By faith Jacob, when dying, blessed each of the sons of Joseph, "bowing in worship over the top of his staff."²⁹ By faith Joseph, at the end of his life, made mention of the exodus of the Israelites and gave instructions about his burial.³⁰

By faith Moses was hidden by his parents for three months after his birth, because they saw that the child was beautiful; and they were not afraid of the king's edict.³¹ By faith Moses, when he was grown up, refused to be called a son of Pharaoh's daughter,³² choosing rather to share ill-treatment with the people of God than to enjoy the fleeting pleasures of sin. He considered abuse suffered for the Christ to be greater wealth than the treasures of Egypt, for he was looking ahead to the reward.³³ By faith he left Egypt, unafraid of the king's anger; for he persevered as though he saw him who is invisible.³⁴ By faith he kept the Passover and the sprinkling of blood, so that the destroyer of the firstborn would not touch the firstborn of Israel.³⁵

By faith the people passed through the Red Sea as if it were dry land, but when the Egyptians attempted to do so they were drowned.³⁶ By faith the walls of Jericho fell after they had been encircled for seven days.³⁷ By faith Rahab the prostitute did not perish with those who were disobedient, because she had received the spies in peace.³⁸

And what more should I say? For time would fail me to tell of Gideon,³⁹ Barak,⁴⁰ Samson,⁴¹ Jephthah,⁴² of David⁴³ and Samuel⁴⁴ and the prophets—who through faith conquered kingdoms,⁴⁵ administered justice, obtained promises, shut the mouths of lions,⁴⁶ quenched raging fire,⁴⁷ escaped the edge of the sword, won strength out of weakness, became mighty in war, put foreign armies to flight.⁴⁸ Women received their dead by resurrection.⁴⁹ Others were tortured, refusing to accept release, in order to obtain a better resurrection. Others suffered mocking and flogging, and even chains and imprisonment.⁵⁰ They were stoned to death,⁵¹ they were sawn in two, they were tempted, they were killed with the sword;⁵² they went about in skins of sheep and goats, destitute, persecuted, tormented—of whom the world was not worthy. They wandered in deserts and mountains, and in caves and holes in the ground.

Yet all these, though they were commended for their faith, did not receive what was promised, since God had provided something better so that they would not, apart from us, be made perfect.⁵³

As the Book of Hebrews makes clear, faith in God and in his commandments and promises is important in Judaism.

Deeds Are Primary in Judaism

Nevertheless, although faith is important, we shall now explore why Judaism treats deeds—behavior—more importantly than faith.

How Is Faith Measured?

Once we recognize that faith is important, how exactly do we measure a person's faith? What does it mean to say that a Jew "firmly believes in the coming of the Messiah"?[54] What if the person generally believes but, like many, questions his or her faith from time to time? And what can we say about a person who has absolute faith in most principles, such as the Divine authorship of the Torah, but a less-than-full faith in others, such as the coming of the Messiah? And what about the agnostic?

The Covenant Was Sealed by a Promise to Do and Obey

A careful reading of the Torah sheds some light on this problem. Before the Revelation on Mount Sinai, God instructed Moses to tell the Israelites, "if you obey my voice and keep my covenant, you shall be my treasured possession out of all the peoples."[55] Note that God stated that the Jewish people were to *obey* him and his Torah ("my covenant"). The response of the Jewish people is also recorded in the Torah. All of them answered together and said, "Everything that the LORD has spoken we will *do*."[56] After the Revelation, the Jewish people had to make the decision whether to reaffirm their acceptance of the Torah. The Torah states that all of the people again answered with one voice and said, "All the words that the LORD has spoken we will *do*."[57] Moses then wrote down all the words of God and took the Torah and read it to the people.[58] Again they said, "All that the LORD has spoken we will we *do, and we will be obedient*."[59]

The covenant with the Jewish people was thus sealed when they promised to *do* and *obey*. The covenant, interestingly enough, was not consummated by their promising to believe. Of course, as the first of the Ten Commandments makes clear, a Jew must believe in God,[60] which itself may be said to be an act of faith. But assuming a Jew has faith in the existence of God, whether a Jew is otherwise observant is simple to determine: Does the person *comply* with God's Torah and his commandments? If the answer is yes, then the person is doing the will of the Creator; if the answer is no, then the person is not. For this reason, the rabbis decreed that if a Jew *complies* with the commandments, even though not *believing* in them, there is still much merit in such compliance.[61] How can someone comply with the commandments even though lacking complete faith in Divine authority?

Doing Without Believing Has Merit

The following example will be helpful in answering the foregoing question: Let us suppose there is a Jewish man who obeys the dietary laws, observes the sabbath, and participates in prayer thrice daily, all of which are required by the Torah's commandments. However, he observes the commandments solely because he wants to please his Torah-observant wife, and not because he fully believes in the Divine origin of the commandments. Certainly such a person is not the ideal: He does, but he has no faith in what he does. Nevertheless, Judaism teaches that there is still much merit in his conduct.[62] Why? Because Judaism emphasizes action and deeds. Yes, faith is important.[63] This was demonstrated by Abraham, Moses, and the many other heroes in the Hebrew Scriptures.[64] But Judaism holds that deeds are actually more important than mere faith.[65] Of course, the ideal is both faith and deeds, but God sealed the covenant with the Jewish people when they promised to do and obey, as Abraham did and obeyed. Indeed, the Jerusalem Talmud states, "It is better that the Jewish people abandon me [God] and continue to observe my laws."[66] Why would God have this? Because, as the Mishnah explains, through observance a person will eventually return to God.[67] In other words, from doing comes believing.

Many Christians are at first amazed that deeds can be considered more important than faith. Indeed, because faith is so important in Christianity,[68] many Christians quite understandably believe that to act without faith is nothing less than hypocrisy. Consider, however, the following hypothetical: A child is severely injured in a car accident. One of the bystanders on the scene happens to be a doctor, who calls the paramedics from his car phone. The doctor is told that the emergency medical team is on the way, but due to heavy traffic cannot arrive for fifteen minutes. The doctor knows that the child will die before the paramedics arrive unless someone administers emergency treatment immediately. The doctor has the skills to keep the child alive, but simply does not want to get involved: He is already late for an important golf game. But then the doctor reconsiders, not for humanitarian reasons, but for publicity reasons. Already reporters and camera crews are on the scene and the doctor thinks that he can get great publicity on the eleven o'clock news ("Doctor Saves Child's Life").

If the doctor is honest with himself, he would let the child die as he has absolutely no humanitarian interest in the child. On the other hand, if the doctor is a hypocrite, treating the child for only selfish reasons, the child lives. True, the ideal would be for the doctor to help the child because he believes in his heart that such a course of conduct is the right thing to do. But if his actions save the child's life, is that not good? Again, the ideal would be for the doctor to do and to believe. But failing that, Judaism believes that merely doing is superior to merely believing. Consequently, if a Jew gives to charity; observes the sabbath; eats only *kosher* food; performs acts of kindness for strangers, widows, and orphans; and otherwise leads a life true to the Torah, then irrespective of any lapses in faith, there is still much merit in what he or she does.[69]

Of course, none of this is to say that Christianity would disapprove of someone doing good deeds even when faith is lacking. The only point that needs to be made here is the difference in degree: Judaism is less concerned about beliefs than deeds, which is different from the Protestant position, but perhaps not that far removed from the Catholic view, as we explain below.

Righteousness Depends on Deeds, Not Beliefs

Judaism teaches that "the righteous of all nations have a share in the World to Come."[70] Whether or not someone is rewarded in the hereafter is dependent on the person's deeds, not beliefs. For this reason Judaism teaches that the World to Come is open not to Jews alone. Anyone may enter. Even a nonbelieving non-Jew can share in the World to Come. How does such a person share in the hereafter? By obeying the Seven Laws of Noah.[71]

Christian Views on Faith and Deeds

Having examined the Jewish view of faith and deeds, we are now prepared to contrast that with the Christian perspective. Initially, we should note that the Gospel declares the importance of faith: "The one who believes and is baptized will be saved; but the one who does not believe will be condemned."[72]

Jesus Recognized the Importance of Deeds

Nevertheless, it would be wrong to believe that deeds have no significance in Christianity. Indeed, Jesus himself taught the importance of deeds:

> *When the Son of Man comes in his glory, and the angels with him, then he will sit on the throne of his glory. All the nations will be gathered before him, and he will separate people one from another as a shepherd separates the sheep from the goats, and he will put the sheep at his right hand and the goats at the left. Then the king will say to those at his right hand, "Come, you that are blessed by my Father, inherit the kingdom prepared for you from the foundation of the world; for I was hungry and you gave me food, I was thirsty and you gave me something to drink, I was a stranger and you welcomed me, I was naked and you gave me clothing, I was sick and you took care of me, I was in prison and you visited me." Then the righteous will answer him, "Lord, when was it that we saw you hungry and gave you food, or thirsty and gave you something to drink? And when was it that we saw you a stranger and welcomed you, or naked and gave you clothing? And when was it that we saw you sick or in prison and visited you?" And the king will answer them, "Truly I tell you, just as you did it to one of the least of these who are members of my family, you did it to me." Then he will say to those at his left hand, "You that are accursed, depart from me into the eternal fire prepared for the devil and his angels; for I was hungry and you gave me no food, I was thirsty and you gave me nothing to drink, I was a stranger and you did not welcome me, naked*

and you did not give me clothing, sick and in prison and you did not visit me." Then they also will answer, "Lord, when was it that we saw you hungry or thirsty or a stranger or naked or sick or in prison, and did not take care of you?" Then he will answer them, "Truly I tell you, just as you did not do it to one of the least of these, you did not do it to me." And these will go away into eternal punishment, but the righteous into eternal life.[73]

Thus, Jesus here teaches that reward or punishment is based upon what people did in their lifetimes, not what they believed.[74]

James Recognized the Importance of Deeds

Similarly, James, the brother of Jesus,[75] also placed great emphasis on deeds:

What good is it, my brothers and sisters, if you say you have faith but do not have works? Can faith save you? If a brother or sister is naked and lacks daily food, and one of you says to them, "Go in peace; keep warm and eat your fill," and yet you do not supply their bodily needs, what is the good of that? So faith by itself, if it has no works, is dead.

But someone will say, "You have faith and I have works." Show me your faith apart from your works, and I by my works will show you my faith. You believe that God is one; you do well. Even the demons believe—and shudder. Do you want to be shown, you senseless person, that faith apart from works is barren? Was not our ancestor Abraham justified by works when he offered his son Isaac on the altar? You see that faith was active along with his works, and faith was brought to completion by the works. Thus the scripture was fulfilled that says, "Abraham believed God, and it was reckoned to him as righteousness,"[76] and he was called the friend of God. You see that a person is justified by works and not by faith alone. Likewise, was not Rahab the prostitute also justified by works when she welcomed the messengers and sent them out by another road? For just as the body without spirit is dead, so faith without works is also dead.[77]

By emphasizing the importance of works, that is, the performance of the Torah's commandments, Jesus and James were teaching basic Jewish doctrine: "Everything that the LORD has spoken we will do."[78]

Paul Emphasized Faith over Deeds

Nevertheless, Paul taught that works alone cannot save a person. According to Paul, salvation can come only from faith that Jesus is the Son of God: "We ourselves are Jews by birth and not Gentile sinners; yet we know that a person is justified not by the works of the law but through faith in Jesus Christ. And we have come to believe in Christ Jesus, so that we might be justified by faith in Christ, and not by doing the works of the law, because no none will be justified by the works of the law."[79] Indeed, Paul framed the problem quite well when he plainly declared, "I do not nullify the grace of God; for if justification comes through the law, then Christ died for nothing."[80] And Paul's position, that salvation comes from having faith in Jesus, became the foundation of Protestantism: Classical Protestant teaching is that salvation is determined solely on the basis of faith, with a person's good works looked upon as an outgrowth of that faith. This is to be contrasted with Catholic teaching, which requires both faith and deeds,[81] but holds that those who do not know Christ through no fault of their own and who follow their consciences to try to do God's will may also achieve eternal salvation.[82]

We, therefore, recognize that on the matter of faith and deeds, Judaism is significantly different from Protestantism since Judaism teaches that deeds are more important than faith, whereas faith is the essence of Protestantism. When comparing Judaism with Catholicism, however, the divide is much smaller, if at all.

In any event, notwithstanding Judaism's emphasis on deeds, if a person performs all of the Torah's 613 *mitzvot* ("commandments"), that alone cannot make the person a Jew. We therefore proceed to discuss who is a Jew.

CHAPTER 12

Who Is a Jew?

Through the centuries, it has been said by both evildoers and good people alike that the Jews are a "race." But such a view is simply incorrect because Jews are found in a variety of racial classifications: Caucasian, Asian, and Black. Furthermore, although a person can be a Jew by birth, one can also become a Jew by choice, that is, by converting to Judaism. Obviously, if being a Jew were solely a matter of blood and genes, conversion would not be possible.

Thus, there are two ways that a person can be Jewish: by birth or conversion. We will examine both in this chapter. We conclude the chapter with a brief discussion of a related matter: the identity of the Messiah.

Matrilineal Descent

Under traditional Jewish law, a person is Jewish if he or she is born to a Jewish mother (who herself either was born to a Jewish mother or became a convert to Judaism before the birth of her child).[1] Similarly, if a person is born to a non-Jewish mother, the person is not Jewish in the absence of a valid conversion to Judaism.

The basis for this rule is found in the Torah. In prohibiting marriages between the children of Israel and the seven nations inhabiting Canaan,[2] the Torah states: "Do not intermarry with them, giving your daughters to their sons or taking their daughters for your sons, for [the non-Jewish husband] will turn away your [grand]children[3] from following me [God], to serve other gods."[4] Based upon this passage, the rabbinical commentators note that the Torah declares two prohibited marriage scenarios: (1) a Jewish woman and a non-Jewish man ("giving your daughters to their sons"), and (2) a Jewish man and a non-Jewish woman ("taking their daughters for your sons"). But it is only in the first case—a Jewish mother and a non-Jewish father—where the Torah is concerned that the child of this "mixed marriage" will be turned away from following God, "for [the non-Jewish husband] will turn away your [grand]children[5] from following me."[6] There is no concern that the offspring who is born of a Jewish man and a non-Jewish woman will be turned away from God and his commandments. Why not? Because such a child is not Jewish. On the other hand, when a child is born of a Jewish woman and a non-Jewish man, there is a concern that such a child will be turned away from God and his Torah. Thus, by implication, such a child (Jewish mother, non-Jewish father) is Jewish.

A Person Cannot Be "Part Jewish"

One often hears someone say, "I am one-quarter Jewish" or "I am part Jewish." In light of the preceding discussion, however, it may now be seen why this is not possible. Under Jewish law, a person is either Jewish or not.[7] If the mother is Jewish, the child is Jewish; if the mother is not Jewish, the child is not Jewish. One cannot be "part Jewish." The following true story is illustrative.

There was a young woman who was raised by her parents as a devout Catholic, had attended a Catholic parochial school, and was at the time attending a Catholic college when she and her friends (also Catholics from the same college) went to Israel for a summer. One day, she and her friends came across several rabbis and began a pleasant discussion with them about Israel and Judaism. In the course of the exchange, the woman told the rabbis that she was "part Jewish." One of the rabbis asked her who in her family was Jewish. The woman responded that it was her grandmother. The rabbi then asked her whether it was her maternal or paternal grandmother who was Jewish. She responded that it was her maternal grandmother. The woman was amazed to learn (from Orthodox rabbis, no less) that if her maternal grandmother was in fact Jewish, both she and her mother were Jewish. Not partly Jewish. Just Jewish.

Devotion to Judaism Is Irrelevant

Let us suppose that a child is born to a Gentile mother and a Jewish father. Let us further suppose that the child is given a Hebrew name, is raised as a Jew, and attends a *Yeshiva* (a school for study of Jewish law, tradition, and custom). As the child becomes an adult, he or she observes the sabbath, eats only *kosher* food, and otherwise lives his or her life as an ultra-Orthodox Jew. Nevertheless, the person is not Jewish. On the other hand, if a person is born to a Jewish mother, even if the person eats non-kosher food, never goes to synagogue, does not celebrate any Jewish holidays, and never sanctifies the sabbath, the person is nonetheless Jewish. And if such a person is female, any child she gives birth to, irrespective of the religion of her husband, is also Jewish.

Some may think it strange that a person born of a Jewish father and a non-Jewish mother is not Jewish (in the absence of a conversion), even if the person is a great Torah scholar and fully observant of all Jewish laws, while one who is born of a Jewish mother is Jewish even if he or she regularly violates numerous laws of the Torah. The following illustration will help to clarify the matter.

A person who is born in the United States is, pursuant to the Constitution, a United States citizen. Such a person may never be concerned with the history of the United States. He or she may never even register to vote, may not know the significance of the Fourth of July, and may not even know, or care to know, who George Washington was. It is even possible that such a person cannot speak a word of English. Yet, this person is a citizen of the United States. On the other hand, a person who is not born in this country—even though he or she may be learned in American history and culture, fluent in the English language, and a great supporter of the United States—is not a citizen in the absence of a "conversion," that is, becoming a United States citizen by naturalization. Why? Because the law says so. And so it is with Judaism.[8]

A Jew Cannot Cease to Be a Jew

What happens—God forbid—if a Jew disavows God and the Torah or converts to another religion? Does that in any way change his or her Jewish identity? The answer is no. Nothing that a Jew does can ever sever his or her Jewish heritage. Thus, if a Jew (whether by birth or conversion) adopted another religion but thereafter left that religion to return to Judaism, no actions by a rabbi or rabbinical court are necessary. Why is this so? Because once a Jew, always a Jew. As the Talmud states, "An Israelite who sins is still an Israelite."[9] Thus, if a Jew converts to another religion, he or she will be looked upon by family and friends as having committed a terrible sin. But the sinner is still a Jew.

Christianity Compared

Christianity is different from Judaism in this regard: No person can become a Christian by birth; he or she must first be baptized into the faith.[10] Moreover, a Christian who subsequently rejects Jesus and converts to another religion is arguably not a Christian any longer, although the validity of the previous baptism would not be nullified.

The Oswald Rufeisen Case

Although, according to Jewish law (*halacha*), a Jew can never do anything to cease being a Jew, the Oswald Rufeisen case is instructive in understanding how Jewish law may conflict with modern Israeli law, which is not generally based on halacha.[11]

In 1942, a Polish Jew by the name of Oswald Rufeisen converted to Catholicism. In 1945 he entered a monastic order and became Brother Daniel. With the defeat of the Nazis (whom Rufeisen had fought against in the Polish underground movement) and the reestablishment of the State of Israel, he sought to emigrate to Israel under the Law of Return. The Law of Return, enacted in the ashes of the Nazi death camps, grants any Jew who wishes to emigrate to Israel automatic citizenship. In his immigration papers, Rufeisen acknowledged that he had converted to Catholicism. Nevertheless, he also demonstrated his love for Israel and his continued identification as a Jew and member of the Jewish community. The Israeli Minister of the Interior refused to grant Rufeisen citizenship on the ground that by converting to another faith, he was no longer a Jew.[12] The case[13] eventually went to the Israeli Supreme Court, which sustained the Minister of the Interior.

Although the court expressed great sympathy for Rufeisen and acknowledged that he was a Jew for purposes of halacha,[14] it held that halacha is not applicable in defining who is a Jew as it relates to the Law of Return. For purposes of the Law of Return, the court decided that the question of who is a Jew is defined from a historical-national viewpoint and the ordinary meaning of the term "Jew." From this perspective, the court found that Rufeisen was no longer a Jew: "[W]hat Brother Daniel is asking us to do is to erase the historical and sanctified significance of the term 'Jew' and to deny all the spiritual values for which our people were killed during various periods in our long dispersion. . . . A sacrifice such as this no one is entitled to ask of us, even one so meritorious as the petitioner. . . ."[15] To be declared a Jew for purposes of the Law of Return, one need not adhere to the laws of halacha, but one who turns to Christianity is deemed removed from the Jewish community.[16]

Thus, for purposes of the Law of Return, a Jew is one born of a Jewish mother or converted to Judaism and who does not profess another faith. Outside the State of Israel, a conversion is valid if a certificate of conversion is issued by any Jewish congregation, whether it be Orthodox, Conservative, Reform, or Reconstructionist.

Patrilineal Descent and Liberal Judaism

The preceding discussion, that a person is a Jew by birth if the person's mother is a Jew, represents the view of the Orthodox and Conservative movements. In Judaism's liberal Reform and Reconstructionist movements, however, a child born to a Jewish father and a non-Jewish mother is Jewish if the child is raised as a Jew, identifies as a Jew, and observes Jewish life-cycle commandments.[17] Both the Conservative and Orthodox movements, however, thoroughly reject patrilineal descent. Why do the Reform and Reconstructionist movements recognize patrilineal descent while the Conservative and Orthodox movements do not? The Reformers and Reconstructionists believe that with the high rate of intermarriage (Jews marrying non-Jews), now in excess of fifty percent, to continue to abide by traditional law (that the child of a non-Jewish mother is not Jewish, even if the child's father is Jewish and the child is raised as a Jew) needlessly drives people out of the Jewish community.[18] Indeed, the Jewish population worldwide at the time of this writing is only about eighteen million,[19] the same number that existed in 1938, the year chosen by many to mark the beginning of the Holocaust—which saw the murder of fully one-third of the Jewish people. The Reformers and Reconstructionists believe that with so few Jews in the world, if a person has a Jewish father and is raised as a Jew, he or she should be considered a Jew. But the rabbis within the Orthodox and Conservative movements take a more basic and traditional approach: Who is a Jew is a matter of Torah law, which cannot be changed.

Conversion: Jews by Choice

Needless to say, even the Orthodox and Conservative rabbis would welcome the person born of a Jewish father and non-Jewish mother if the person wanted to convert to Judaism. But traditionally, Jews have not actively sought to convert non-Jews since Judaism teaches that all righteous people, irrespective of beliefs,[20] go to heaven.[21] As the rabbis of old taught, "The righteous of all nations have a share in the World to Come."[22]

A person who is not Jewish but who strongly identifies with the Jewish people and is desirous of keeping the Torah's commandments may, of course, convert to Judaism. By some estimates, three percent of American Jews are converts (converts often refer to themselves as "Jews by choice") and their numbers are expected to grow to as much as ten percent in the coming decades. In any event, conversion is a process which requires much learning under the auspices of a rabbi. An Orthodox conversion may take a year or more of learning. A Reform conversion is typically shorter in duration. A rabbinical court (*beth din*) must be convened in order to effect a conversion.

A traditional conversion culminates with the man undergoing circumcision[23] and immersion in a ritual bath called a *mikvah*. For a woman, the conversion is culminated only with immersion in the mikvah. Once a person converts to Judaism, he or she has the same obligations to comply with the 613 commandments as does one who is a Jew by birth. As such, a convert to Judaism is as Jewish as one who is born of a Jewish mother. In fact, it is prohibited to talk about the proselyte's past,[24] lest the convert feel that he or she is not fully part of the Jewish people. As the Torah states: "The alien who resides with you shall be to you as the citizen among you; you shall love the alien as yourself, for you were aliens in the land of Egypt: I am the LORD your God."[25] That converts are as Jewish as those born into the religion is beautifully told in the story of Ruth.

Ruth the Proselyte

There was a Jewish couple by the name of Naomi and Elimelech who, along with their two sons, settled in the land of Moab.[26] Sometime thereafter, one son married Orpah; the other married Ruth.[27] Both Orpah and Ruth were not Jews, but Moabites.[28] The Moabites were a pagan tribe[29] who did not treat Israel kindly after the Exodus from Egypt.[30] After some time, Naomi's husband and sons died.[31] Naomi thereupon decided to return to Israel.[32] She then bade each of her daughters-in-law to return to their own people: "Go back each of you to your mother's house. May the LORD deal kindly with you, as you have dealt with the dead and with me."[33] But both Orpah and Ruth refused to leave Naomi, desiring to return with her to Israel.[34] Whereupon Naomi lovingly replied, "Turn back, my daughters, go your way. . . ."[35] Orpah then kissed Naomi farewell, "but Ruth clung to her."[36]

Now for a third time Naomi tried to dissuade Ruth from coming with her.[37] But Ruth would not leave, and made a passionate plea to Naomi: "Do not press me to leave you or to turn back from following you! Where you go, I will go: where you lodge, I will lodge; your people shall be my people, and your God my God. Where you die, I will die—there will I be buried. May the LORD do thus and so to me, and more as well, if even death parts me from you!"[38] Ruth did not wish merely to go with Naomi to Israel, but to accept upon herself all of the commandments of the Jewish people. With this Ruth converted to Judaism.

From the foregoing dialogue, two touching themes emerge, which we will now discuss.

Prospective Proselytes to Be Dissuaded from Converting

By tradition, when a person contacts a rabbi and seeks to convert to Judaism, the rabbi is duty-bound to attempt three times to dissuade the person from converting, just as Naomi attempted to dissuade Ruth from converting.[39] Why is this the case? Because, as previously mentioned,[40] one does not need to be a Jew in order to go to heaven; a Gentile who obeys the Seven Laws of Noah is assured of a place in the World to Come. Further, while a Noachide (a non-Jew ethical monotheist) has only seven commandments (or categories of commandments) to be concerned with, a Jew has many more.[41] As such, only a person who is truly desirous of becoming a Jew and accepting the "yoke of the Torah"[42] should convert. It is better for one to be a Noachide-practicing Gentile than a non-observant Jew.

Of course, once a prospective convert makes a clear commitment to accept the Torah and become part of the Jewish people, he or she is welcomed with open arms.[43]

Proselytes Are Jews in Every Respect

The story of Ruth has a second theme: Once a Gentile converts to Judaism, he or she is fully accepted and is as much a Jew as one who was born to a Jewish mother.[44] How do we deduce this from the account of Ruth? Not only was Ruth a non-Jew, but she was from the tribe of Moab. As stated earlier, this tribe not only practiced idolatry,[45] but was cruel to Israel: The Moabites did not offer the Israelites bread and water,[46] or even allow them to pass through the land of Moab after the Exodus from Egypt.[47] Because the Moabites were so lacking in compassion to their Jewish cousins (the Moabites were descended from Lot, the nephew of Abraham),[48] God forbade the males of the Moabites[49] from ever converting to Judaism and, thus, entering into the congregation of marriage with the Jewish people.[50]

Notwithstanding the scorn that Israel had for the tribe of Moab, and the fact that Ruth was a member of that tribe, she was fully accepted into the Jewish community. Indeed, when Boaz, a relative of Ruth's deceased husband, married Ruth, the Jewish people and the elders of Bethlehem declared, "May the LORD make the woman who is coming into your house like Rachel and Leah, who together built up the house of Israel. May you produce children in Ephrathah and bestow a name in Bethlehem; and, through the children that the LORD will give you by this young woman, may your house be like the house of Perez, whom Tamar bore to Judah."[51] And soon thereafter, Ruth gave birth to a son who was named Obed. Obed became the father of Jesse, who was the father of David.[52] The Messiah will be descended from the line of David.[53]

That converts to Judaism are fully Jews is thus made clear from the Book of Ruth: A convert from the ignominious tribe of Moab would become the great-grandmother of King David and the ancestor of the Messiah.

The Identity of the Messiah

We conclude this chapter on a related matter: the identity of the Messiah. As it is written by the prophet, "On that day the root of Jesse [the father of King David] shall stand as a signal to the peoples; the nations shall inquire of him, and his dwelling shall be glorious."[54] Consequently, the traditional Jewish view is that the Messiah must be Jewish and must be able to trace his lineage back to King David. For this reason, the Gospel goes to great lengths to establish that Jesus was Jewish (through his mother Mary) and able to trace his lineage back to David, and even beyond.[55] The Gospel thus serves to give Jesus the necessary bona fides to establish his claim to the Messianic throne. Of course, Christians accept Jesus' lineage and Messianic kingship while Jews do not.[56]

CHAPTER 13

Judaism as a Way of Life

We have seen in the previous chapters that Judaism is both a religion and a legal system. But Judaism is more than a religion and a legal system. It is a way of life, too, for observant Jews as well as for non-observant Jews.

A Way of Life for Observant Jews

Judaism is a way of life for the observant Jew because being observant means that virtually every hour of every day is surrounded by ritual, the purpose of which is to be reminded of the omnipresence of God and to make him and his commandments the center of one's life. For example, there are blessings to be recited upon awakening in the morning; there are three daily prayer services to recite; there are foods that cannot be eaten;[1] as well as many other commandments for which the observant Jew is thankful to be able to perform.

Yearly Cycle

Being an observant Jew also means recognizing that life is affected by yearly cycles. For example, in September is *Rosh Hashanah* ("Head of the

Year," that is, the New Year),[2] which commemorates the creation of the universe and humankind and is a time for prayer, introspection, charity, and repentance. Ten days later is *Yom Kippur* ("Day of Atonement"),[3] a day[4] of complete fasting which culminates the Ten Days of Repentance. In the fall, *Sukkot* ("Tabernacles") is celebrated,[5] and Jews live in temporary booths to commemorate the forty years the Jewish people spent traveling in the desert after the Exodus from Egypt. In December is *Hanukkah* ("Dedication"),[6] which commemorates the victory of the Jewish people over the Syrians in 165 B.C.E. and the rededication of the Temple, which the Syrians had previously profaned in their attempt to destroy Judaism. With the spring thaw comes Passover and participation in the Passover *seder* (the Passover meal),[7] a law that has been followed continuously for every year since the first Passover in the year 1312 B.C.E., when the Israelites went out from Egypt.[8] Seven weeks later is the holiday of *Shavuot* ("Weeks"),[9] which commemorates the Revelation on Mount Sinai and the giving of the Ten Commandments.[10] In July or August falls *Tisha B'Av* (literally, the "Ninth Day of [the Hebrew month of] Av"),[11] the day that the First Temple was destroyed by the Babylonians in 586 B.C.E. and the Second Temple by the Romans in 70 C.E. Tisha B'Av is commemorated by a day of fasting and reading from the Book of Lamentations. And so, the cycle of the Jewish year goes on and on.

Life Cycle

Being an observant Jew also means celebrating major life-cycle events. For example, it means marrying under the *chuppah* ("marriage canopy") beneath the nighttime stars;[12] circumcising one's son on the eighth day of his young life;[13] preparing for the *Bar Mitzvah* (literally, "Son of the Commandment") of one's son when he reaches adulthood at age thirteen, or the *Bat Mitzvah* ("Daughter of the Commandment") of one's daughter when she reaches twelve;[14] paying a *shiva* call (visiting the house of someone who is mourning the death of a family member); and saying *Kaddish* (the memorial prayer for the dead) daily for the first eleven months following the death of one's parent.

Kiddush Hashem: To Sanctify the Divine Name

One should not believe, however, that ritual is the only concern for the observant Jew; there is also a constant concern to comply with strict rules of ethical behavior. Indeed, contrary to popular misconceptions,[15] an observant Jew must always conduct himself or herself with the utmost modesty,[16] honesty,[17] and integrity.[18] When a Jew acts in a manner that causes non-Jews to admire the Jewish religion, this is called *Kiddush Hashem* ("Sanctification of God's Name"). But for a Jew to conduct himself or herself in a manner that will cause others to speak poorly of the Jewish people is *Chillul Hashem* ("Desecration of God's Name").[19] Moreover, as part of this ethical behavior, a Jew is required to assist non-Jews as well as Jews.[20] For example, the Torah states: "Every third year you shall bring out the full tithe of your produce for that year, and store it within your towns; the Levites, because they have no allotment . . . as well as the resident aliens . . . may come and eat their fill so that the LORD your God may bless you in all the work that you undertake."[21] Consistent with this is the Talmudic teaching, "We support the poor of the Gentiles along with the poor of Israel."[22]

A Way of Life for Jews Not Fully Observant

But what of those Jews who are not fully observant? Many Jews who are not Orthodox (only ten percent of American Jews are) nevertheless participate in at least some rituals. For example, it is estimated that fully ninety percent of all Jews celebrate Passover. Virtually all have their sons circumcised. Many light the Friday-night candles to usher in the sabbath.[23] And although many Jews may eat prohibited foods[24] outside their home, a good number keep *kosher* (use food and utensils that are in compliance with Jewish law) inside their homes. Many also donate time and money to charitable causes, fulfilling an important commandment in Judaism.[25] For these Jews, Judaism is still very much a way of life.

A Way of Life for "Secular" Jews, Too

And what of those who are best described as "secular" Jews (that is, Jews who do not abide by any of the ritual laws of Judaism)? Can it still be said of them that Judaism is a way of life? To this, the answer is yes. Irrespective of the degree of observance, being Jewish means remembering the past twenty centuries of persecutions, expulsions, pogroms, and death camps that one's ancestors and family were subjected to, and being vigilant to help make sure that it does not happen again, to the Jewish community or to others. For example, during the 1950s and 1960s, many prominent Jewish lawyers gave their time, energy, and money to actively support this nation's young civil rights movement. Many "Freedom Riders," Northerners who went to the South to participate in civil disobedience, were Jewish college students who put themselves in harm's way to end segregation. Some paid with their lives.

A Common Bond Among All Jews

Whether one is an Orthodox Jew or a Reform Jew, a secular Jew or any other type of Jew, being Jewish means feeling a special type of rage when an Arab terrorist blows up a bus in Tel Aviv packed with Israeli men, women, and children. (Before detonating a bomb, terrorists have never asked whether the intended victims keep *kosher*.) It also means supporting the United Jewish Appeal to help settle Jews who have emigrated from Ethiopia to Israel. And it means wanting to whack some fool when he says the Holocaust never happened.

Irrespective of the degree of observance, being Jewish means feeling like you belong when you enter a synagogue, even if you have not been to one in many years. Being Jewish means having a warm feeling remembering your grandfather going to synagogue. Being Jewish means still thinking of yourself as a Jew, irrespective of how observant (or nonobservant) you may be. As the Talmud teaches, "An Israelite who sins is still an Israelite."[26] Indeed, even Jews who have converted to other religions still consider themselves part of the Jewish community. One would think that a person who converts would want to sever his ties to Judaism. But such is not the case. For example, the Archbishop of Paris, Cardinal Jean-Marie Lustiger, who was born of Jewish parents and converted to Catholicism during the Holocaust, continues to strongly identify himself as a Jew. Why is this? Why does a Jew converted to Catholicism still identify with the Jewish people? Why do even agnostics continue to identify themselves as Jews? Because Judaism is more than a religion and a legal system. It is also a way of life.

A Duty to "Repair the World"

Wherever a Jew may be in his or her level of observance, being Jewish means being part of a link to those who stood at the base of Mount Sinai and accepted the responsibility to make the world a better place, what in Hebrew is called *tikkun ha-olam* ("repairing the world"). As Jesus himself said of the Jewish people, his people:

> *You are the salt of the earth; but if salt has lost its taste, how can its saltiness be restored? It is no longer good for anything, but is thrown out and trampled under foot.*
>
> *You are the light of the world. A city built on a hill cannot be hid. No one after lighting a lamp puts it under the bushel basket, but on the lampstand, and it gives light to all in the house. In the same way, let your light shine before others, so that they may see your good works and give glory to your Father in heaven.*[27]

Appendix 1

Orthodox Judaism and Traditional Christianity: A Comparison

SUBJECT	JUDAISM	CHRISTIANITY
(1) Monotheism	One God Absolute unity Personal	One God Absolute unity Personal
(2) Trinitarian Monotheism	Not recognized	Fundamental to Christianity
(3) Messiah	Has yet to come Will come once Not yet identified A mere mortal	Already came Will come a second time Jesus of Nazareth Second Person of the Holy Trinity
(4) Torah (Written Law)	Divine Revelation Perfect doctrine Immutable	Divine Revelation Good doctrine Perfected by the Gospel
(5) Mishnah (Oral Law)	Divine Revelation Perfect doctrine Elucidates the Torah	Not recognized Not recognized Not recognized
(6) New Covenant	Not recognized Not recognized Not recognized	Divine Revelation Perfect doctrine Elucidates the Torah
(7) Salvation	For all humanity Requires righteousness	For all humanity[1] Righteousness requires grace
(8) Original Sin	Not recognized	Fundamental to Christianity
(9) Vicarious Atonement	Not recognized	Fundamental to Christianity
(10) Afterlife	Recognized	Recognized
(11) Resurrection of the Dead	Recognized	Recognized

Appendix 2

A Summary of the 613 Commandments of the Torah as Redacted by Maimonides

This appendix contains a brief summary of each of the 613 commandments of the Torah as redacted by the twelfth-century scholar, Rabbi Moses ben Maimon (Maimonides) in his work, *Book of the Commandments* (see selected bibliography and suggested reading). Omitted here are the details of each commandment, many of which are quite complex and which Maimonides explains in *Book of the Commandments*. Of the 613 commandments, 248 are stated in the positive and 365 in the negative.

The two lists immediately below provide an overview of the topics covered by the 248 positive and 365 negative commandments. The corresponding numbers of the commandments are in parentheses. This overview is not part of Maimonides' original work. Nevertheless, it is useful in understanding his apparent organization.

Topics of the 248 Positive Commandments

- God (1-19).
- Holy Temple, Priesthood, and sacrifices (20-95).
- Ritual impurity and purification (96-113).
- Donations (114-133).
- Sabbatical and Jubilee Years (134-142).
- Food (143-152).

- ◆ Holidays (153-171).
- ◆ Jewish state (172-184).
- ◆ Idolatry (185-189).
- ◆ War and community (190-209).
- ◆ Family (210-223).
- ◆ Criminal law (224-231).
- ◆ Civil law (232-248).

Topics of the 365 Negative Commandments

- ◆ Idolatry (1-59).
- ◆ God and the Holy Temple (60-88).
- ◆ Sacrifices (89-157).
- ◆ Priests, Levites, and related matters (158-171).
- ◆ Diet (172-209).
- ◆ Agriculture and land (210-228).
- ◆ Business and the poor (229-272).
- ◆ Justice (273-319).
- ◆ Sabbath and holidays (320-329).
- ◆ Forbidden relationships and related matters (330-361).
- ◆ Kings (362-365).

Of the 613 commandments, many are presently not operative. For example, those that deal with the Holy Temple have been suspended because the Temple does not exist at this time. Similarly, the laws relating to kings of Israel are not now in effect. According to traditional Jewish belief, all 613 of these laws will once again become operative when the Messiah arrives, reestablishes the Davidic kingship, and ushers in the Final Redemption of the Jewish people and the world.

The positive commandments preceded by an asterisk (*) are those which, according to Maimonides, continue to bind the Jewish people (in the absence of the Temple and the Great Sanhedrin). Maimonides did not compile a similar list for the negative commandments, however. Perhaps it was because he felt that all of the negative commandments are always operative. But if that was his view, it was not unanimously held by all Jewish scholars. For example, the eighteenth-century sage Rabbi Israel Meir haCohen believed that only certain negative commandments continue to bind the Jewish people, and I have taken the liberty to share his view with the reader: The negative commandments preceded by an asterisk (*) are those, according to Rabbi haCohen, which remain in force for the Jewish people.

The first time a new or uncommon term appears in appendix 2, it has been italicized and can be found in the glossary at the back of this book. Each commandment is followed by its Biblical source in parentheses.

The 248 Positive Commandments

1. *   Believe in God (Exod. 20:2).
2. *   Believe in the Unity of God (Deut. 6:4).
3. *   Love God (Deut. 6:5).
4. *   Fear God (Deut. 6:13).
5. *   Worship God (Exod. 23:25; Deut. 6:13 and 13:5).
6. *   Cleave to God (Deut. 10:20).
7. *   Swear only by God's Name (Deut. 10:20).
8. *   Walk in God's ways (Deut. 28:9).
9. *   Sanctify God's Name (Lev. 22:32).
10. *   Read the *Shema* daily, morning and night (Deut. 6:7).
11. *   Study the *Torah* and teach others (Deut. 6:7).
12. *   Wear *tefillin* (phylactery) on the head (Deut. 6:8).
13. *   Wear tefillin on the arm (Deut. 6:8).
14. *   Wear *tzitzit* (garment of fringes) (Num. 15:38).
15. *   Attach a *mezuzah* to the door (Deut. 6:9).
16.   Assemble every seventh year to hear the Torah read (Deut. 31:12).
17.   The king must write a Torah scroll (Deut. 17:18).
18. *   Every man must acquire a Torah scroll for himself (Deut. 31:19).
19. *   Say grace after meals (Deut. 8:10).
20.   Build the Temple (Exod. 25:8).
21.   Revere the Temple (Lev. 19:30).
22.   Guard the Temple (Num. 18:14).
23.   *Levites* must perform certain services in the Temple (Num. 18:33).

24.   *Priests* must wash their hands and feet upon performing services (Exod. 30:19).

25.   Priests must daily light the lamps of the Temple (Exod. 27:21).

26. * Priests must bless Israel (Num. 6:23).

27.   Priests must set the showbread before the *Ark* of the Covenant (Exod. 25:30).

28.   Priests must burn incense twice daily on the altar of the Temple (Exod. 30:7).

29.   Priests must keep the fire burning continually on the altar (Lev. 6:6).

30.   Priests must remove the ashes daily from the altar (Lev. 6:3).

31.   Ritually unclean persons must be kept out of the Temple (Num. 5:2).

32. * Israel must honor its Priests (Lev. 21:8).

33.   Priests must wear special garments (Exod. 28:4-42).

34.   Priests must carry the Ark upon their shoulders (Num. 7:9).

35.   The *High Priest* must be anointed with a special oil (Exod. 30:31).

36.   Priests must weekly rotate their duties (Deut. 18:6-8).

37.   Priests must ritually defile themselves for certain deceased relatives (Lev. 21:2-3).

38.   The High Priest must marry only a virgin (Lev. 21:13).

39.   Make a continual burnt-offering twice daily (Num. 28:3).

40.   The High Priest must offer a meal-offering twice daily (Lev. 6:13).

41.   Make an additional offering on every sabbath (Num. 28:9).

42.   Offer a sacrifice on the first of every month (Num. 28:11).

43.   Offer a sacrifice on each of the seven days of *Passover* (Lev. 23:36).

44.   Make an offering of barley on the second day of Passover (Lev. 23:10).

45.   On *Shavuot*, make an additional offering (Num. 28:26-27).

46.   Bring two loaves of bread as an offering on Shavuot (Lev. 26:17).

47.   Make an additional offering on *Rosh Hashanah* (Num. 29:1-2).

48.   Make an additional offering on *Yom Kippur* (Num. 29:7-8).

49.   Perform the service on Yom Kippur (Lev. 16:1-34).

50.   An additional offering must be made on *Sukkot* (Num. 29:13).

51.   Make an additional offering on *Shemini Atzeret* (Num. 29:36).

52.   Go to the Temple three times a year to make an offering (Exod. 23:14).

53.   Go to the Temple during the *Pilgrim Festivals* (Exod. 34:23 and Deut. 16:16).

54. * Rejoice on the Pilgrim Festivals (Deut. 16:14).

55.   Slaughter the *Passover-offering* on the fourteenth day of *Nisan* (Exod. 12:6).

56.   Eat the roasted Passover-offering (Exod. 12:8).

57.   Slaughter the *Second Passover-offering* if previously unable to offer it (Num. 9:11).

58.   Eat the roasted Second Passover-offering (Num. 9:11).

59.   Blow trumpets for the Festival sacrifices and in times of trouble (Num. 10:9-10).

60.   Offered cattle must be at least eight days old (Lev. 22:27).

61.   Offer only unblemished sacrifices (Lev. 22:21).

62.   Salt all offerings (Lev. 2:13).

63.   Bring a burnt-offering in the manner indicated (Lev. 1:2-3).

64.   Bring a sin-offering in the manner indicated (Lev. 6:18).

65.   Bring a guilt-offering in the manner indicated (Lev. 7:1).

66.   Bring a peace-offering in the manner indicated (Lev. 3:1).

67.   Bring a meal-offering in the manner indicated (Lev. 2:1 and 6:7).

68.   The *Sanhedrin* that errs must bring an offering (Lev. 4:13).

69.   Bring a sin-offering for unintentional sin (Lev. 4:27).

70.   One who may have committed sin brings a suspensive-offering (Lev. 5:17-19).

71.   Bring a guilt-offering for specified sins (Lev. 5:15, 21-25, and 19:20-21).

72.   The offering may sometimes be according to the sinner's means (Lev. 5:1-11).

73. * Confess sin to God (Num. 5:6-7).

74.   A man suffering a flux must bring an offering (Lev. 15:13-16).

75.   A woman suffering a flux must bring an offering (Lev. 15:28-29).

76.   A woman must bring an offering after giving birth (Lev. 12:6).

77.   A healed leper must bring an offering (Lev. 14:10).

78.   Tithe cattle (Lev. 27:32).

79.   Make an offering of the firstborn of certain animals (Exod. 13:2 and Deut. 15:19).

80.   Redeem your firstborn son (Exod. 22:28).

81.   Redeem the firstborn of an ass with a lamb (Exod. 34:20).

82.   If the owner does not redeem it, break the neck of the ass (Exod. 13:13).

83.   Bring an offering for each of the three Pilgrim Festivals (Deut. 12:5-6).

84.   All offerings must take place in the Temple only (Deut. 12:14).

85.   Offerings from outside Israel must be brought to the Temple, too (Deut. 12:26).

86.   Redeem blemished offerings (Deut. 12:15).

87.   An animal exchanged for an offering is also holy (Lev. 27:33).

88.   Priests must eat the residue of meal-offerings (Lev. 6:9).

89.   Priests must eat the meat of sin-offerings and guilt-offerings (Exod. 29:33).

90.   Burn consecrated offerings that have become ritually unclean (Lev. 7:19).

91.   Burn the remnant of consecrated offerings (Lev. 7:17).

92.   A *Nazirite* must let his hair grow (Num. 6:5).

93.   A Nazirite must shave his head when his obligations are fulfilled (Num. 6:18).

94.   *   All vows and oaths must be fulfilled (Deut. 23:24).

95.   A vow or oath can be revoked only in accordance with law (Num. 30:3).

96.   Touching a carcass renders a person unclean (Lev. 11:8, 24).

97.   Touching any one of eight reptiles renders a person unclean (Lev. 11:29-31).

98.   Food becomes unclean when it comes in contact with impure objects (Lev. 11:34).

99.   A menstruant woman is ritually unclean (Lev. 15:19-24).

100. Women after childbirth are ritually unclean for a period of days (Lev. 12:2).

101. A leper is ritually unclean (Lev. 13:3).

102. Garments of a leper are ritually unclean (Lev. 13:51).

103. The house of a leper is ritually unclean (Lev. 14:44).

104. A man with a flux is ritually unclean (Lev. 15:2).

105. The semen of a man with a flux is ritually unclean (Lev. 15:16).

106. A woman suffering from a flux is ritually unclean (Lev. 15:19).

107. A human corpse is ritually unclean (Num. 19:14).

108. Observe the laws of sprinkling water (Num. 19:13, 21).

109. Observe the law of immersion to be cleansed of spiritual impurity (Lev. 15:16).

110. A leper is to be cleansed according to law (Lev. 14:2).

111. A leper must shave off all hair from the head (Lev. 14:9).

112. A male leper must rend his garments to be distinguishable (Lev. 13:45).

113. The ashes of the red heifer are to be used for ritual purification (Num. 19:2-9).

114. A person may be valued as a Temple donation (Lev. 27:2-8).

115. An unclean beast may be valued as a Temple donation (Lev. 27:11-12).

116. A house may be valued as a Temple donation (Lev. 27:14).

117. A field may be valued as a Temple donation (Lev. 27:16, 22-23).

118. Restitution plus one-fifth must be made for negligent use of Temple property (Lev. 5:16).

119. The fruit of fourth-year fruits may be eaten only in Jerusalem (Lev. 19:24).

120. Leave the corners of your fields for the poor (Lev. 19:9).

121. Leave the gleanings of the field for the poor (Lev. 23:22).

122. Leave the forgotten sheaves for the poor (Deut. 24:19).

123. Leave defective grape clusters for the poor (Lev. 19:10).

124. Leave the gleanings of the grapes for the poor (Lev. 19:10).

125. Separate the first-fruits and bring them to the Temple (Exod. 23:19).

126. Set aside the great heave-offering (Deut. 18:4).

127. Give a tithe of the produce to the Levites (Lev. 27:30 and Num. 18:24).

128. Give a second tithe and bring it to Jerusalem (Deut. 14:22).

129. The Levites must give a tenth of their tithe to the Priests (Num. 18:26).

130. Set aside a tithe for the poor as indicated (Deut. 14:28).

131. Make a declaration to God when separating the various tithes (Deut. 26:13).

132. Make a declaration to God when bringing the first-fruits to the Temple (Deut. 26:5).

133. Set aside a cake from every portion of dough and give it to the Priest (Num. 15:20).

134. In the *Sabbatical Year*, ownership of the land's produce is renounced and is available to all (Exod. 23:11).

135. Rest the land during the Sabbatical Year (Exod. 34:21).

136. Sanctify the *Jubilee Year* (Lev. 25:10).

137.   Sound the *shofar* on Yom Kippur in the Jubilee Year (Lev. 25:9).

138.   All land reverts to ancestral owners in the Jubilee Year (Lev. 25:24).

139.   In a walled city, the seller can buy back a house within one year (Lev. 25:29-30).

140.   Count and announce the years of the Jubilee Year (Lev. 25:8).

141.   Annul all debts in the Sabbatical Year (Deut. 15:3).

142.   Exact a debt from an idolater in the Sabbatical Year (Deut. 15:3).

143.   *   Upon slaughtering an animal, give the Priest his share (Deut. 18:3).

144.   Give the first of the fleece to the Priest (Deut. 18:4).

145.   Distinguish between things devoted to God and to Priests (Lev. 27:21, 28).

146.   *   In order to eat an animal, it must be slaughtered according to law (Deut. 12:21).

147.   *   Cover up the blood of a bird or animal after slaughter (Lev. 17:13).

148.   Release the mother bird when taking its nest (Deut. 22:7).

149.   *   Examine beasts to determine whether they are *kosher* (Lev. 11:2).

150.   *   Examine fowl to determine whether they are kosher (Deut. 14:11).

151.   Examine locusts to determine whether they are kosher (Lev. 11:21).

152.   *   Examine fish to determine whether they are kosher (Lev. 11:9).

153.   The Sanhedrin determines the first of each month and seasons (Exod. 12:2 and Deut. 16:1).

154.   *   Rest on the sabbath (Exod. 23:12).

155.   *   Proclaim the sanctity of the sabbath (Exod. 20:8).

156.   *   Remove all leaven from one's domain on the day before Passover (Exod. 12:5).

157.   *   Recount the departure from Egypt on the first night of Passover (Exod. 13:8).

158.   *   Eat unleavened bread on the first night of Passover (Exod. 12:18).

159.   *   Rest on the first day of Passover (Exod. 12:16).

160.   *   Rest on the seventh day of Passover (Exod. 12:16).

161.   *   Starting from the second day of Passover, count off forty-nine days (Lev. 23:35).

162.   *   Rest on Shavuot (Lev. 23:21).

163.   *   Rest on Rosh Hashanah (Lev. 23:24).

164.   *   Fast on Yom Kippur (Lev. 16:29).

165. * Rest on Yom Kippur (Lev. 16:29, 31).

166. * Rest on the first day of Sukkot (Lev. 23:35).

167. * Rest on the eighth day of Sukkot (Lev. 23:36).

168. * Dwell in a booth during Sukkot (Lev. 23:42).

169. * Take the *four spices* and rejoice with them on Sukkot (Lev. 23:40).

170. * Hear the sound of the shofar on Rosh Hashanah (Num. 29:1).

171. Give half a shekel to the Temple annually (Exod. 30:12-13).

172. * Obey a prophet (Deut. 18:15).

173. Appoint a king (Deut. 17:15).

174. Obey the *Great Sanhedrin* (Deut. 17:11).

175. * Follow the majority if there is a division of opinion (Exod. 23:2).

176. Appoint judges and officers of the court in every town (Deut. 16:18).

177. Judges must treat litigants equally in court (Lev. 19:15).

178. Whoever has evidence to give must testify in court (Lev. 5:1).

179. Judges must examine the testimony of witnesses carefully (Deut. 13:15).

180. Punish witnesses who testify falsely (Deut. 19:19).

181. Decapitate a heifer if a murder victim is found in a field and the killer is unknown (Deut. 21:4).

182. Establish cities of refuge (Deut. 19:3).

183. Assign cities to the Levites, who have no ancestral land (Num. 35:2).

184. * Build a fence around your roof and remove sources of danger (Deut. 22:8).

185. Destroy idol-worship (Deut. 12:2, 7:5).

186. Destroy an apostate city (Deut. 13:17).

187. Destroy the seven Canaanite nations if they do not accept peace (Deut. 20:17).

188. Blot out the offspring of *Amalek* (Deut. 25:19).

189. Remember what Amalek did to Israel (Deut. 25:17).

190. Wage non-obligatory wars only as provided for in the Torah (Deut. 20:11-12).

191. Appoint a Priest for wartime duties (Deut. 20:2).

192. Keep the military camp in sanitary condition (Deut. 23:14-15).

193. Provide each soldier with a shovel (Deut. 23:14).

194. A thief must restore what he took from the victim, plus one-fifth (Lev. 5:23).

195. * Give charity to the needy (Deut. 15:8 and Lev. 25:35-36).

196.   Lavish gifts on a Hebrew slave when he is set free (Deut. 15:14).

197. * Lend money to an Israelite without interest (Exod. 22:24).

198.   Lend money to a foreigner with interest (Deut. 23:21).

199.   Restore a pledge to a needy owner (Deut. 24:13 and Exod. 22:25).

200.   Pay wages on time (Deut. 24:15).

201.   Allow a worker to eat of the produce with which he is working (Deut. 23:25-26).

202.   Unload a beast that has fallen under its burden (Exod. 23:5).

203.   Help a person to load a burden on his beast or on himself (Deut. 22:4).

204.   Return lost property to its owner (Deut. 22:1 and Exod. 23:4).

205.   Rebuke the sinner (Lev. 19:17).

206. * Love your neighbor (Lev. 19:18).

207. * Love the stranger (Deut. 10:19).

208. * Have just weights and measures (Lev. 19:36).

209. * Honor scholars and the aged (Lev. 19:32).

210. * Honor your parents (Exod. 20:12).

211. * Respect your parents (Lev. 19:3).

212. * Procreate in marriage (Gen. 1:28).

213. * Marry according to law (Deut. 24:1).

214. * A bridegroom must devote himself to his wife for the first year (Deut. 24:5).

215. * Male children must be circumcised (Gen. 17:10 and Lev. 12:3).

216.   If a man dies childless, his brother must marry his widow (Deut. 25:5).

217.   The brother does not marry his sister-in-law if she releases him (Deut. 25:9).

218.   A man who violates a virgin must marry her and never divorce her (Deut. 22:29).

219.   A man who defames his bride must be punished (Deut. 22:18-19).

220.   A seducer is punished according to law (Exod. 22:15-23).

221.   A woman taken captive in a war must be treated according to law (Deut. 21:11).

222.   A man who divorces his wife must do so by a bill of divorcement (Deut. 24:1).

223.   A woman suspected of adultery must submit to the required test (Num. 5:15-27).

224.   Certain transgressors of the law are to be flogged (Deut. 25:2).

225. Those who kill accidentally are to be exiled to a city of refuge (Num. 35:25).
226. Certain transgressors of the law are to be beheaded (Exod. 21:20).
227. Certain transgressors of the law are to be strangled (Exod. 21:16).
228. Certain transgressors of the law are to be put to death by burning (Lev. 20:14).
229. Certain transgressors of the law are to be put to death by stoning (Deut. 21:22).
230. The bodies of certain transgressors are to be hung after execution (Deut. 21:22).
231. Those executed by the court must be buried the same day (Deut. 21:23).
232. Hebrew slaves must be released according to law (Exod. 21:2).
233. The master or his son must marry his Hebrew maidservant (Exod. 21:8).
234. If the master or his son does not marry her, she must be freed (Exod. 21:8).
235. An alien slave must be treated according to law (Lev. 25:46).
236. Pay compensation for tortious conduct (Exod. 21:18).
237. Apply applicable law when an ox causes injury (Exod. 21:28).
238. If a pit causes injury, applicable law is administered (Exod. 21:33-34).
239. Thieves are to be punished according to law (Exod. 21:37-22:3).
240. Render judgment for damages caused by cattle (Exod. 22:4).
241. Render judgment for damages caused by fire (Exod. 22:5).
242. Unpaid bailees are to be judged according to appropriate law (Exod. 22:6-8).
243. Paid bailees are to be judged according to appropriate law (Exod. 22:9-12).
244. Borrowers are to be judged according to appropriate law (Exod. 22:13).
245. Render judgment in disputes involving sales (Lev. 25:14).
246. Render judgment in other types of litigation (Exod. 22:8).
247. Save the life of one being pursued (Deut. 25:12).
248. Comply with the laws of inheritance (Num. 27:8).

The 365 Negative Commandments

1. * Do not believe in the existence of any but the One God (Exod. 20:3).

2. * Do not make images for yourself to worship (Exod. 20:4).
3. * Do not make images for another to worship (Lev. 19:4).
4. * Do not make images for any other purpose (Exod. 20:20).
5. * Do not bow down to idols (Exod. 20:5).
6. * Do not worship idols (Exod. 20:5).
7. * Do not sacrifice children to *Molech* (Lev. 18:21).
8. * Do not practice necromancy (Lev. 19:31).
9. * Do not worship spirits (Lev. 19:31).
10. * Do not take a serious interest in idolatry (Lev. 19:4).
11. * Do not erect a pillar to worship God (Deut. 16:22).
12. * Do not prostrate yourself on pillared stones (Lev. 20:11).
13.   Do not plant trees in the Temple (Deut. 16:21).
14. * Do not swear by an idol (Exod. 23:13).
15. * Do not summon people to idolatry (Exod. 23:13).
16. * Do not summon an individual Jew to idolatry (Deut. 13:12).
17. * Do not love one who teaches idolatry (Deut. 13:9).
18. * Do not relax hatred for one who teaches idolatry (Deut. 13:9).
19. * Do not pity one who teaches idolatry (Deut. 13:9).
20.   Do not defend one who teaches idolatry (Deut. 13:9).
21.   Do not suppress evidence against one who teaches idolatry (Deut. 13:9).
22. * Do not obtain any benefit from the ornaments of idols (Deut. 7:25).
23.   Do not rebuild an apostate city (Deut. 13:17).
24.   Do not derive any benefit from the property of an apostate city (Deut. 13:18).
25. * Do not derive any benefit from anything connected with idolatry (Deut. 7:26).
26. * Do not prophesy in the name of an idol (Deut. 18:20).
27. * Do not prophesy falsely in the name of God (Deut. 18:20).
28. * Do not listen to one who prophesies in the name of an idol (Deut. 13:3-4).
29.   Do not pity a false prophet (Deut. 18:22).
30. * Do not adopt the customs of idolaters (Lev. 20:23).
31. * Do not practice divination (Lev. 19:26 and Deut. 18:10).
32. * Do not practice astrology (Deut. 18:10).
33. * Do not practice soothsaying (Deut. 18:10).
34. * Do not practice sorcery (Deut. 18:10-11).
35. * Do not practice charming (Deut. 18:10-11).

36.   * Do not consult a necromancer (Deut. 18:10-11).

37.   * Do not consult a sorcerer (Deut. 18:10-11).

38.   * Do not seek information from the dead (Deut. 18:10-11).

39.   * Women must not wear men's clothing (Deut. 22:5).

40.   * Men must not wear women's clothing (Deut. 22:5).

41.   * Do not make tattoos on your body (Lev. 19:28).

42.   * Do not wear a garment of wool and linen (Deut. 22:11).

43.   * Do not shave the sides of your head (Lev. 19:27).

44.   * Do not shave the sides of your beard (Lev. 19:27).

45.   * Do not make cuttings in your flesh for your dead (Deut. 16:1, 4 and Lev. 19:28).

46.   * Do not settle in the land of Egypt (Deut. 17:16).

47.   * Do not accept opinions contrary to the Torah (Num. 15:39).

48.   Do not make a covenant with the seven Canaanite nations (Exod. 23:32 and Deut. 7:2).

49.   Do not spare the seven Canaanite nations if they adhere to idolatry (Deut. 20:16).

50.   * Do not show mercy to idolaters (Deut. 7:2).

51.   Do not allow idolaters to dwell in the Land of Israel (Exod. 23:33).

52.   * Do not marry a non-Jew (Deut. 7:3).

53.   A Jewish woman must not marry an Ammonite or Moabite, even though they be proselytes (Deut. 23:4).

54.   Do not refuse to marry proselytes who are descended from Esau (Deut. 23:8).

55.   Do not refuse to marry proselytes who are Egyptians (Deut. 23:8).

56.   Do not offer peace to the nations of Ammon and Moab (Deut. 23:7).

57.   * Do not destroy fruit trees while besieging an enemy city (Deut. 20:9).

58.   Do not fear an enemy (Deut. 7:21).

59.   * Do not forget the evil of Amalek (Deut. 25:19).

60.   * Do not blaspheme God's Holy Name (Lev. 24:16).

61.   * Do not violate an oath (Lev. 19:12).

62.   * Do not swear a vain oath (Exod. 20:7).

63.   * Do not profane God's Name (Lev. 22:32).

64.   Do not test God (Deut. 6:16).

65.   * Do not destroy synagogues or sacred books (Deut. 12:4).

66.   *   Do not leave the body of an executed criminal hanging overnight (Deut. 21:23).

67.   Do not be lax in guarding the Temple (Num. 18:5).

68.   The High Priest cannot enter the Temple indiscriminately (Lev. 16:2).

69.   A Priest with a blemish cannot enter the Temple (Lev. 21:23).

70.   A Priest with a blemish cannot officiate in the Temple (Lev. 21:17).

71.   A Priest with even a temporary blemish cannot officiate in the Temple (Lev. 21:18).

72.   Levites and Priests must not interchange their duties (Num. 18:3).

73.   Do not render a decision or enter the Temple while intoxicated (Lev. 10:9-11).

74.   Non-Priests cannot officiate in the Temple (Num. 18:4).

75.   A ritually unclean Priest cannot officiate in the Temple (Lev. 22:2).

76.   A Priest who has immersed himself but is still unclean cannot officiate in the Temple (Lev. 21:6).

77.   No unclean person can enter the Temple (Num. 5:3).

78.   *   No unclean person can enter the camp of the Levites (Temple Mount) (Deut. 23:11).

79.   Do not build the Altar of stones which have been touched by iron (Exod. 20:25).

80.   Do not build steps to go up to the Altar (Exod. 20:26).

81.   Do not extinguish the fire from the Altar (Lev. 6:6).

82.   Do not offer indiscriminate sacrifices on the Altar (Exod. 30:9).

83.   *   Do not manufacture oil which was prepared by Moses (Exod. 30:32).

84.   Do not make improper use of the oil prepared by Moses (Exod. 30:32).

85.   *   Do not manufacture incense like that used in the Temple (Exod. 30:37).

86.   Do not remove the staves from their rings in the Ark (Exod. 25:15).

87.   Do not remove the breastplate from the *Ephod* of the High Priest (Exod. 28:28).

88.   Do not tear the edge of the High Priest's robe (Exod. 28:32).

89.   Do not offer any sacrifice outside the Temple (Deut. 12:13).

90.   Do not slaughter holy offerings outside the Temple (Lev. 17:3-4).

91.   Do not dedicate blemished animals for the Altar (Lev. 22:20).

92.   Do not slaughter blemished animals in sacrifice (Lev. 22:22).

93. Do not sprinkle the blood of blemished animals upon the Altar (Lev. 22:24).

94. Do not burn the parts of a blemished animal upon the Altar (Lev. 22:22).

95. Do not sacrifice an animal that has even a temporary blemish (Deut. 17:1).

96. Do not offer a blemished sacrifice of a Gentile (Lev. 22:25).

97. Do not inflict a blemish on an offering (Lev. 22:21).

98. Do not offer leaven or honey upon the Altar (Lev. 2:11).

99. Do not offer a sacrifice without salt (Lev. 2:13).

100. Do not offer an animal that was the hire of a harlot or the price of a dog (Deut. 23:19).

101. * Do not slaughter the mother and its young on the same day (Lev. 22:28).

102. Do not put olive oil upon the meal-offering of a sinner (Lev. 5:11).

103. Do not bring frankincense with the meal-offering of a sinner (Lev. 5:11).

104. Do not mix olive oil with the meal-offering of a suspected adulteress (Num. 5:15).

105. Do not put frankincense on the meal-offering of a suspected adulteress (Num. 5:15).

106. Do not substitute sacrifices (Lev. 27:10).

107. Do not change one type of holy offering for another (Lev. 27:26).

108. * Do not redeem the firstborn of permitted animals (Num. 18:17).

109. Do not sell the tithe of a herd of cattle (Lev. 27:33).

110. Do not sell property that its owner has declared devoted (Lev. 27:28).

111. Do not redeem land that its owner has declared devoted (Lev. 27:28).

112. Do not sever the head of a bird offered as a sin-offering (Lev. 5:8).

113. Do not work an animal dedicated as a sacrifice (Deut. 15:19).

114. Do not shear an animal dedicated as a sacrifice (Deut. 15:19).

115. Do not slaughter the Paschal lamb while leaven remains in your possession (Exod. 34:25).

116. Do not leave overnight the sacrificial portions of the Passover-offering (Exod. 23:18).

117. Do not leave overnight any of the meat of the Passover-offering (Exod. 12:10).

118. Do not allow any part of the voluntary festive-offering to remain until the third day (Deut. 16:4).

119. Do not allow any of the meat of the Second Passover-offering to remain until morning (Num. 9:12).

120. Do not allow any of the meat of a thanksgiving-offering to remain until morning (Lev. 22:30).

121. Do not break any of the bones of the Passover-offering (Exod. 12:46).

122. Do not break any of the bones of the Second Passover-offering (Num. 9:12).

123. Do not remove the meat of the Passover-offering from the house where it is being eaten (Exod. 12:46).

124. Do not bake the residue of a meal-offering with leaven (Lev. 6:10).

125. Do not eat the Passover-offering boiled or raw (Exod. 12:9).

126. Do not allow a resident alien to eat of the Passover-offering (Exod. 12:45).

127. Do not allow an uncircumcised person to eat of the Passover-offering (Exod. 12:48).

128. Do not allow an apostate Israelite to eat of the Passover-offering (Exod. 12:43).

129. Do not allow a ritually unclean person to eat holy things (Lev. 12:4).

130. Do not allow anyone to eat the meat of unclean consecrated offerings (Lev. 7:19).

131. Do not eat the meat of offerings left beyond the time allowed for its eating (Lev. 19:6-8).

132. Do not eat the meat of an offering rendered unfit through improper intentions (Lev. 7:18).

133. One not a Priest is forbidden to eat of the heave-offering (Lev. 22:10).

134. The servant of a Priest is forbidden to eat of the heave-offering (Lev. 22:10).

135. An uncircumcised Priest is forbidden to eat of the heave-offering (Lev. 22:10).

136. A ritually unclean Priest is forbidden to eat of the heave-offering (Lev. 22:4).

137. The daughter of a Priest married to a non-Priest cannot eat holy foods (Lev. 22:12).

138. Do not eat the meal-offering of a Priest (Lev. 6:16).

139. Priests are forbidden to eat the meat of sin-offerings whose blood must be sprinkled in the Temple (Lev. 6:23).

140. Do not eat offerings that have become invalid through a blemish (Deut. 14:3).

141. Do not eat the second tithe of corn outside Jerusalem (Deut. 12:17).

142. Do not eat the second tithe of wine outside Jerusalem (Deut. 12:17).

143. Do not eat the second tithe of oil outside Jerusalem (Deut. 12:17).

144. Do not eat the unblemished firstling outside Jerusalem (Deut. 12:17).

145. Do not eat the sin-offering and the guilt-offering outside the Temple court (Deut. 12:17).

146. Do not eat the meat of a burnt-offering (Deut. 12:17).

147. Do not eat of certain offerings before the dashing of their blood on the Altar (Deut. 12:17).

148. A Priest is forbidden to eat first-fruits outside Jerusalem (Deut. 12:17).

149. One not a Priest is forbidden to eat of certain holy offerings (Exod. 29:33).

150. Do not eat the second tithe that has become ritually unclean (Deut. 26:14).

151. Do not eat the second tithe when in mourning (Deut. 26:14).

152. Do not spend the redemption money of the second tithe for anything other than food and drink (Deut. 26:14).

153. Do not eat produce that is not tithed (Lev. 22:15).

154. Do not change the order of separating the various tithes (Exod. 22:28).

155. * Do not delay in the payment of offerings and vows (Deut. 23:22).

156. Do not go to the Temple for the Pilgrim Festival without an offering (Exod. 23:15).

157. * Do not go back on your word (Num. 30:3).

158. * A Priest is forbidden to marry a harlot (Lev. 21:7).

159. * A Priest is forbidden to marry a woman of marred priestly status (Lev. 21:7).

160. * A Priest is forbidden to marry a divorcee (Lev. 21:7).

161. The High Priest is forbidden to marry a widow (Lev. 21:14).

162. The High Priest is forbidden to take a widow as a concubine (Lev. 21:15).

163. A Priest with loose hair is forbidden to enter the Temple (Lev. 10:6).

164.   A Priest wearing torn clothing is forbidden to enter the Temple (Lev. 10:6).

165.   An officiating Priest is forbidden to leave the Temple (Lev. 10:7).

166.   *   An ordinary Priest is forbidden to make himself ritually impure by coming in contact with a corpse, save Scriptural exceptions (Lev. 21:1).

167.   The High Priest is forbidden to be under a roof with a corpse (Lev. 21:11).

168.   The High Priest is forbidden to come into contact with a corpse (Lev. 21:11).

169.   The Levites are forbidden to take a portion in the Land of Israel (Deut. 18:1).

170.   The Levites are forbidden to share in the spoils of war (Deut. 18:1).

171.   *   Do not make yourself bald as a sign of mourning (Deut. 14:1).

172.   *   Do not eat unclean animals (Deut. 14:7).

173.   *   Do not eat unclean fish (Lev. 11:11).

174.   *   Do not eat unclean fowl (Lev. 11:13).

175.   *   Do not eat winged swarming insects (Deut. 14:19).

176.   *   Do not eat anything that swarms upon the earth (Lev. 11:41).

177.   *   Do not eat any creeping thing that breeds in decayed matter (Lev. 11:41).

178.   *   Do not eat anything that breeds in seeds or fruit (Lev.11:42).

179.   *   Do not eat any swarming thing (Lev. 11:43).

180.   *   Do not eat an animal that has died naturally (Deut. 14:21).

181.   *   Do not eat an animal that was killed by other animals (Exod. 22:30).

182.   *   Do not eat a limb torn from a living animal (Deut. 12:23).

183.   *   Do not eat the sinew of an animal (Gen. 32:33).

184.   *   Do not eat blood (Lev. 7:26).

185.   *   Do not eat certain types of fat of a clean animal (Lev. 7:23).

186.   *   Do not cook meat together with milk (Exod. 23:19).

187.   *   Do not eat meat cooked in milk (Exod. 34:26).

188.   Do not eat an ox that was stoned, even if it was slaughtered beforehand (Exod. 21:28).

189.   *   Do not eat bread made from the grain of a new crop before the end of the sixteenth day of the month of Nisan (the second day of Passover) (Lev. 23:14).

190.   *   Do not eat roasted grain of a new crop before the end of the sixteenth day of the month of Nisan (Lev. 23:14).

191.   * Do not eat fresh ears of grain before the end of the sixteenth day of the month of Nisan (Lev. 23:14).

192.   * Do not eat the fruit of young trees during the first three years (Lev. 19:23).

193.   * Do not eat the produce of a vineyard sown with different kinds of seeds (Deut. 22:9).

194.   * Do not drink wine used in connection with idolatry (Deut. 32:38).

195.   * Do not eat or drink to excess (Lev. 19:26 and Deut. 21:21).

196.   * Do not eat on Yom Kippur (Lev. 23:29).

197.   * Do not eat leaven on Passover (Exod. 13:3).

198.   * Do not eat anything containing leaven on Passover (Exod. 13:20).

199.   * Do not eat leaven after the middle of the fourteenth day of the month of Nisan (the day before Passover) (Deut. 16:3).

200.   * Do not allow leaven to be seen during the seven days of Passover (Exod. 13:7).

201.   * Do not possess leaven during the seven days of Passover (Exod. 12:19).

202.   A Nazirite is forbidden to drink wine (Num. 6:3).

203.   A Nazirite is forbidden to eat fresh grapes (Num. 6:3).

204.   A Nazirite is forbidden to eat dried grapes (Num. 6:3).

205.   A Nazirite is forbidden to eat the seeds of grapes (Num. 6:4).

206.   A Nazirite is forbidden to eat the peel of grapes (Num. 6:4).

207.   A Nazirite is forbidden to make himself ritually unclean for his dead (Num. 6:7).

208.   A Nazirite is forbidden to make himself ritually unclean by entering a house containing a corpse (Lev. 21:11).

209.   A Nazirite is forbidden to shave (Num. 6:5).

210.   Do not reap the whole of a field (Lev. 9:9).

211.   Do not gather ears of corn that fell during the harvest (Lev. 19:10).

212.   Do not gather the grape-clusters not fully grown (Lev. 19:10).

213.   Do not gather single fallen grapes (Lev. 19:10).

214.   Do not return to take in a forgotten sheaf (Deut. 24:19).

215.   * Do not sow diverse kinds of seeds in one field (Lev. 19:19).

216.   * Do not sow diverse kinds of seeds in a vineyard (Deut. 22:9).

217.   * Do not mate animals of different species (Lev. 19:19).

218.   * Do not work two different kinds of animals together (Deut. 22:10).

219.   * Do not muzzle an animal working in a field to prevent it from eating (Deut. 25:4).

220.　　Do not cultivate the ground in the Sabbatical Year (Lev. 25:4).

221.　　Do not prune trees in the Sabbatical Year (Lev. 25:4).

222.　　Do not reap in the usual manner anything that grows of itself in the Sabbatical Year (Lev. 25:5).

223.　　Do not gather fruit which has grown in the Sabbatical Year as in an ordinary year (Lev. 25:5).

224.　　Do not cultivate the soil in the Jubilee Year (Lev. 25:11).

225.　　Do not reap that which has grown without cultivation in the Jubilee Year as in an ordinary year (Lev. 25:11).

226.　　Do not gather fruit that has grown without cultivation in the Jubilee Year as in an ordinary year (Lev. 25:11).

227.　　Do not permanently sell land in Israel (Lev. 25:23).

228.　　Do not sell or change the land of the Levites (Lev. 25:33).

229.　　Do not financially forsake the Levites (Deut. 12:19).

230.　*　Do not demand payment of debts in the Sabbatical Year (Deut. 15:2).

231.　　Do not withhold a loan because it will be annulled in the Sabbatical Year (Deut. 15:9).

232.　*　Do not fail to give to the poor (Deut. 15:7).

233.　　Do not send away a Hebrew slave empty-handed when he completes his period of servitude (Deut. 15:13).

234.　*　Do not demand payment from a debtor when you know he cannot repay (Exod. 22:24).

235.　*　Do not lend at interest to a fellow Jew (Lev. 25:37).

236.　*　Do not borrow at interest from a fellow Jew (Deut. 23:20).

237.　*　Do not participate in a transaction involving interest between Jews (Exod. 22:24).

238.　*　Do not delay in payment of wages to employees (Lev. 19:13).

239.　*　Do not take a pledge from a debtor by force (Deut. 24:10).

240.　*　Do not keep a pledge from a debtor when he needs it (Deut. 24:12).

241.　*　Do not take a pledge from a widow (Deut. 24:17).

242.　*　Do not take as a pledge cooking utensils (Deut. 24:6).

243.　*　Do not kidnap a Jew (Exod. 20:13).

244.　*　Do not steal (Lev. 19:11).

245.　*　Do not commit robbery (Lev. 19:13).

246.　*　Do not deceitfully alter land boundaries (Deut. 19:14).

247.　*　Do not engage in fraud (Lev. 19:13).

248. * Do not repudiate debts (Lev. 19:11).

249. * Do not swear falsely regarding another's property (Lev. 19:11).

250. * Do not wrong one another in business (Lev. 25:14).

251. * Do not wrong one another by speech (Lev. 25:17).

252. * Do not wrong a stranger by speech (Exod. 22:20).

253. * Do not wrong a stranger in business (Exod. 22:20).

254. Do not return a foreign fugitive slave who has escaped to the Land of Israel (Deut. 23:16).

255. Do not wrong a foreign fugitive slave who has escaped to the Land of Israel (Deut. 23:17).

256. * Do not afflict fatherless children or widows (Exod. 22:21).

257. Do not make a Hebrew slave perform menial tasks (Lev. 25:39).

258. Do not sell a Hebrew slave in a public auction (Lev. 25:42).

259. Do not be cruel to a Hebrew slave (Lev. 25:43).

260. Do not allow a heathen to mistreat a Hebrew slave (Lev. 25:43).

261. Do not sell a Hebrew maidservant (Exod. 21:8).

262. * A man who marries his Hebrew maidservant must not mistreat her (Exod. 21:10).

263. Do not sell a woman captured in war (Deut. 21:14).

264. Do not treat a woman captured in war as a slave (Deut. 21:14).

265. * Do not scheme to acquire another's property (Exod. 20:17).

266. * Do not covet another's property (Deut. 5:18).

267. * An employee is forbidden to cut down standing crops for his own consumption (Deut. 23:26).

268. * An employee is forbidden to pick for his own consumption more fruit than he can eat (Deut. 23:25).

269. * Do not ignore another's lost property (Deut. 22:3).

270. * Do not refuse to help a man or beast trapped under a burden (Exod. 23:5).

271. * Do not cheat anyone by using false weights or measures (Lev. 19:35).

272. * Do not even keep false weights (Deut. 25:13).

273. * A judge is forbidden to commit injustice (Lev. 19:15).

274. * A judge is forbidden to accept bribes (Exod. 23:8).

275. * A judge is forbidden to favor a litigant (Lev. 19:15).

276. * A judge is forbidden to give an unjust verdict because of fear (Deut. 1:17).

277. * A judge is forbidden to favor the poor (Lev. 19:15).

278. * A judge is forbidden to discriminate against the wicked (Exod. 23:6).

279.   A judge is forbidden to pity the convicted (Deut. 19:13).

280. * A judge is forbidden to deny justice to strangers and orphans (Deut. 24:17).

281. * A judge is forbidden to listen to one litigant without the other being present (Exod. 23:1).

282.   A court is forbidden to convict a defendant in a capital case by a majority of one (Exod. 23:2).

283.   A judge is forbidden to rely on another judge's opinion, unless he is convinced it is correct (Exod. 23:2).

284. * Do not appoint a judge who is unlearned in the law (Deut. 1:17).

285. * Do not give false testimony (Exod. 20:16).

286. * A judge is forbidden to accept testimony from a wicked person (Exod. 23:1).

287. * A judge is forbidden to accept testimony from a litigant's relative (Deut. 24:16).

288. * Do not convict a defendant on the basis of the testimony of one witness (Deut. 19:15).

289. * Do not murder (Exod. 20:13).

290.   Do not convict a defendant on the basis of only circumstantial evidence (Exod. 23:7).

291.   A witness is forbidden to act as a judge or advocate in a capital case (Num. 35:30).

292.   Do not execute a murderer in the absence of a trial and due process (Num. 35:12).

293.   Do not spare the life of a pursuer (one who runs after another to commit murder or rape) (Deut. 25:12).

294.   Do not punish someone who commits a sin while under duress (Deut. 22:26).

295.   Do not accept a ransom for a murderer (Num. 35:31).

296.   Do not accept a ransom for a manslayer (Num. 35:32).

297. * Do not neglect to save the life of a person in danger (Lev. 19:16).

298. * Do not leave obstacles on public or private property (Deut. 22:8).

299. * Do not mislead another by giving incorrect advice (Lev. 19:14).

300. * Do not administer excessive corporal punishment to a convicted defendant (Deut. 25:2-3).

301. * Do not bear tales (Lev. 19:16).

302. * Do not hate another in your heart (Lev. 19:17).

303. * Do not shame another (Lev. 19:17).

304. * Do not take vengeance on another (Lev. 19:18).

305. * Do not bear a grudge (Lev. 19:18).

306. * Do not take the dam with her young (Deut. 22:6).

307.   Do not shave the hair around a leprous scab (Lev. 13:33).

308.   Do not conceal other signs of leprosy (Deut. 24:8).

309.   Do not cultivate an area in which the victim of an unknown murderer was found and the ritual of breaking the heifer's neck was therefore performed (Deut. 21:4).

310.   Do not allow a sorcerer to live (Exod. 22:17).

311.   Do not force a bridegroom to serve in the military during his first year of marriage (Deut. 24:5).

312. * Do not rebel against the teachings of the authorities who transmitted the law (Deut. 17:11).

313. * Do not add to the law (Deut. 13:1).

314. * Do not detract from the law (Deut. 13:1).

315. * Do not curse a judge (Exod. 22:27).

316.   Do not curse a ruler (Exod. 22:27).

317. * Do not curse any Jew (Lev. 19:14).

318. * Do not curse your parents (Exod. 21:17).

319. * Do not strike your parents (Exod. 21:15).

320. * Do not work on the sabbath (Exod. 20:10).

321. * Do not journey on the sabbath (Exod. 16:29).

322.   Do not carry out the punishment of a criminal on the sabbath (Exod. 35:3).

323. * Do not do work on the first day of Passover (Exod. 12:16).

324. * Do not do work on the seventh day of Passover (Exod. 12:16).

325. * Do not do work on Shavuot (Lev. 23:21).

326. * Do not do work on Rosh Hashanah (Lev. 23:25).

327. * Do not do work on the first day of Sukkot (Lev. 23:35).

328. * Do not do work on the eighth day of Sukkot (Lev. 23:36).

329. * Do not do work on Yom Kippur (Lev. 23:28).

330. * A man is forbidden to have intercourse with his mother (Lev. 18:7).

331. * A man is forbidden to have intercourse with his stepmother (Lev. 18:8).

332. * A man is forbidden to have intercourse with his sister (Lev. 18:9).

333. * A man is forbidden to have intercourse with his half-sister (Lev. 18:11).

334. * A man is forbidden to have intercourse with his son's daughter (Lev. 18:10).

335. * A man is forbidden to have intercourse with his daughter's daughter (Lev. 18:10).

336. * A man is forbidden to have intercourse with his daughter (Lev. 18:10).

337. * A man is forbidden to have intercourse with any woman and her daughter (Lev. 18:17).

338. * A man is forbidden to have intercourse with any woman and her son's daughter (Lev. 18:17).

339. * A man is forbidden to have intercourse with any woman and her daughter's daughter (Lev. 18:17).

340. * A man is forbidden to have intercourse with his father's sister (Lev. 18:12).

341. * A man is forbidden to have intercourse with his mother's sister (Lev. 18:13).

342. * A man is forbidden to have intercourse with his father's brother's wife (Lev. 18:14).

343. * A man is forbidden to have intercourse with his daughter-in-law (Lev. 18:15).

344. * A man is forbidden to have intercourse with his brother's wife (Lev. 18:18).

345. * A man is forbidden to have intercourse with his wife's sister during his wife's lifetime (Lev. 18:18).

346. * A man is forbidden to have intercourse with a menstruous woman (Lev. 18:19).

347. * Do not commit adultery (Lev. 18:20).

348. * A man is forbidden to have intercourse with an animal (Lev. 18:23).

349. * A woman is forbidden to have intercourse with an animal (Lev. 18:23).

350. * A man is forbidden to have intercourse with a man (Lev. 18:22).

351. * A man is especially forbidden to have intercourse with his father (Lev. 18:7).

352. * A man is especially forbidden to have intercourse with his uncle (Lev. 18:14).

353. * A man is forbidden to have intimate physical contact with any woman with whom intercourse is prohibited (Lev. 18:6).

354. * A *mamzer* is forbidden to marry a Jew (Deut. 23:3).

355. * A man is forbidden to have intercourse with any woman not his wife (Deut. 23:18).

356.   *   A divorced woman is forbidden to remarry her first husband if, after divorcing her first husband, she married a second husband (Deut. 24:4).

357.   *   A childless widow is forbidden to marry anyone other than her late husband's brother (but see Positive Commandment 217) (Deut. 25:5).

358.   A man who rapes a woman and subsequently marries her is forbidden to divorce her (Deut. 22:29).

359.   A man is forbidden to divorce his wife after having slandered her (Deut. 22:19).

360.   *   A eunuch is forbidden to marry a Jew (Deut. 23:2).

361.   *   Do not castrate a male of any species, man or beast (Lev. 22:24).

362.   Do not elect as king anyone who is not Jewish and descended from Jews (Deut. 17:15).

363.   A king is forbidden to own many horses (Deut. 17:16).

364.   A king is forbidden to have many wives (Deut. 17:16).

365.   A king is forbidden to accumulate much wealth (Deut. 17:17).

Appendix 3

Organization and Summary of the Babylonian Talmud

The Talmud is comprised of the Mishnah (the oral law) and the Gemara (the rabbinical commentary to the Mishnah). The Mishnah is divided into six sections or "orders." Each order is further divided into texts or "tractates." There are sixty-three tractates in the Mishnah. In the Babylonian Talmud, thirty-seven of the tractates have a Gemara.

The following material gives the reader a broad summary of the organization of the six orders of the Mishnah and its sixty-three tractates. An asterisk (*) indicates that there is a Gemara for that tractate in the Babylonian Talmud. The Biblical source, where applicable, follows in parentheses.

First Order: Zeraim ("Seeds")

1. *Berakoth* ("Benedictions").* Liturgy.

2. *Peah* ("Corners"). Corners of the field (Lev. 19:9-10).

3. *Damai* ("Doubtful"). Crops purchased from a person who may not have tithed to the Priest.

4. *Kilayim* ("Mixtures"). Diverse seeds (Deut. 22:9-11).

5. *Shebiith* ("Seven"). The Sabbatical Year (Exod. 23:10-11).

6. *Terumoth* ("Heave-offerings"). The heave-offering (Lev. 22:10-14).

7. *Maaseroth* ("Tithes"). Tithes of the Levite (Num. 18:21).

8. *Maaser Sheni* ("Second Tithe"). The second tithe (Deut. 14:22).

9. *Hallah* ("Dough"). The dough-offering (Num. 15:17-21).

10. *Orlah* ("Uncircumcision"). Fruits of young trees (Lev. 19:23-25).

11. *Bikkurim* ("First-fruits"). First-fruits brought to the Temple (Deut. 26:1ff.).

Second Order: Moed ("Season")

1. *Shabbat* ("Sabbath").* The sabbath.

2. *Erubin* ("Amalgamations").* The boundaries which may not be exceeded on the sabbath.

3. *Pesahim* ("Passovers").* Passover (see glossary).

4. *Shekalim* ("Shekels"). The annual tax paid to the Temple.

5. *Yoma* ("The Day").* The Day of Atonement (*Yom Kippur*) (see glossary).

6. *Sukkah* ("Booth").* The Feast of Tabernacles (*Sukkot*) (see glossary).

7. *Yom Tob* ("Festival").* Laws regarding festivals.

8. *Rosh Hashanah* ("New Year").* The Jewish New Year (see glossary).

9. *Taanith* ("Fast").* Public fast days.

10. *Megillah* ("Scroll").* Public reading of the Scroll of Esther on the holiday *Purim* (see glossary) (Esth. 9:28).

11. *Moed Katan* ("Minor Feast").* Intermediate days of the festivals of Passover and the Feast of Tabernacles.

12. *Hagigah* ("Festival-offering").* Sacrifices offered on the three Pilgrim Festivals (see glossary) of Passover, the Feast of Weeks, and the Feast of Tabernacles (Deut. 16:16).

Third Order: Nashim ("Women")

1. *Yebamoth* ("Levirate Marriage").* The marriage of a childless sister-in-law (Deut. 25:5-10) and forbidden marriages (Lev. 18).

2. *Ketuboth* ("Marriage Contracts").* Marriage contracts and obligations.

3. *Nedarim* ("Vows").* Making and annulling vows, especially those involving women (Num. 30:3ff.).

4. *Nazir* ("Nazirite").* Vows of the Nazirite (see glossary) (Num. 6).

5. *Sotah* ("Suspected Adulteress").* The wife suspected of adultery (Num. 5:12ff.).

6. *Gittin* ("Divorces").* Divorce (Deut. 24:1ff.).

7. *Kiddushin* ("Sanctification").* Marriage.

Fourth Order: Nezikin ("Damages")

1. *Baba Kama* ("First Gate").* Damages to property and persons.

2. *Baba Metzia* ("Middle Gate").* Civil law.

3. *Baba Bathra* ("Last Gate").* Real estate law and inheritance.

4. *Sanhedrin* ("Court").* Courts, procedure, and criminal law.

5. *Makkoth* ("Flagellation").* Punishment by flagellation (Deut. 25:2) and cities of refuge (Num. 35:10ff.).

6. *Shebuoth* ("Oaths").* Oaths made privately and in court.

7. *Eduyoth* ("Testimonies"). Testimonies of rabbis (see glossary) regarding decisions of earlier rabbinical authorities.

8. *Abodah Zarah* ("Idol Worship").* Heathen practices.

9. *Pirke Aboth* ("Chapters of the Fathers"). Ethical teachings.

10. *Horayoth* ("Decisions").* Erroneous court decisions.

Fifth Order: Kodashim ("Sanctities")

1. *Zebahim* ("Sacrifices").* The system of sacrifices in the Temple.

2. *Menahoth* ("Meal-offerings").* The meal-offering (Lev. 2).

3. *Hullin* ("Profane Things").* The slaughter of animals and dietary law.

4. *Beckhoroth* ("Firstborns").* The firstborn of humans and animals (Exod. 13:12ff.; Num. 18:15ff.).

5. *Arakhin* ("Estimations").* Vows of estimation (Lev. 27).

6. *Temurah* ("Substitution").* The substituted-offering (Lev. 27:10, 33).

7. *Kerithoth* ("Excisions").* Punishment of extirpation (Lev. 18:29).

8. *Meilah* ("Trespass").* Sacrileges (Lev. 5:15-16).

9. *Tamid* ("Continual-offering").* The daily-offering (Num. 28:3-4).

10. *Middoth* ("Dimensions"). The dimensions and architecture of the Temple.

11. *Kinnim* ("Birds' Nests"). The bird-offering (Lev. 1:14 and 5:7).

Sixth Order: Tohoroth ("Purities")

1. *Kelim* ("Vessels"). Ritual uncleanness of utensils (Lev. 9:33ff.).

2. *Oholoth* ("Tents"). Defilement caused by being in the same tent or under the same roof with a corpse (Num. 9:14-15).

3. *Negaim* ("Plagues"). Concerning leprosy (Lev. 13-14).

4. *Parah* ("Cow"). The red heifer (Num. 19).

5. *Tohoroth* ("Purities"). Ritual impurities that last until sunset (Lev. 11:24ff.).

6. *Mikvoth* ("Baths"). Ritual bathing (Lev. 15:11ff.).

7. *Niddah* ("Menstruant").* The menstruant (Lev. 12:2-8 and 15:19-31).

8. *Makshirin* ("Preparations"). Liquids that make food become ritually unclean (Lev. 11:34-38).

9. *Zabim* ("Fluxes"). Uncleanness caused by running issues (Lev. 15:2-18).

10. *Tevul Yom* ("Immersed at Daytime"). Ritual uncleanness after immersion and before sunset (Lev. 22:6-7).

11. *Yadayim* ("Hands"). Ritual uncleanness of the hands.

12. *Uktzin* ("Stalks"). Uncleanness transmitted by plants and fruits.

Notes

Notes for Introduction

1. In all frankness, it must be admitted that there is also a conspicuous absence of materials available to Jews who want to learn about Christianity, not for purposes of conversion, but for purposes of acquiring knowledge.

2. Matt. 5:17.

3. See, for example, Matt. 16:1. Cf. Luke 13:31.

4. See, for example, Matt. 5:19.

5. See Lev. 19:27.

6. Luke 2:21.

7. Luke 2:46.

8. See, for example, Matt. 26:18.

9. See chapter 7.

10. Cf. Matt. 23:15, "Woe to you, scribes and Pharisees, hypocrites! For you cross sea and land to make a single convert. . . ."

11. *Mishneh Torah*, *Laws of Repentance*, 3:5. (See glossary, "Mishneh Torah.")

12. Mal. 2:10.

Notes for Chapter 1

1. Gen. 2:17.

2. Gen. 3:16-19.

3. Gen. 3:21.

4. Gen. 3:23.

5. Cf. Gen. 4:3.

6. See Gen. Rabbah 38:14. Cf. Deut. 4:19. (Genesis Rabbah is part of the *Midrash Rabbah*. See glossary.)

7. Cf. Deut. 4:28.

8. Cf. Deut. 18:10 and Jer. 7:31.

9. Cf. Isa. 13:16.

10. Cf. 2 Kings 23:7.

11. Mishnah Abodah Zarah 11:1. (See glossary, "Mishnah.")

12. Cf. 2 Kings 17:27-28.

13. Cf. 2 Kings 17:29-33.

14. Cf. Jer. 2:28.

15. Cf. Jer. 14:22.

16. Cf. Jer. 11:12.

17. Cf. Isa. 45:20.

18. 1 Kings 14:15.

19. Gen. 6:5-6.

20. Gen. 6:8.

21. Gen. 6:18-20.

22. Gen. 6:22.

23. Gen. 8:20.

24. See Gen. 11:1-9.

25. Gen. Rabbah 38:13. According to one rabbinical source, Abraham was, astonishingly, only three years old at the time. Alternatively, another states that he was ten; some hold that he was forty-eight. See Gen. Rabbah 64:4.

26. Gen. Rabbah 38:13.

27. Ibid.

28. God sent the angel Gabriel to deliver Abraham from the fiery furnace. Talmud Pesahim 118a.

29. Gen. Rabbah 39:14. In the tradition of Jewish modesty, Abraham taught the men and Sarah taught the women (Gen. Rabbah 84:4). Currently, among the Conservative, Reform, and Reconstructionist movements (see text, below, for discussion), men and women may learn together. In the Orthodox movement, however, men and women continue to learn separately in the traditional manner: Men typically learn with men and women learn with women.

30. See, for example, Gen. 1:16 and 5:13.

31. Gen. Rabbah 18:13.

32. The clause "the persons whom they had acquired in Haran" refers to the many who abandoned paganism and took up the ethical monotheism that they learned from Abraham (Gen. Rabbah 39:14).

33. Gen. 12:1-5.

34. See Gen. 17:5.

35. Gen. 17:15.

36. Gen. 17:7-27.

37. Gen. 17:19.

38. Ibid.

39. Both Jews and Christians suffered at the hands of the Almohads.

40. Rambam also wrote a treatise detailing the 613 commandments of the Torah (see chapter 4). The reader will find a summary of Rambam's redaction of the 613 commandments in appendix 2.

41. The reader should note that the Conservative, Reform, and Reconstructionist movements (discussed in the text below) may also be said to trace their heritage back before the time of Jesus, as all the movements of modern-day Judaism are historical outgrowths of the Pharisaic movement (see chapter 9). In this regard, all branches of Judaism may be said to trace their heritage back to before the time of Jesus. Nevertheless, the beliefs and practices of the Orthodox movement are the most traditional and, in this sense, closest to those of the Pharisaic movement. The differences found in the beliefs and practices of the various movements within modern-day Judaism are discussed throughout this book (but see especially this chapter and chapters 12 and 13).

42. Not all Orthodox communities sing the Thirteen Principles. Thus, the reader may now clearly see that not only are there four major movements within Judaism (Orthodox, Conservative, Reform, and Reconstructionist), but that there are "sub-movements" within movements. For example, within the Orthodox movement, there are the modern-Orthodoxy, Hasidim, and Musar sub-movements, to name just a few. While a discussion of the differences among these sub-movements is beyond the scope of this book, the reader should know that all of the sub-movements within Orthodoxy accept the Thirteen Principles of Faith.

43. See chapter 7 for a discussion on conversion to Judaism, and why Judaism does not actively seek converts.

44. See Exod. 3:14, "God said to Moses, 'I AM WHO I AM.' He said further, 'Thus you shall say to the Israelites, 'I AM has sent me to you.' "

45. Gen. 1:1.

46. Isa. 45:7.

47. See glossary.

48. See chapter 6.

49. Talmud Sanhedrin 38a.

50. Ps. 33:9.

51. See, for example, Gen. 2:15-17 and Exod. 3:7-12.

52. Ps. 33:9.

53. Ps. 46:6.

54. Ps. 102:12, 24-27.

55. Ps. 145:13.

56. Ps. 90:2.

57. Ps. 97:9.

58. Ps. 135:6.

59. Ps. 68:19.

60. Cf. Deut. 6:4. The English translation that is given in the text is not from the New Revised Standard Version but is, in my opinion, closer in meaning to the original Hebrew. The translation in the New Revised Standard Version is "Hear, O Israel: The Lord is our God, the Lord alone."

61. 2 Cor. 13:14; Gal. 4:4-6.

62. Cf. Acts 13:42-46.

63. Talmud Sanhedrin 44a.

64. See Deut. 29:14-15 ("I am making this covenant, sworn by an oath, not only with you who stand here with us today before the LORD our God, but also with those who are not here with us today"), which makes it clear that when the covenant between God and Israel was sealed at Sinai, it bound not only those who were alive at that time, but also those who were yet to be born.

65. Job 9:11.

66. Job 23:8-9.

67. Deut. 4:12-16.

68. Cf. Exod. Rabbah 3:12. (Exodus Rabbah is part of the *Midrash Rabbah*. See glossary.)

69. Deut. 11:12.

70. Exod. 16:3.

71. Isa. 45:15.

72. John 1:1.

73. John 1:14.

74. Mark 6:49.

75. Matt. 8:3.

76. Matt. 27:35.

77. Ps. 97:9.

78. Hab. 3:6.

79. Isa. 48:12.

80. Exod. 20:3.

81. See Ezek. 8:14.

82. Deut. 18:10.

83. Judg. 13:16. See also Talmud Shabbat 12b (prayer directed to angels is not useful because they cannot understand the vernacular of a language).

84. Exod. 20:4.

85. Ps. 145:18. Although the Bible gives us many illustrations of individuals acting as intercessors on behalf of others (for example, Abraham praying for Sodom, Gen. 18:23-33), these actions should not be taken to mean that an intermediary is necessary. Indeed, in the final analysis, whether God grants the petition is dependent not on the intercessor but on the merits of the one for whom prayer is made (see Ezek. 14:14, 20).

86. Exod. 20:2 (emphasis added).

87. Ps. 145:18-19.

88. See also Thirteen Principles of Faith, Principle 10, below.

89. See, for example, Amos 3:8.

90. See, for example, Ezek. 12:28.

91. Gen. 20:7.

92. Deut. 34:10.

93. Cf. Exod. 7:1.

94. Exod. 15:20.

95. 1 Kings 18:36.

96. 2 Kings 9:1.

97. These prophets authored the books of the Bible which bear their names.

98. Isa. 42:9.

99. See Dan. 8:26.

100. See Matt. 5:17.

101. 1 Pet. 1:9-12. See also chapter 8 of this book.

102. Deut. 34:10.

103. See Exod. 32:30-33.

104. See, for example, Gen. 28:10-16.

105. Exod. 33:11.

106. The term "Torah" is defined and discussed in Principle 8, below. See also glossary.

107. See chapter 5.

108. See chapter 4.

109. Mishnah Aboth 1:1.

110. Deut. 5:33.

111. Ps. 18:30.

112. Ps. 19:7.

113. Deut. 4:2.

114. See chapter 4.

115. Although some Biblical scholars have opined that Paul was the author of Hebrews, most now discount his authorship. It is not known who the author was.

116. Heb. 9:11-15.

117. See, for example, 2 Cor. 3:1-18.

118. Christians do, of course, devote significant time to studying Genesis and Exodus because these books are essential for an understanding of salvation and Israel. But Christians do not typically study the balance of the Torah (Pentateuch) with the degree of intensity that Jews do. One reason for this is that the Torah contains hundreds of laws that bind the Jewish people, but which do not bind non-Jews (see chapters 4 and 7).

119. See, for example, Isa. 53:3.

120. See *Catechism of the Catholic Church*, ¶129.

121. Ps. 19:7-9.

122. See Isa. 49:6; Luke 2:32; Matt. 5:13-16.

123. See Gen. 9:1-7. The Noachide Covenant is discussed in chapter 7 of this book.

124. Gen. 17:13.

125. See Gal. 3:17. See also *Catechism of the Catholic Church*, ¶129.

126. Deut. 4:31.

127. Ps. 139:2.

128. Matt. 6:8.

129. Ps. 139:23.

130. Exod. 20:2 (emphasis added).

131. Cf. Prov. 15:26.

132. See chapter 3.

133. Ps. 136:1.

134. Isa. 45:21.

135. Prov. 21:12.

136. See Prov. 21:15.

137. Eccles. Rabbah 7:16:1. (Ecclesiastes Rabbah is part of the *Midrash Rabbah*. See glossary.)

138. Prov. 13:13.

139. See, for example, Ps. 91:16.

140. Ps. 92:7.

141. Ps. 19:11.

142. Deut. 30:15-19.

143. See chapters 4 and 7. See also appendix 2.

144. Cf. Gal. 3:10. See also chapter 9 for a discussion of the views of Paul of Tarsus.

145. Ps. 136:1.

146. Ps. 136:17.

147. Exod. 20:17.

148. See Lev. 11:7.

149. Lev. 26:3-5 (emphasis added).

150. Mark 16:16.

151. Lev. 26:5, above.

152. See chapter 11.

153. But see Talmud Rosh Hashanah 28b for the proposition that proper intention to perform a commandment is not a requirement. See also chapter 11 of this book.

154. See chapter 6. See also glossary.

155. Mishnah Aboth 1:3.

156. See Talmud Sanhedrin 90a.

157. Deut. 11:12.

158. Gen. 19:16.

159. Isa. 45:21.

160. 2 Sam. 2:6.

161. Talmud Yebamoth 71a. See also Talmud Sanhedrin 56a.

162. Isa. 11:6.

163. Cf. John 18:36.

164. See Matt. 24:27-31.

165. Matt. 28:19.

166. See Thirteen Principles of Faith, Principles 2 and 3, earlier in this chapter.

167. Gen. 35:18.

168. Dan. 12:2, 13.

169. "We look for the resurrection of the dead, and the life of the world to come."

Notes for Chapter 2

1. *B.C.E.* stands for Before the Common Era and is commonly used by Jewish writers in place of the *B.C.* designation. Similarly, *C.E.* stands for the Common Era and is used in place of the *A.D.* abbreviation.

2. See Exod. 20:3.

3. Deut. 16:18-20.

4. See Matt. 26:57. Cf. John 18:12-24, where it appears that Jesus was questioned by an informally convened body. See also text below and chapter 4.

5. A few states do not have intermediate Courts of Appeal. In such states, the appeal of a Superior Court case goes directly to the state Supreme Court.

6. In California, one can become an attorney in the manner of Abraham Lincoln by studying under an attorney and then taking the bar exam.

7. Exod. 20:13. Jewish criminal law is not presently operative, not even in the modern State of Israel. See discussion later in this chapter; see also chapter 4.

8. Deut. 24:14-15.

9. Lev. 19:10.

10. Exod. 20:8-11.

11. Exod. 20:3.

12. Lev. 23:26-32.

13. Lev. 12:3.

14. See chapter 4.

15. Mishnah Rosh Hashanah 2:9.

16. Mishnah Sanhedrin 1:1-6.

17. Mishnah Sanhedrin 1:1.

18. Talmud Sanhedrin 17a. Amazingly, according to the Talmud, all courts in Israel had to have judges who knew many different languages. The reason for this was to allow the judges to hear the testimony of any litigant or witness without the assistance of an outside translator.

19. Knowledge of the law was only one qualification. Judges also had to be ethical and beyond reproach. They also had to have children. It was believed that a person who does not have children does not have the same compassion and insight as one who does. See Talmud Sanhedrin 36a.

20. Mishnah Sanhedrin 1:1-2.

21. Mishnah Sanhedrin 1:1.

22. Mishnah Sanhedrin 4:1.

23. Talmud Sanhedrin 2b.

24. Mishnah Sanhedrin 1:4.

25. Mishnah Sanhedrin 3:8.

26. Talmud Sanhedrin 6a.

27. Mishnah Sanhedrin 1:5.

28. Mishnah Sanhedrin 11:2.

29. *Mishneh Torah, Sanhedrin* 5:1.

30. Mishnah Sanhedrin 1:5.

31. Talmud Sanhedrin 88b.

32. Mishnah Sanhedrin 1:5. See also Deut. 13:1-5.

33. Mishnah Sanhedrin 1:5. See also Deut. 13:12-18.

34. Mishnah Sanhedrin 1:5.

35. Mishnah Sanhedrin 11:2. Cf. Exod. 23:2.

36. Mishnah Sanhedrin 1:5.

37. Exod. 18:22.

38. Matt. 26:59; Mark 14:55; Luke 22:66.

39. John 18:15. See also Mark 14:54; cf. Luke 22:66.

40. Mishnah Sanhedrin 11:2. When the Temple was destroyed by the Romans, the Great Sanhedrin was eventually moved. See next section of text below.

41. Mark 14:64.

42. See Luke 22:54.

43. See 14 *Encyclopaedia Judaica* 836-839.

44. Acts 4, 6:12-15, and 23:1-11.

45. Acts 5:33-41.

46. The plural of *beth din*.

47. See Deut. 24:1-3.

48. As did Rambam in his *Mishneh Torah*. See chapter 1.

49. In ancient times, rabbis earned their living by having an occupation. Thus, one sage was a baker, another a gravedigger. The tradition that a rabbi had a congregation, which paid him to teach and give advice, came into existence only in the Middle Ages. Some have said that the evolution of the rabbinate into a full-time job may have been influenced by the way in which priests functioned in parishes.

50. Traditionally, rabbis were men only. Currently, among all but the Orthodox, they may also be women. But even in the Orthodox movement there is pressure by feminists to ordain women. Indeed, it is reported that a woman in Israel is learning with an Orthodox rabbi, who is apparently willing to ordain her as a rabbi in the Orthodox movement when she satisfies all of her educational requirements. See also text below.

51. Some hold that the synagogue was in place even before the destruction of the First Temple. (See 15 *Encyclopaedia Judaica* 580, citing 1 Sam. 1:10ff.) In any event, whenever the synagogue did come into existence, it became a popular place for community prayer. In fact, by the time the Romans destroyed the Second Temple in the first century C.E., there were literally hundreds of synagogues just in Jerusalem. Because of the synagogue, Judaism was able to continue, even without the Temple.

52. See, for example, John 1:38.

53. Mic. 6:8. See also Gen. 18:9 and Gen. Rabbah 18:2.

54. See note 50 above.

Notes for Chapter 3

1. Exod. 19:16-18.

2. Exod. 20:1.

3. Exod. 31:18.

4. Exod. 12:37. That millions of Israelites witnessed the Revelation is readily deduced from the Torah, which states that 600,000 men—not counting the women and children—left Egypt in the Exodus. Moreover, according to tradition, the soul of every Jew who would ever be born (including those Gentiles who would convert to Judaism) also witnessed the Revelation. See Deut. 5:3. Many Christian and non-Orthodox Jewish scholars, however, interpret the number stated in the Torah in a symbolic, not literal, manner.

5. Exod. 20:2.

6. See chapter 1, Thirteen Principles of Faith, Principle 1. See also appendix 2, Positive Commandment 1.

7. Ps. 145:9.

8. Ps. 6.

9. Ps. 139:14.

10. Prov. 30:8; cf. Matt. 6:11.

11. Gen. 25:21.

12. See Ps. 51.

13. Exod. 20:3-6.

14. See appendix 2, Negative Commandment 1.

15. See appendix 2, Negative Commandments 3 and 4.

16. Cf. Num. 5:14, where "jealousy" is used in the context of marital infidelity. These are the only two situations where the Torah uses the term "jealousy."

17. See chapter 1, Thirteen Principles of Faith, Principles 3 and 11.

18. Cf. Exod. 20:5.

19. 2 Sam. 7:22.

20. Prov. 13:21. See also chapter 1, Thirteen Principles of Faith, Principle 11.

21. Deut. 24:16.

22. See chapter 1, Thirteen Principles of Faith, Principles 8 and 9.

23. Talmud Sanhedrin 27b. Cf. Prov. 1:8.

24. See Gen. 6:3.

25. Rashi, Judaism's commentator *par excellence*, states that this passage shows that the reward for complying with God's commandments is at least five hundred times greater than the punishment for not. Rashi's commentary is found in virtually all Hebrew-language editions of Jewish Bibles (Old Testament). See also glossary.

26. Exod. 20:7.

27. See appendix 2, Negative Commandment 62. Cf. Matt. 5:33-37.

28. Cf. Exod. 20:19, "And [the Israelites] said to Moses, 'You speak to us, and we will listen; but do not let God speak to us, or we will die.'"

29. Cf. Talmud Makkoth 24a.

30. Exod. 20:8-11.

31. See Jer. 32:17, 27.

32. See chapter 1, Thirteen Principles of Faith, Principles 3 and 11.

33. Gen. 1:5.

34. Talmud Shabbat 34b.

35. Cf. *Code of Jewish Law* 75:1.

36. Cf. Neh. 10:31.

37. Exod. 31:17.

38. See Deut. 5:3.

39. Asher Ginzberg (1856-1927), quoted in Nathan Ausubel, *The Book of Jewish Knowledge*, page 374. (See selected bibliography and suggested reading.)

40. Mark 2:27.

41. Mechilta, Ki Theesa. The *Mechilta* is an ancient rabbinical commentary on the Book of Exodus. *Ki Theesa* is a section of Exodus.

42. See Gen. 48:20.

43. See Num. 6:24-26.

44. Prov. 31:10-31.

45. See chapter 6. See also glossary.

46. Cf. Talmud Berakoth 57b.

47. Exod. 20:12.

48. See, for example, Gen. 47:30-31. See also Talmud Kiddushin 30b.

49. Talmud Kiddushin 30b.

50. Exod. 20:13.

51. See, for example, Exod. 22:2.

52. Gen. Rabbah 34:13. For the heartrending account of Rabbi Channina, who, while being tortured by the Romans, refused to end his own life prematurely by even a few seconds, see Talmud Abodah Zarah 18a.

53. Talmud Sanhedrin 78a and Talmud Pesahim 54b. See also Deut. 32:39.

54. Gen. 9:5.

55. Ibid. Cf. Mishnah Sanhedrin 10:3.

56. Mishnah Aboth 3:15.

57. Talmud Baba Metzia 59a.

58. Matt. 5:21-22.

59. Mishnah Oholoth 7:6.

60. Ibid.

61. Cf. Mishnah Sanhedrin 72b. See also *Mishneh Torah, Laws of Homicide* 1:9.

62. See, for example, *Catechism of the Catholic Church*, ¶2270, citing Jer. 1:5 and Ps. 139:15.

63. Exod. 20:14.

64. See Mishnah Kiddushin 3:12.

65. See, for example, Deut. 23:2, King James Version. In the New Revised Standard Version, in lieu of the term "bastard," the translation given is "Those born of an illicit union." This translation is more consistent with the Jewish view, as is explained in the text below.

66. Talmud Yebamoth 49a.

67. *Mishneh Torah, Laws of Prohibited Intercourse* 15:1. See also note 65 above.

68. See Mishnah Kerithoth 1:1.

69. The basis for this rule is found in Deut. 23:2, which states, "Those born of an illicit union shall not be admitted to the assembly of the LORD. Even to the tenth generation, none of their descendants shall be admitted to the assembly of the LORD." The "assembly of the LORD" refers to the assemblage of marriage with a Jew (although, as stated in the text, it is permissible for a mamzer to marry a convert to Judaism).

70. Ibid.

71. Cf. Deut. 24:16.

72. Lev. Rabbah 32:7, citing Eccles. 4:1 ("Again I saw all the oppressions that are practiced under the sun. Look, the tears of the oppressed—with no one to comfort them! On the side of their oppressors there was power—with no one to comfort them."). Leviticus Rabbah is part of the *Midrash Rabbah*. (See glossary.)

73. Talmud Yebamoth 22b.

74. Tosefta, Talmud Yebamoth 45b. The *Tosefta* is a collection of ancient rabbinical teachings that supplement the Mishnah.

75. Matt. 5:27.

76. Matt. 5:27-28.

77. See Prov. 6:24-28.

78. *Code of Jewish Law* 152:1.

79. See Prov. 7:5.

80. Exod. 20:15.

81. For example, see Rashi, commentary to Exod. 20:13.

82. Exod. 21:16.

83. Exod. 21:12.

84. Lev. 20:10.

85. Exod. 20:13.

86. Exod. 20:14.

87. Exod. 22:1, 7.

88. See, for example, Sforno (see glossary), commentary to Exod. 20:13.

89. See Exod. 22:1, 7.

90. Exod. 20:16.

91. See discussion of the sixth commandment above.

92. Cf. Prov. 14:5, 25.

93. See Deut. 19:19.

94. Talmud Shebuoth 31a.

95. Sforno, commentary to Exod. 20:13.

96. Cf. Prov. 16:28.
97. See Ps. 15:1-2.
98. Exod. 20:17.
99. Exod. 20:2.
100. Exod. 20:4-5.
101. Exod. 20:7.
102. Exod. 20:8.
103. Exod. 20:12.
104. Exod. 20:13-16.
105. Cf. Talmud Rosh Hashanah 28b.
106. See Mic. 2:2 (emphasis added). Cf. Isa. 29:13.
107. See chapter 1.
108. Mishnah Aboth 2:13.
109. See chapter 11.
110. Ps. 19:12.
111. Prov. 24:8, 9.
112. Matt. 5:27-28.
113. See Matt. 9:4.
114. Talmud Berakoth 61a.
115. Cf. Prov. 20:9.
116. Exod. 20:1-17.
117. Deut. 5:6-21.
118. Exod. 20:8.
119. Deut. 5:12.
120. Talmud Rosh Hashanah 27a.
121. See appendix 2, Positive Commandment 155.
122. See appendix 2, Negative Commandment 320.
123. See end of chapter 2.

Notes for Chapter 4

1. Exod. 12:29-51.
2. Exod. 20.
3. Gen. 12:7 and 13:15.
4. See chapter 3.
5. See chapter 1, Thirteen Principles of Faith, Principle 8.
6. Exod. 20:13.
7. Exod. 21:14.
8. Exod. 21:12.
9. Deut. 19:15; cf. Matt. 26:60.
10. See Deut. 19:5.

11. Exod. 21:12-13.

12. Exod. 21:12.

13. Num. 35:12.

14. Deut. 16:20.

15. Exod. 21:13.

16. Lev. 18:6-18.

17. Although not expressly stated, a man is forbidden to have relations with his daughter. This is deduced from the Torah: "You shall not uncover the nakedness of a woman and her daughter" (Lev. 18:17). Additionally, a female who consents to intercourse with a prohibited male is just as guilty (Talmud Yebamoth 84b), except, of course, where the female is too young to give consent.

18. See Lev. 20:11-21.

19. Lev. 20:11.

20. Lev. 18:30.

21. Lev. 18:22.

22. Lev. 20:13.

23. Lev. 20:15-16.

24. See Gen. 4:1.

25. Exod. 22:1.

26. Exod. 22:4.

27. See Lev. 24:12 and Num. 15:34.

28. See, for example, Exod. 21:12.

29. Exod. 21:12-13.

30. Exod. 22:1.

31. Deut. 25:2.

32. Deut. 25:3.

33. See Exod. 21:13.

34. See Matt. 26:28.

35. See, for example, Lev. 24:23.

36. Lev. 19:18.

37. Deut. 21:22-23.

38. Cf. Acts 5:30 and 10:39.

39. Cf. Gal. 3:13.

40. See chapter 2.

41. 384 U.S. 436 (1966).

42. Exod. 21:18-19.

43. Exod. 21:35-36.

44. Exod. 22:6.

45. See Exod. 21:24.

46. See chapter 6.

47. Exod. 23:6.

48. Exod. 23:7-9.

49. See chapter 2.

50. Deut. 25:13-15.

51. Deut. 15:1.

52. Lev. 25:8-34. Thus, the "sale" of real estate was in fact a long-term lease, subject to a maximum term of fifty years.

53. Deut. 24:14-15.

54. Lev. 25:14.

55. Exod. 22:21.

56. Exod. 22:22.

57. Exod. 22:23-24.

58. Deut. 24:19.

59. Exod. 22:25.

60. Deut. 14:28.

61. Lev. 19:14.

62. Lev. 19:18.

63. Rabbinical commentary to Lev. 19:18, cited in A. Cohen, *Everyman's Talmud*, page 212. (See selected bibliography and suggested reading.) See also Mishnah Aboth 1:12; cf. Matt. 5:43.

64. See Gen. 2:21-25.

65. Deut. 24:5.

66. Deut. 24:1-2; cf. Matt. 1:18-19.

67. Cf. Exod. 21:10.

68. Num. 27:8-11.

69. Mishnah Baba Bathra 9:1.

70. See Deut. 23:17.

71. Num. 1:3.

72. Deut. 20:19-20.

73. Deut. 20:10-11.

74. Deut. 20:12.

75. Cf. Deut. 20:18.

76. See chapter 1.

77. Cf. Isa. 13:16.

78. Deut. 21:10-14.

79. Exod. 21:10.

80. Prov. 3:17.

81. See chapter 5.

82. Exod. 12:1-15, 19-20.

83. This is according to the Synoptic Gospels (Matthew, Mark, and Luke). See, for example, Matt. 26:18.

84. Deut. 16:9-11.

85. See Acts 2:1-47 and 20:16.

86. Deut. 16:13-15.

87. Lev. 23:42-43.

88. Lev. 23:24.

89. Exod. 19:16.

90. Cf. Exod. 20:18 ("all the people witnessed the thunder and lightning"). The passage as quoted in the text is the traditional Jewish understanding of the passage, and is discussed in the text immediately below.

91. Lev. 23:27-28.

92. Rom. 3:28. The position that faith alone can save an individual is a fundamental principle of Protestantism, but is rejected by Catholicism. See *Catechism of the Catholic Church*, ¶¶1263 and 1459.

93. Exod. 20:8.

94. Deut. 6:8; cf. Matt. 23:5. See also glossary.

95. Num. 15:38. See also glossary.

96. Cf. Isa. 3:17.

97. Lev. 17:10.

98. Lev. 11:3.

99. Lev. 11:4-7.

100. Lev. 11:44. A fuller explanation of the reasons for the dietary laws is presented in chapter 5 of this book.

101. Deut. 18:10.

102. See chapter 1.

103. Talmud Makkoth 23b. See also appendix 2 for Maimonides' redaction of the 613 commandments. In addition to the 613 commandments found in the Torah, there are also many hundreds of other laws found in the body of oral law known as the *Mishnah*. The Mishnah is discussed in chapter 5.

104. See chapter 1, Thirteen Principles of Faith, Principle 8.

Notes for Chapter 5

1. See chapter 1.

2. See chapter 1, Thirteen Principles of Faith, Principle 8.

3. See Deut. 30:10 and 31:9, 24.

4. See chapter 1, Thirteen Principles of Faith, Principle 8.

5. See chapter 4, end. See also appendix 2 for Maimonides' redaction of the 613 commandments.

6. See, for example, Exod. 20:22.

7. See, for example, Lev. 1:2.

8. See, for example, 2 Chron. 17:9.

9. Luke 2:24, 39.

10. See, for example, Josh. 23:6.

11. Exod. 24:4.

12. Of course, as stated in the text above, the Orthodox view is that there are absolutely no errors in the Torah. See chapter 1, Thirteen Principles of Faith, Principle 9.

13. Deut. 30:19.

14. See Mishnah Aboth 1:18, quoting Isa. 60:21.

15. Ps. 19:7.

16. Ps. 119:141-144, 150-152. See also chapter 1, Thirteen Principles of Faith, Principle 9.

17. John 14:6.

18. See chapter 7.

19. Lev. 19:19.

20. Lev. 11:7.

21. See chapter 1, Thirteen Principles of Faith.

22. Maimonides, *The Commandments*, Negative Commandment 42. (See selected bibliography and suggested reading.) See also appendix 2, Negative Commandment 42.

23. Recanti (see glossary), commentary to Gen. 4:3-4.

24. See, for example, Num. 19.

25. See discussion in text above.

26. Ps. 18:30.

27. See views of Maimonides and Recanti in text above.

28. Lev. 11:7.

29. Exod. 20:13.

30. See chapter 1, Thirteen Principles of Faith, Principle 12.

31. Lev. 11:44.

32. Exod. 20:8-11.

33. Deut. 12:21.

34. Exod. 21:12.

35. Exod. 21:24.

36. See chapter 1, Thirteen Principles of Faith, Principle 8.

37. Ps. 18:30.

38. Jer. 32:17, 27.

39. Isa. 48:5.

Notes for Chapter 6

1. See chapter 1, Thirteen Principles of Faith, Principle 8.

2. See text below. See also glossary.

3. See text below. See also glossary.

4. See text below. See also glossary.

5. See Matt. 15:2 and Mark 7:3, 5. See also Matt. 15:3, 6 ("your tradition"), Mark 7:8 ("the tradition of men"), and Mark 7:9 ("your own tradition"). It is not fully clear if by the "tradition of the elders," the Gospels meant only the Mishnah (oral law), or also the rabbinical debates on the oral law that had been underway since the second century B.C.E. Although it seems that Jesus did not support the oral law, it is my position that he did. And to the extent he disagreed with the rabbis on debating the Mishnah, such spirited debate is simply a part of Jewish learning and Judaism. See text below. See also chapter 9.

6. Mishnah Aboth 1:1.

7. See chapter 9 for discussion of the Pharisees. See also glossary.

8. See appendix 3 for a list of all sixty-three tractates of the Mishnah, as well as a summary of their contents.

9. See chapter 5, end.

10. Mishnah Shabbat 7:1. The thirty-nine categories of work are those types of labor that were used in building the Sanctuary in the desert. See Exod. 35:1 and Talmud Shabbat 49b. The thirty-nine categories are: (1) sowing; (2) plowing; (3) reaping; (4) binding sheaves; (5) threshing; (6) winnowing; (7) sorting; (8) grinding; (9) sifting; (10) kneading; (11) baking; (12) shearing sheep; (13) washing wool; (14) beating wool; (15) dyeing wool; (16) spinning; (17) weaving; (18) making two loops; (19) weaving two threads; (20) separating two threads; (21) tying a knot; (22) loosening a knot; (23) sewing two stitches; (24) tearing in order to sew two stitches; (25) hunting a gazelle (that is, a deer), and (26) slaughtering, (27) flaying, (28) salting, (29) curing, and (30) scraping it and (31) cutting its skin; (32) writing two letters of the alphabet; (33) erasing in order to write two letters of the alphabet; (34) building a structure; (35) pulling down a structure; (36) extinguishing a fire [but, as will be seen in the text immediately following, the laws of the sabbath are suspended in order to save life]; (37) lighting a fire; (38) striking with a hammer; and (39) moving something from one domain to another. The reader should note that these thirty-nine rules are major categories; many derivative rules flow from them. For example, a car may not be driven on the sabbath because when the ignition turns on, a spark is generated (see no. 37, lighting a fire).

11. Mishnah Shabbat 2:5 and Mishnah Yoma 8:6.

12. See generally Mishnah Hullin.

13. See generally Mishnah Sanhedrin.

14. Mishnah Baba Kama 8:1.

15. See selected bibliography and suggested reading.

16. Mishnah Sanhedrin 10:1-4.

17. See chapter 1.

18. See, for example, Luke 2:46.

19. See, for example, Exod. 21:24.

20. See Mishnah Baba Kama 8:1.

21. See appendix 3.

22. In 1240, Pope Gregory IX ordered the Talmud to be "burned at the stake." These instructions were subsequently conveyed to the kings of France, Spain, England, and Portugal. In June 1242, twenty-four wagon loads of Jewish books (including thousands of volumes of the Talmud) were put to fire in a public burning in Rome. Confiscation of the Talmud subsequently took place by Louis IX (1247 and 1248). A public burning took place in 1319 in Toulouse; another occurred in Paris. Others took place in

southern Italy in 1270. During the Counter-Reformation, on September 9, 1553 (the Jewish New Year), a pyre was constructed in Rome which was used to destroy thousands of seized Jewish books, which included many volumes of the Talmud. The confiscation of Hebrew books continued in Italy (including the Papal States) as late as the eighteenth century. Outside of France and Italy, however, it appears that the European monarchy did not take such dire action against the Talmud, although the Talmud was subject to government censorship for passages deemed disrespectful to Christianity. Thus, nowhere in Europe was the Talmud fully secure. Indeed, the last public burning of the Talmud of this era took place in Poland in 1757. There, as a result of a "disputation" between Catholic and Jewish leaders, one thousand copies of the Talmud were set afire. See 15 *Encyclopaedia Judaica* 768-771.

23. See, for example, Matt. 15:2 and 24:3, and Mark 12:28.

Notes for Chapter 7

1. Exod. 19:3-8.

2. Num. Rabbah 14:10. (Numbers Rabbah is part of the *Midrash Rabbah*. See glossary).

3. Exod. 24:7. God knew that Israel would accept the Torah. But if the Torah was offered to Israel first, the other nations of the world would have complained: They too would have accepted the Torah had it first been offered to them. To prevent these nations from ever making such a complaint, God first offered the Torah to all the other nations of the world before he offered it to Israel. Only after the other nations rejected the Torah did God offer it to Israel. See A. Cohen, *Everyman's Talmud*, page 63 and sources cited therein. (See selected bibliography and suggested reading.) Of course—and this is most significant—the laws of the Torah (including the Ten Commandments) are available to all individuals who seek to live a righteous life. See chapter 8 of this book.

4. Talmud Sanhedrin 59a. Cf. Rom. 2:14.

5. Lev. 11:7.

6. Exod. 20:8.

7. Gen. 17:9-14.

8. Exod. 20:13.

9. Exod. 20:14.

10. Talmud Sanhedrin 56a.

11. Talmud Sanhedrin 56a-60a.

12. Gen. 9:1-7.

13. See Talmud Sanhedrin 56b. See also Gen. 3:19.

14. Ibid.

15. See Talmud Sanhedrin 57b.

16. See Gen. 2:24.

17. Talmud Sanhedrin 57a.

18. Talmud Sanhedrin 56b.

19. See Talmud Sanhedrin 74b.

20. See Exod. 21:12-14.

21. See Num. 35:11-12.

22. For an excellent treatment on the subject, see A. Lichtenstein, *The Seven Laws of Noah*. (See selected bibliography and suggested reading.)

23. Lev. 19:11.

24. Lev. 19:13.

25. Deut. 19:14.

26. Exod. 20:17.

27. Exod. 20:15.

28. Lev. 19:35-36.

29. Exod. 20:14.

30. Lev. 18:6-18.

31. Lev. 18:22.

32. Many commandments are not presently operative for a variety of reasons. A significant number of commandments relate to the Holy Temple. See, for example, Lev. 1, dealing with offerings. Because the Temple no longer stands and has yet to be rebuilt, these commandments have been, by necessity, suspended. Various other laws are also not presently operative. See, for example, Lev. 25:8-34, the law of the Jubilee, which is not operable in the absence of all twelve tribes living in the land originally parceled out to them (see Josh. 13-21). Orthodox Judaism teaches that when the Messiah comes, the Temple will be rebuilt and the twelve tribes will once again inhabit the Land of Israel. At such time, these and all of the commandments will be operative. See also appendix 2.

33. See A. Lichtenstein, *The Seven Laws of Noah*, in note 22 above.

34. See Talmud Sanhedrin 56a.

35. Gen. 17:2-7.

36. Talmud Yoma 28b.

37. Gen. 26:5.

38. See Deut. 6:1.

39. See Gen. Rabbah 95:3.

40. Gen. Rabbah 39:14. Cf. Mishnah Aboth 1:1.

41. See Gen. 12:5.

42. See Gen. Rabbah 39:14.

43. Tosefta Sanhedrin 13:2, interpreting Ps. 9:17.

44. See chapter 11.

45. *Mishneh Torah, Laws of Kings* 8:11.

46. 1 Cor. 13:6.

47. Matt. 5:21-22.

48. Matt. 5:27-28.

49. Heb. 13:18.

50. Cf. Matt.1:11-13.

51. Matt. 12:31-32.

52. Rev. 21:8 and 22:15.

53. See Deut. 6:4.

54. See chapter 1 for a discussion of the evils of idolatrous polytheism.

55. As mentioned earlier, a Jew cannot practice Judaism and subscribe to a Trinitarian view of God. Such a person is practicing Christianity. See chapter 1, Thirteen Principles of Faith, Principles 2 and 12.

56. Gal. 2:11.

57. Gal. 2:13.

58. Matt. 13:55. See also note 75, chapter 11.

59. Gal. 2:11.

60. Gal. 2:21.

61. Acts 15:24-29.

Notes for Chapter 8

1. See chapter 1, Thirteen Principles of Faith, Principle 8. See also chapter 5.

2. Gen. 1 and 2.

3. Gen. 3.

4. Gen. 4.

5. Gen. 5.

6. Gen. 6-9.

7. Gen. 10.

8. Gen. 11.

9. Gen. 12-23.

10. Gen. 24-26.

11. Gen. 27-35.

12. Gen. 37-50.

13. Exod. 1.

14. Exod. 2-3.

15. Exod. 12.

16. Exod. 20.

17. See note 1.

18. See chapter 5.

19. Esther 4:16.

20. Isa. 56:1.

21. Ps. 16:1.

22. Prov. 19:1.

23. The festivals are *Rosh Hashanah*, *Yom Kippur*, *Sukkot*, *Shemini Atzeret*, the first and last days of *Passover*, and *Shavuot*. See chapter 4 for a discussion of Jewish holidays. See also glossary.

24. For example, the New Revised Standard Version.

25. The Torah is also read on Monday and Thursday during morning synagogue services. Whenever the Torah is read publicly in the synagogue, it is done so from a scroll. Cf. Isa. 34:4.

26. The numbering by chapter and verse was made by Christian redactors, but has since been adopted by most Jewish publishers too for the sake of uniformity.

27. Isa. 42:5.

28. Gen. 6:5.

29. Isa. 43:8-10.

30. See note 1.

31. This is not to suggest that Christians do not study the Torah. Indeed, the Book of Genesis is most significant to Christians, for it is there where one reads of the Creation, the fall of humankind, the beginnings of Israel, etc. The Book of Exodus is also important for its account of the Exodus and the giving of the Ten Commandments (to which Christianity subscribes) on Mount Sinai. Still, Jews study the texts of the Torah with a special intensity. One reason for this is because Jews are bound by the hundreds of commandments of the Torah and Christians are not. (See chapter 7.)

32. The teaching of the Roman Catholic Church is that Jesus fulfilled or transcended the law of the Torah (Old Testament), but did not revoke it. See *Catechism of the Catholic Church*, ¶¶128-130, 1953. On the other hand, some Protestant denominations take the position that the old covenant of the Torah was actually superseded or made obsolete by the New Testament. See, for example, Ronald F. Youngblood, gen. ed., *Nelson's New Illustrated Bible Dictionary*, page 307. (See selected bibliography and suggested reading.) See also Heb. 8:13 ("In speaking of 'a new covenant,' he has made the first one obsolete. And what is obsolete and growing old will soon disappear"). See also chapter 9 of this book.

33. See chapter 9 for a discussion of Jesus' fulfilling the law.

34. Isa. 43:10.

35. Isa. 9:6.

36. See, for example, Isa. 7:14 and 53:1-12; Mic. 5:2; 2 Sam. 7:12; and Ps. 69:8, 31:5, 16:10 and 110:1.

37. See chapter 1, Thirteen Principles of Faith, Principle 12.

38. Deut. 27:8.

39. Talmud Sotah 32a.

40. See chapter 6.

Notes for Chapter 9

1. See chapter 1.

2. See chapter 2.

3. See chapters 3 and 4.

4. Matt. 5:17-19.

5. See text at note 4.

6. See chapter 4, end.

7. See glossary for a brief description of these movements.

8. See chapter 6.

9. Matt. 15:2.

10. Matt. 15:17.

11. Matt. 12:34.

12. In Luke 11:38, a Pharisee accuses Jesus himself of not complying with the handwashing requirement. We discuss this matter in the text below.

13. Mishnah Yadayim 1:1ff.

14. Matt. 15:2 (emphasis added). See also Mark 7:1-23. The "tradition of the elders" refers to the oral law, what would come to be known as the Mishnah. See chapter 6.

15. The Sadducees ceased to exist after the destruction of the Temple in the year 70 C.E. The Pharisees endured, however, becoming the ancestors of modern-day Judaism.

16. Matt. 23:2-3. The balance of the passage quoted in the text is "but do not do as they do, for they do not practice what they teach."

17. See chapter 6, end.

18. Mishnah Aboth 1:1.

19. See text at note 4.

20. See chapter 8.

21. The "Twelve Minor Prophets" are so named based on the length of their books, not their stature. See chapter 8. Many Jews simply refer to these books as the "Twelve Prophets," to avoid even the slightest implication of a diminished status.

22. Luke 24:27. See also Rom. 1:2.

23. See text at note 4.

24. See text at notes 6-8.

25. See chapters 5 and 6.

26. Ps. 18:30.

27. Cf. Ps. 19:7.

28. 1 John 3:20.

29. Exod. 20:13.

30. Matt. 5:21-22. The reader will recall that Judaism teaches that publicly humiliating someone is deemed to be murder in a figurative sense, and that one who commits such a sin has no share in the World to Come. See chapter 3, the sixth commandment. Jesus' teaching was undoubtedly influenced by this instruction.

31. Exod. 20:14.

32. Matt. 5:27-28. Judaism too teaches that one must not look upon a woman in a lewd manner. The Talmud, for example, admonishes a man to not walk behind a woman who is crossing a stream since she, not knowing that a man is in back of her, may pick up her dress to keep it from getting wet. Once again (see note 30) we see how Jesus' teaching was impacted by his Jewish heritage and education. See Luke 2:46 and 24:27.

33. Lev. 19:18.

34. Matt. 5:43. "You have heard that it was said, 'You shall love your neighbor and hate your enemy,' " quoting in part from Lev. 19:18, "You shall not take vengeance or bear a grudge against any of your people, but you shall love your neighbor as yourself: I am the LORD." But nowhere does the Torah teach causeless hatred. Cf. Exod. 23:4, "When you come upon your enemy's ox or donkey going astray, you shall bring it back." Of course, there are times when hatred is appropriate. As it is written, "The LORD loves those who hate evil" (Ps. 97:10). See also Ps. 139:19-22.

35. Matt. 26:18.

36. Deut. 14:1-21; cf. Matt. 15:11.

37. Luke 4:16.

38. See Exod. 12:1-20 and 20:8.

39. Matt. 12:9-13.

40. Matt. 12:1.

41. Matt. 15:2. Cf. Luke 11:38.

42. Matt. 12:9-10.

43. Matt. 12:10.

44. Mishnah Shabbat 2:5. See also Deut. 30:16, where it is provided, "If you obey the commandments of the LORD your God that I am commanding you today, by loving the LORD your God, walking in his ways, and observing his commandments, decrees, and ordinances, then you shall live and become numerous, and the LORD your God will bless you in the land that you are entering to possess." See also Lev. 18:5, where it states, "You shall keep my statutes and my ordinances; by doing so one shall live: I am the LORD." From these passages the rabbis taught that one is to live by the Torah and not die by it. Thus, to save life, a person is not merely permitted to violate any of the Torah's commandments, but actually required to do so, with four exceptions: idolatry, blasphemy, incest, and murder. See Talmud Yoma 85b and Talmud Sanhedrin 74a-b. Under no circumstances, not even to save one's own life, may a person engage in these prohibitions. It is for this reason that countless multitudes of Jews throughout history have accepted death rather than succumb to forced conversions. See, for example, the heartrending account of Hannah and her seven sons in 2 Macc. 7.

45. Matt. 12:13.

46. Matt. 12:1.

47. Talmud Yoma 85b.

48. Matt. 12:3-4; see Lev. 24:9.

49. 1 Sam. 21:4, 8.

50. See text at note 44.

51. Matt. 12:2 (emphasis added).

52. Deut. 24:16. Compare with Lev. 19:14 ("You shall not revile the deaf or put a stumbling block before the blind"), which is interpreted by Maimonides and other rabbis to mean that one may not cause another to sin. In this regard, it is said that all Jews are responsible for the spiritual well-being of others. Indeed, the Talmud expressly teaches *Kol Yisrael arevim zeh ha-zeh* ("All Jews are responsible for each other") (Talmud Sanhedrin 16b).

53. Matt. 15:2.

54. Matt. 15:11.

55. See Lev. 11:1-47.

56. See chapter 1, Thirteen Principles of Faith, Principle 9. See also chapters 5 and 6.

57. Matt. 5:18.

58. Matt. 5:29.

59. Lev. 19:28.

60. See text at note 9.

61. In Mark, only some of Jesus' disciples are charged with having violated the handwashing requirement: "They [the Pharisees] noticed that some of his disciples were eating with defiled hands, that is, without washing them" (Mark 7:2).

62. See Matt. 15:2.

63. Matt. 15:3-20.

64. Cf. Luke 11:38, discussed in the text below.

65. Cf. Acts 10:9-15.

66. Luke 11:37-38.

67. Matt. 15:2.

68. Mark 7:2.

69. James Strong, *A Concise Dictionary of the Words in the Greek Testament; With Their Renderings in the Authorized Version*, included in *The New Strong's Exhaustive Concordance of the Bible*, page 50. (See selected bibliography and suggested reading.)

70. Luke 11:38.

71. Strong, *A Concise Dictionary of the Words in the Greek Testament; With Their Renderings in the Authorized Version*, page 18.

72. Matt. 3:6.

73. Immersion would be appropriate in a situation where no pitcher is available, such as when one is out in the wilderness and the only source of water is a stream. See *Code of Jewish Law* 40:7.

74. In Matthew and Mark, it was a group of Pharisees who criticized Jesus' disciples because they did not wash (Matt. 15:1 and Mark 7:1), but in Luke it was only one Pharisee who questioned Jesus' failure to immerse (Luke 11:38). This is significant because it indicates that the Pharisee in Luke had acted alone; he did not have the weight of the Jewish community behind him, unlike the Pharisees in Matthew and Mark. See text immediately following this note.

75. Matt. 26:59.

76. See Matt. 12:1-8, discussed in text at notes 42-44.

77. Num. 15:32-36.

78. Matt. 26:65.

79. This four-letter name of God is often referred to as the *Tetragrammaton*, which is Greek and means "four letters." In Judaism, the Tetragrammaton, often referred to simply as "the Name," is never pronounced as written. In formal prayer, it is pronounced *Adonoy*. In everyday speech it is pronounced *Hashem*, which in Hebrew means "the Name."

80. Cf. Matt. 26:64-65.

81. See Acts 5:34-39.

82. Although Jesus did not violate the law, some of his actions were nonetheless scandalous by Pharisaic standards. For example, he ate with sinners (Luke 5:30) and allowed a woman of ill repute to wash his feet (Luke 7:38). By so doing, Jesus ignored rabbinical principles of modesty and propriety (see, for example, Ps. 26:5 and 5:3-14). As a consequence, he brought rebuke from the Pharisees (Luke 7:39).

83. Cf. Matt. 9:2-3, where the scribes attack Jesus, apparently for forgiving sins.

84. John 10:30; cf. chapter 1, Thirteen Principles of Faith, Principles 2 and 3.

85. John 14:6; cf. chapter 1, Thirteen Principles of Faith, Principle 5. See also Deut. 13:1-3.

86. See Exod. 20:3.

87. In the Gospel of Luke (22:70-71) and John (19:7), Jesus is convicted for claiming to be the "Son of God." But as discussed in the text above, this is not blasphemy, the crime that Jesus was found guilty of in Matthew (26:65). While the Hebrew Scriptures use the term "Son of God" or similar terms, it is never meant in a literal sense. See, for example, Deut. 14:1 and 32:8; Job 1:6; and Jer. 3:19. To Jews, a literal rendering of "Son of God" would not even make sense. See chapter 1, Thirteen Principles of Faith, Principles 2-4.

88. There are two alternative explanations for why Jesus was not prosecuted for statements that he made ("The Father and I are one" and "I am the way, and the truth, and the life. No one comes to the Father except through me"). One explanation (and it must be emphasized that this explanation is clearly at odds with traditional Christian teachings) is that Jesus did not mean his words to be taken in a literal sense, and those who heard him knew this. Another explanation (which is consistent with traditional Christian teachings) is that Jesus did indeed intend his words to be taken in a literal sense, but the Sanhedrin did not prosecute him for having uttered these words because the court did not believe that it could convict him of false prophecy (Deut. 18:20) or other wrongdoing in light of the many procedural protections Jewish law gives to those charged with crimes (see, for example, Deut. 19:15). Of course, the Gospels indicate that the Sanhedrin eventually did convict Jesus of criminal wrongdoing, and the procedural protections were thus to no avail. See also John 7:30 and 10:39, where the authorities tried to arrest Jesus, but were not successful.

89. Luke 4:16-19, quoting from Isa. 61:1-2.

90. See text at note 4.

91. Luke 4:16.

92. Matt. 26:18.

93. *Catechism of the Catholic Church*, ¶¶1965-1986. It is also in this sense according to the Catholic Church and others that "Christ is the end of the law" (Rom. 10:4) (see text below for discussion).

94. Matt. 5:18.

95. Cf. Matt. 28:20.

96. Ps. 119:44.

97. Matt. 5:19; cf. Matt. 26:28.

98. For a discussion of the "Greatest Commandments," see chapter 10.

99. Matt. 23:14.

100. Talmud Sotah 22b refers to hypocritical and ostentatious Pharisees as a "plague."

101. Cf. Matt. 23:23.

102. Josephus, *Antiquities of the Jews*, 13:10:6.

103. Talmud Shabbat 31a. Cf. Matt. 7:12. See also chapter 10 of this book.

104. See Luke 23:50-53; John 3:1-21; and Acts 5:34-39. Moreover, in Luke's Gospel, the Pharisees even warn Jesus that Herod wants to kill him (Luke 13:31).

105. Acts 22:3 and 23:6; see also Phil. 3:5.

106. See chapter 2.

107. See, for example, Mic. 3.

108. Cf. Exod. 32:33.

109. Rom. 10:4.

110. See also Rom. 8:3 and Col. 2:14.

111. See, for example, Ronald F. Youngblood, gen. ed., *Nelson's New Illustrated Bible Dictionary*, page 307. (See selected bibliography and suggested readings.)

112. See, for example, Gen. 17:19 and Luke 3:34; Num. 24:17 and Matt. 1:2; and Isa. 9:7 and Luke 1:32.

113. Rom. 10:4.

114. *Catechism of the Catholic Church*, ¶1953.

115. See chapter 5.

116. During the second century, Marcion of Pontus called for the rejection of the Old Testament. Although his movement had a substantial following for a while, he was excommunicated as a heretic. The Roman Catholic Church expressly renounces "Marcionism." See *Catechism of the Catholic Church*, ¶123.

117. See, for example, *Catechism of the Catholic Church*, ¶121.

118. See discussion in text above.

119. Gal. 3:13.

120. See also Gal. 3:10.

121. Exod. 22:21-27.

122. Deut. 19:15-21.

123. Deut. 5:19 and 22:1-4.

124. Deut. 25:1-3.

125. Gal. 1:13.

126. See chapter 5.

127. Rom. 7:12.

128. 1 Cor. 9:19-23.

129. Phil. 1:12-19.

130. Gal. 1:1.

131. See chapter 1.

132. See Gal. 3 and 1 Cor. 10:1-2.

133. See chapter 7.

134. Gal. 3:10; see also Jas. 2:10.

135. Deut. 27:15-26.

136. Deut. 27:15.

137. Deut. 27:19.

138. Deut. 27:21.

139 Deut. 27:22.

140. Deut. 27:25.

141. Nachmonides (see glossary), commentary to Deut. 27:26.

142. Cf. Jas. 2:10.

143. See Exod. 34:5-7, which in Judaism is referred to as the "Thirteen Attributes of God's Mercy."

144. Cited in R. Isaacs, *Mitzvot: A Sourcebook for the 613 Commandments*, page 60. (See selected bibliography and suggested reading.)

145. Gen. 2:17.

146. Gen. 3:6.

Notes for Chapter 10

1. See chapter 3 for discussion of the Ten Commandments.

2. See chapter 4 for discussion.

3. Exod. 20:13.

4. Lev. 11:7.

5. Exod. 21:14.

6. Cf. Deut. 25:1-3.

7. See chapter 5.

8. Deut. 22:11.

9. Deut. Rabbah 6:2. (Deuteronomy Rabbah is part of the *Midrash Rabbah*. See glossary.)

10. The Torah only infrequently mentions the reward for observing a particular commandment: "Honor your father and your mother, so that your days may be long in the land that the LORD your God is giving you" (Exod. 20:12); "Give liberally . . . for on this account the LORD your God will bless you in all your work and in all that you undertake" (Deut. 15:10); "If you come on a bird's nest, in any tree or on the ground, with fledglings or eggs, with the mother sitting on the fledglings or on the eggs, you shall not take the mother with the young. Let the mother go, taking only the young for yourself, in order that it may go well with you and you may live long" (Deut. 22:6-7); and "You shall have only a full and honest weight; you shall have only a full and honest measure, so that your days may be long in the land that the LORD your God is giving you" (Deut. 25:15).

11. See chapter 1, Thirteen Principles of Faith, Principle 11.

12. Mishnah Aboth 1:3.

13. Matt. 22:36.

14. Matt. 22:37-40.

15. Deut. 6:5.

16. Lev. 19:18.

17. Deut. 6:4-9 and 11:13-21; Num. 15:37-41.

18. Cf. Deut. 6:4. The reader should note that the translation given in the book is my own, and is one that is most familiar to Jews. The translation of Deut. 6:4 in the New Revised Standard Version is: "Hear, O Israel: The LORD is our God, the LORD alone." It is my opinion that this latter translation does not sufficiently emphasize the "oneness" of God, the significance of which is explained in the text immediately below.

19. See chapter 1, Thirteen Principles of Faith, Principle 2.

20. Of course, Christians also recognize the One God. (See Matt. 28:19 and 2 Cor. 13:14.) But the Trinitarian view of God is not part of, and is inconsistent with, Judaism. See note 19.

21. Deut. 6:5.

22. See Exod. 33:20; cf. John 1:1, 14.

23. Mishnah Aboth 1:3.

24. Deut. 10:12-13.

25. Ps. 119:1-8.

26. Cf. Luke 4:16-22.

27. See Matt. 5:17.

28. Lev. 19:18.

29. Deut. 30:11-14.

30. In the original Hebrew, the love of God (Deut. 6:5) is direct (*ais Hashem*)— "love God." The love of one's neighbor (Lev. 19:18) is indirect (*lerayahchaw*), however— "love to your neighbor." Of course, there are denominations within Christianity which understand the Bible from a literal perspective. In such case, one must indeed love another as oneself.

31. See authorities cited in N. Scherman and M. Zlotowitz, eds., *The Stone Edition, The Chumash*, pages 661-662. (See selected bibliography and suggested reading.)

32. Matt. 22:37-40.

33. Matt. 5:17-19.

34. Mic. 6:8.

35. Isa. 56:1.

36. See chapter 9, text at note 103.

37. Talmud Shabbat 31a. Cf. Matt. 7:12, "In everything do to others as you would have them do to you; for this is the law and the prophets."

38. See chapter 5.

39. Deut. 4:2.

40. Matt. 5:19.

41. That Judaism does not subscribe to the doctrine of Original Sin is made clear in the morning prayer service, which includes a passage from the Talmud: "My God, the soul which you have given me is pure." Talmud Berakoth 60b. Cf. Gen. 3:6-24.

42. See Lev. 19:2.

Notes for Chapter 11

1. See chapter 1.

2. Principle 1.

3. Principle 2.

4. Principle 3.

5. Principle 4.

6. Principle 5.

7. Principle 6.

8. Principle 7.

9. Principle 8.

10. Principle 9.

11. Principle 10.

12. Principle 11.

13. Principle 12.

14. Principle 13.

15. Talmud Hullin 5a.

16. Mishnah Sanhedrin 10:1.

17. Talmud Sanhedrin 11a.

18. See Gen. 4:2-10.

19. Meaning that Enoch did not die, but was taken up to heaven while living; see Gen. 5:21-24.

20. See Gen. 6:13-22.

21. See Gen. 12:1-9.

22. See Gen. 17:17-19.

23. See Gen. 22:17.

24. See Gen. 23:4.

25. See Gen. 22:1-10.

26. See Gen. 21:12.

27. See Gen. 22:11-18.

28. See Gen. 27:27-29, 38-40.

29. See Gen. 48:1, 8-22.

30. See Gen. 50:24-25.

31. See Exod. 1:16, 22 and 2:2.

32. See Exod. 2:10-11.

33. From the Jewish perspective, Moses would suffer for God, but not the Messiah, since Judaism does not subscribe to the Trinitarian view of God. See chapter 1, Thirteen Principles of Faith, Principle 2.

34. See Exod. 12:50-51.

35. See Exod. 12:21-23.

36. See Exod. 14:21-31.

37. See Josh. 6:12-20.

38. See Josh. 2:1, 9-14 and 6:22-25.

39. See Judg. 6-8.

40. See Judg. 4-5.

41. See Judg. 13-16.

42. See Judg. 11-12.

43. See 1 Sam. 16:1, 13.

44. See 1 Sam. 1:20.

45. See 2 Sam. 8:1-3.

46. See Dan. 6:22.

47. See Dan. 3:19-27.

48. See Judg. 15:8.

49. See 1 Kings 17:17-24.

50. See Jer. 20:2.

51. See 2 Chron. 24:21.

52. See 1 Kings 19:10 and Jer. 26:23.

53. Heb. 11:1-40.

54. See chapter 1, Thirteen Principles of Faith, Principle 12.

55. Exod. 19:5.

56. Exod. 19:8 (emphasis added).

57. Exod. 24:3 (emphasis added).

58. Exod. 24:4.

59. Exod. 24:7 (emphasis added).

60. Exod. 20:2.

61. Similarly, a Gentile who complies with the Seven Laws of Noah merits credit even if not believing in their Divine authorship. Maimonides called such a person a "wise Gentile" (which is to be contrasted with a "righteous Gentile," that is, one who complies with the Noachide Laws and believes in their Divine authorship). See *Mishneh Torah, Laws of Kings* 8:11. See also chapter 7 of this book for a discussion of the Noachide Laws.

62. Talmud Rosh Hashanah 28b.

63. Hab. 2:4.

64. See Heb. 11:1-40, in text, at note 53, above.

65. Mishnah Aboth 1:17.

66. Jerusalem Talmud, Mishnah Hagigah 8:1.

67. See Mishnah Aboth 4:2.

68. See, for example, John 3:16: "For God so loved the world that he gave his only Son, so that everyone who *believes* in him may not perish but have eternal life" (emphasis added). Cf. Matt. 25:31-46, discussed below in text. See also *Catechism of the Catholic Church*, ¶847, which teaches that those who do not "know Christ" through no fault of their own may nonetheless achieve eternal salvation by seeking God sincerely and trying to do his will as their consciences allow them.

69. See Talmud Pesahim 8a-b and Talmud Baba Bathra 10b, where it is stated that if a person gives to charity for selfish reasons, the giver is nonetheless "fully righteous."

70. Tosefta Sanhedrin 13:2.

71. See note 61.

72. Mark 16:16. See also John 3:16 (quoted in note 68). Cf. *Catechism of the Catholic Church*, ¶161 (salvation comes only by believing in Jesus Christ) with ¶847 (those who through no fault of their own do not know Christ may nevertheless achieve eternal salvation). See also text, end of this chapter, for a discussion of Paul's views on faith.

73. Matt. 25:31-46.

74. Cf. John 3:16 (quoted in note 68) and Mark 16:16 (quoted in text at note 72).

75. Matt. 13:55. For those who believe that Jesus was Mary's only child (which is traditional Christian doctrine), James was not actually Jesus' brother. From such a perspective, one of two alternatives is possible: (1) James was the son of Joseph, making James Jesus' stepbrother; or (2) through Mary, James was a collateral relative of Jesus, such as a cousin, and the Gospel's use of the term "brother" is meant only to denote some type of distant familial relationship between James and Jesus.

76. Gen. 15:6, quoted also by Paul in Rom. 4:9 and Gal. 3:6. See below for discussion of Paul's view of faith versus deeds.

77. James 2:14-26.

78. Exod. 19:8.

79. Gal. 2:15-16; see also 3:1-29.

80. Gal. 2:21. Even if one takes the position that deeds alone do save (which is, of course, the Jewish view), it may still be said that Jesus did not die in vain since he brought a form of ethical monotheism to the idolatrous non-Jews (see Matt. 4:12-16; cf. 15:21-28). Nevertheless, such a posture is not the traditional Christian view.

81. *Catechism of the Catholic Church*, ¶¶1425 and 1446.

82. *Catechism of the Catholic Church*, ¶847.

Notes for Chapter 12

1. If a child is born to a proselyte (a new convert), it is of no consequence that the mother was not Jewish at the time of conception so long as the mother had converted to Judaism by the time of delivery.

2. The commentaries explain that the Torah's prohibition against Jews marrying Canaanites is not limited to those Gentiles who are the descendants of the Canaanites. Rather, it extends to all non-Jews.

3. In the New Revised Standard Version, the text reads, "for *that* will turn away your *children*. . . ." (Deut. 7:4, emphasis added.) I believe, however, that the more correct and understandable translation is as indicated in brackets in the text: "[the non-Jewish husband] will turn away your [grand]children. . . ." The "that" which is referred to is the non-Jewish husband of the Jewish wife, and the "children" are in fact grandchildren, as is explained in the text below. See also note 5 below.

4. Deut. 7:3-4.

5. That the religion of the grandchildren is the concern is obvious: We start with a Jewish couple (which we will call the "first generation"). This couple has a daughter (the "second generation"). The daughter marries a Gentile (also of the second generation). The Jewish daughter and her Gentile husband have a child (the "third generation"). It is the religion of this child (the third generation and the grandchild of the first generation) with which the Torah is concerned.

6. Deut. 7:4.

7. In the years portending the Holocaust, Nazi legislation proclaimed someone a Jew even though the person was not Jewish under *halacha* (Jewish law). Pursuant to Article 5 of the Reich Citizenship Law, a Jew was defined as one descended from at least three "fully Jewish" grandparents. Article 2 defined a person descended from one "fully Jewish" grandparent as "partly Jewish." Even though they were not Jewish according to the halacha, those individuals classified as Jews under the Nazi legislation often suffered along with their Jewish relatives.

8. Deut. 7:3-4.

9. Talmud Sanhedrin 44a.

10. Matt. 28:19.

11. As a general proposition, modern Israeli law is based on Turkish and English law. This is because Turkey controlled Palestine for centuries, until 1922, when it was ceded to England as a consequence of World War I. Nevertheless, Jewish law is the law of the land in the modern State of Israel with respect to matters of family law (marriage and divorce), and in those instances when English and Turkish law is silent. See chapter 2.

12. Cf. Talmud Sanhedrin 44a ("An Israelite who sins is still an Israelite").

13. *Rufeisen v. Minister of the Interior*, 16 P.D. 2428 (1962).

14. Talmud Sanhedrin 44a.

15. 3 *Encyclopaedia Judaica* 209-210.

16. See also the case of *Beresford v. Minister of the Interior*, 43(iv) P.D. 793 (1989), which held that one who was born a Jew but became a member of a Messianic congregation (e.g., Jews for Jesus) was not eligible to seek automatic Israeli citizenship under the Law of Return (but could become a naturalized citizen under the Citizenship Law).

17. Commandments dealing with the cycles of life include marriage, birth, and death. See chapter 13 for a brief discussion.

18. The rabbis of the Reform and Reconstructionist movements also do not believe that Deut. 7:3-4 is meant to exclude from the Jewish community those born of a Jewish father.

19. According to some, the number of Jews today stands at only fourteen million.

20. When I say that "all righteous people, irrespective of beliefs, go to heaven," I mean to include all who practice some form of ethical monotheism: Judaism or the Seven Laws of Noah. (See chapter 7.) I obviously exclude idolaters, however, since idolatry denies God and has traditionally been involved with hideous practices. (See chapter 1.)

21. See Luke 10:30-37; cf. Matt. 25:31-46. See also chapter 11 of this book.

22. Tosefta Sanhedrin 13:2.

23. In the United States, most male newborns who are not Jewish are circumcised by physicians in hospitals before they are discharged. Consequently, a man who has previously undergone a non-ritual circumcision has a small drop of blood taken from him as a symbolic circumcision.

24. Talmud Yebamoth 22a.

25. Lev. 19:34. According to some of the commentators, this passage from the Torah relates to Gentiles who live in the Land of Israel and adopt the Seven Laws of Noah. See chapter 7 for a discussion of the Noachide Laws.

26. Ruth 1:1-2.

27. Ruth 1:4.

28. Ibid.

29. 1 Kings 11:7.

30. Judg. 11:17-18.

31. Ruth 1:3 and 5.

32. Ruth 1:6.

33. Ruth 1:8.

34. Ruth 1:10.

35. Ruth 1:12.

36. Ruth 1:14.

37. Ruth 1:15.

38. Ruth 1:16-17.

39. Ruth 1:8, 11, 15. Cf. Talmud Yebamoth 49a.

40. See chapter 7.

41. It is often said that Jews have 613 commandments to obey whereas Gentiles have only seven, but this is not fully precise. Of the 613 commandments of the Torah, many are presently not operative. With respect to the Seven Noachide Laws, it is more accurate to look at them as seven categories of laws. Consequently, Gentiles who obey the Seven Laws of Noah actually have more than sixty laws to obey. (See chapter 7 for a discussion.) Still, a Gentile has many fewer commandments than does a Jew.

42. See Prov. 1:9; cf. Matt. 11:29-30.

43. Lev. Rabbah 2:9.

44. There are, however, several traditional limitations on proselytes, all of which have absolutely no significance today: A proselyte cannot be appointed to public office (Talmud Yebamoth 45b), nor can a proselyte be a judge in a criminal case (Talmud Sanhedrin 36b). This is based upon the Scriptural decree, "One of your own community you may set as king over you; you are not permitted to put a foreigner over you, who is not of your own community" (Deut. 17:15). It is important for the reader to understand that this limitation does not in any way imply anything negative about a proselyte. Judaism recognizes that different people have different duties. Thus, for example, while only a man can be the Messiah, it would be fully incorrect to infer from this that women may be treated disrespectfully (see Prov. 31:10-31). Similarly, although a Priest is required to perform a special blessing (see appendix 2, Positive Commandment 26), that in no way implies an inferiority of those who are not Priests.

45. 1 Kings 11:17.

46. Deut. 23:4.

47. Judg. 11:17-18.

48. Gen. 11:27-31 and 19:16-37.

49. According to the commentators, only the males acted without compassion; the women did not. It was for this reason that only the males of the Moabites could not convert to Judaism and enter into the congregation of marriage with the Jewish people. Ruth could convert and marry Boaz, a Jew, because the injunction in Deuteronomy (see text at next note) did not apply to females.

50. Deut. 23:3.

51. Ruth 4:11-12.

52. Ruth 4:17.

53. Isa. 11:10. See also next section of text for a discussion of Jesus' lineage.

54. Isa. 11:10.

55. Matt. 1:1-16; cf. Luke 3:23-37.

56. See chapter 1, Thirteen Principles of Faith, Principle 12.

Notes for Chapter 13

1. For example, observant Jews do not eat cheeseburgers. The reason for this is based upon the Torah's prohibition of the mixing of meat and dairy products: "You shall not boil a kid in its mother's milk" (Exod. 23:19).

2. Lev. 23:24.

3. Lev. 23:26-32.

4. All Jewish days begin at sunset and end the following evening. (See chapter 3, text at note 33.) Consequently, the fast for Yom Kippur extends more than twenty-four hours.

5. Lev. 26:33-43.

6. The holiday of Hanukkah was instituted well after the Hebrew Bible had been closed to further books. For fascinating reading about the story of Hanukkah, see 1 and 2 Maccabees, which is omitted from the King James Version but which is included in the New Revised Standard Version, and is a part of the Roman Catholic canon and included in the Apocrypha of some Protestant Bibles.

7. Lev. 23:4-8.

8. See Exod. 12-14.

9. Lev. 23:15-22.

10. Cf. Deut. 16:9-11.

11. Cf. 2 Kings 25:8-9 and Jer. 52:12-13.

12. See Gen. 15:5.

13. See Gen. 17.

14. The Bat Mitzvah for girls is identical to the Bar Mitzvah for boys in the Conservative, Reform, and Reconstructionist movements. Within the Orthodox movement, however, there are noticeable differences. The most significant difference is that on the day of the Bat Mitzvah, girls do not read from the Torah at the sabbath morning service as boys do for their Bar Mitzvah. The principal reason for the Orthodox position is founded on the requirement that women conduct themselves in a modest manner, and being the center of attention at a Torah reading ceremony is not conducive to modesty. In some Orthodox congregations, however, the girl may read from the Torah in the presence of women only.

15. See, for example, Shakespeare's *Merchant of Venice*, a terribly anti-Semitic play that portrays Jews in their mythically evil role as heartless moneylenders.

16. See, for example, Deut. 23:17, "None of the daughters of Israel shall be a temple prostitute; none of the sons of Israel shall be a temple prostitute." See also Prov. 2:16.

17. See, for example, Lev. 19:11, "You shall not steal; you shall not deal falsely; and you shall not lie to one another."

18. See, for example, Lev. 19:35-36, "You shall not cheat in measuring length, weight, or quantity. You shall have honest balances, honest weights, an honest ephah, and an honest hin: I am the LORD your God, who brought you out of the land of Egypt."

19. Cf. Lev. 22:32.

20. See, for example, Lev. 19:33-34.

21. Deut. 14:28-29.

22. Talmud Gittin 61a.

23. See Exod. 20:8.

24. See, for example, Lev. 11.

25. See, for example, Deut. 15:7-11. The Hebrew word for charity is *tzeduckaw*, which is a derivation of the Hebrew word *tzedek*, meaning "justice." One talmudic dictum declares, "Charity is equal to all the other commandments combined." Talmud Baba Bathra 9a.

26. Talmud Sanhedrin 44a.

27. Matt. 5:13-16.

Note for Appendix 1

1. Catholicism teaches that salvation is available to non-Christians. Protestantism teaches that salvation is available to all who have faith in Jesus.

Glossary

Aggadah (lit. "narration"). The nonlegal aspects of the Talmud and other rabbinical literature. It is to be contrasted with the legal aspects, *halacha*.

Amalek. A son of Esau's son, Elphaz (Gen. 36:2), and the ancestor of the Amalekites, the enemies of Israel. The Amalekites attacked the Israelites without cause soon after the Exodus from Egypt (Exod. 17:8-16) and remained enemies of Israel. The Torah commands the Jewish people to "Remember what Amalek did to you on your journey out of Egypt" (Deut. 25:17).

Ark. A wooden chest which contained the two tablets of the Ten Commandments (Exod. 25:10ff. and 37:1ff.). It was sacred to Israel and was eventually housed in the First Temple, in an area known as the Holy of Holies. After the First Temple was destroyed by the Babylonians in 586 B.C.E., the whereabouts of the Ark and the tablets of the Ten Commandments became uncertain. The Talmud indicates that either the prophet Jeremiah hid the Ark and the Ten Commandments or they were taken to Babylon (Talmud Yoma 53b-54a). Present-day synagogues have replicas of the Ark which house scrolls of the Torah.

Beth Din (lit. "house of judgment"). A three-judge court and the equivalent of the local superior court found in the United States. After the destruction of the Sanhedrin, the beth din endured and continues to this day in every Jewish community.

Conservative Judaism. A movement within Judaism which arose in the nineteenth century, shortly after the birth of the Reform movement. The Conservative movement is more conservative than the liberal Reform movement in its interpretation and application of the law, but less so than the Orthodox movement.

Day of Atonement. See *Yom Kippur*.

Deuteronomy Rabbah. See *Midrash Rabbah*.

Ephod. An apronlike garment worn by the High Priest (Exod. 28:6ff., 28:25ff., and 39:2ff.).

Essenes. A movement within Judaism from the second century B.C.E. to the first century C.E. It was a monastic-like order, whose members stressed ritual purity, celibacy, and secret teachings. Some believe that Jesus was an Essene, but such a position is highly questionable since, unlike the Essenes, Jesus thrust himself into the general Jewish community, in the manner of Pharisaic Judaism.

Exodus Rabbah. See *Midrash Rabbah*.

Feast of Tabernacles. See *Sukkot*.

Feast of Weeks. See *Shavuot*.

Four Spices. Four different plants used during the *Sukkot* (Feast of Tabernacles) holiday. The spices consist of branches of palm trees, willows, citrons, and myrtles. The first two plants are derived expressly from the Biblical text (Lev. 23:40); the latter two are from the Talmud (Talmud Sukkot 32b-33a).

Gemara (lit. "completion"). A part of the Talmud. The Talmud consists of the Mishnah (the oral law) and the Gemara, the rabbinical debate on the law which took place from 200 B.C.E. to 500 C.E. The Gemara became the foundation for additional laws not found in the Torah or the Mishnah. The Gemara is not, however, limited to discussions of law. The Gemara also has a significant amount of material dealing with Biblical characters, science, medicine, philosophy, and ethics.

Genesis Rabbah. See *Midrash Rabbah.*

Great Sanhedrin. See *Sanhedrin.*

Halacha (lit. "to walk"). Rabbinic literature which deals with Jewish law. The foundation of the halacha is the 613 commandments of the Torah, as well as the many other laws found in the Mishnah (oral law).

Hanukkah (lit. "dedication"). An eight-day holiday in December which commemorates the victory of the Jewish people over the invading Syrians and the subsequent rededication of the Temple in 165 B.C.E. After the Syrian forces were routed from Jerusalem, the Jews cleansed and repaired the Temple, which the Syrians had desecrated. To mark the rededication, it was necessary to light the Temple's candelabrum with consecrated oil, but only a small amount could be found. Expected to last only one day, the oil burned for eight days. From that time on, the holiday has been celebrated for eight days. A history of this war can be found in 1 and 2 Maccabees.

Hashem (lit. "the name"). One of the many names for God and used when God manifests his attribute of mercy. In the New Revised Standard Version of the Bible (as well as many other editions), it is translated as "LORD" (see, for example, Exod. 19:3). In formal prayer, the word is pronounced *Adonoy.*

High Priest. See *Priests/High Priest.*

Jubilee Year. An institution of the Torah wherein every fifty years, all Jewish slaves were released and all ancestral land reverted to the heirs of the family (Lev. 25:8ff.). Thus, however financially difficult a Jew's life may have become, the Jubilee Year gave assurance of a fresh start. Because the Jubilee Year depended upon all twelve tribes living in the Land of Israel, the law of the Jubilee went into suspense after the Babylonian exile. Under traditional (Orthodox) belief, the Jubilee Year will once again become operative when the Messiah arrives and the Final Redemption unfolds, during which time all Jews will once again live in the Land of Israel. None of the other movements of Judaism believe in an individual who will be the Messiah.

Kiddush (lit. "sanctification"). A prayer recited on sabbaths and holidays, over a cup of wine, to consecrate the holiness of the day. The basis for Kiddush is found in the Torah: "Remember the Sabbath day, to keep it holy" (Exod. 20:8). The ancient rabbis interpreted this passage as "remember it [the sabbath day] over wine" (Talmud Pesahim 106a). Kiddush consists of two parts: the blessing over the wine and the benediction of the day. The blessing of the wine, which is always the same for whenever Kiddush is said, is: "Blessed are you, Lord our God, King of the universe, who brings forth the fruit of the vine."

Kosher (lit. "fit"). In its most narrow sense, foods which comply with the Biblical and rabbinical dietary laws. The basis for these laws is found in the Bible (Lev. 11; Deut. 14:3-20). The word usually used in English-language editions of the Bible to denote animals which are "fit" is "clean"; in contrast, words indicating animals which are not fit are "unclean," "abhorrent," or an "abomination." In its broadest sense, the term "kosher" also refers to the fitness of an individual to participate in Jewish religious activities, as well as to the fitness of an object for use in ritual practices.

Lesser Sanhedrin. See *Sanhedrin*.

Levites. Jews who are descendants of Levi, the third son of Jacob, one of Judaism's Three Patriarchs. To the Levites went the honor of serving in the Sanctuary and, after its construction by King Solomon, the Temple. In addition to assisting the Priests, the Levites also were the gatekeepers of the Temple and its musicians. To this very day, virtually all Jewish men know whether they are Priests, Levites, or commoners. In the Orthodox community of today, Levites still perform a functionary role by washing the hands of the Priests before they recite the Priestly blessing in the synagogue.

Leviticus Rabbah. See *Midrash Rabbah*.

Maimonides (*Moses ben Maimon*). A great Jewish physician, philosopher, and rabbi who lived in the twelfth century, also known as "Rambam" (an acronym for Rabbi Moses ben Maimon). Maimonides' major work is a fourteen-volume code of Jewish law called the *Mishneh Torah* ("Relearning the Law"). He also authored the *Thirteen Principles of Faith* (see chapter 1 of this book).

Mamzer. Often translated as "bastard" (Deut. 23:2, King James Version), but the Hebrew meaning is much more narrow since it includes only a child born of an adulterous or incestuous union (see Lev. 18:7-10, 12-18). Thus, for example, a child born of a union between a single Jewish woman and a single Jewish man who are not related to each other (as defined in Lev. 18, above) is not a mamzer and has absolutely no taint in any respect whatsoever. On the other hand, a mamzer is tainted: A mamzer (and his or her descendants) is forbidden to marry a Jew who is not also a mamzer (Deut. 23:2). Only the Orthodox movement, however, currently recognizes and applies the law with respect to the mamzer. In any event, outside of the marriage prohibition, a mamzer is Jewish in every respect and has no other restrictions.

Mezuzah (lit. "doorpost"). A small scroll of parchment which contains selected passages from the Torah (Deut. 6:4-9 and 11:13-21) and which is typically encased in a wooden or metal capsule. The parchment must be made from the hide of a clean (kosher) animal. The mezuzah is attached to the right-handed doorpost of doorways that meet certain requirements. The reason for attaching the mezuzah is to comply with the commandment "[A]nd write them on the doorposts of your house and on your gates" (Deut. 6:9 and 11:20).

Midrash Rabbah ("Great Commentary"). A multivolume rabbinical commentary on the five books which comprise the Torah (Genesis, Exodus, Leviticus, Numbers, and Deuteronomy) and several other books of the Bible (Lamentations, Ecclesiastes, Ruth, Song of Songs, and Esther), composed between 500 and 1000 C.E. The essence of the Midrash Rabbah is nonlegal narratives (*aggadah*), which expound upon and explain Biblical verses.

Mikvah (lit. "gathering"). A ritual bath used for spiritual cleansing (see Lev. 11:36). In ancient times, the mikvah was an integral part of Jewish life. Today, it is used mainly in the Orthodox community by married women after they complete their menstrual period. Immersion in the mikvah is also required for converts to Judaism in the Orthodox and Conservative movements. The mikvah itself must be constructed in a specified manner and contain a minimum amount of water gathered from particular sources, such as rainwater or water from the sea or a river. Immersion in a flowing body of water, such as the sea or a river, also satisfies the requirements for ritual purification (see 2 Kings 5:10). An entire tractate of the Talmud is devoted to the laws of the mikvah. The Christian rite of baptism is derived from the ritual immersion of Judaism (cf. Matt. 3:6).

Mishnah (lit. "oral instruction"). The oral law which, according to Jewish tradition, explains and elucidates the written law (Pentateuch), and which was as much a part of the Revelation at Sinai as was the written law. The Mishnah was handed down orally from Moses to succeeding generations until it was reduced to writing by Rabbi Judah the Prince in 200 C.E. Rabbi Judah put the oral law to writing because he feared that it would become forgotten as a result of the destruction of the Jewish state by the Romans in 135 C.E. The Mishnah and the Gemara together comprise the Talmud. The oral law is referred to in the New Testament as the "tradition of the elders" (Matt. 15:2).

Mishneh Torah. See *Maimonides*.

Mitzvah (lit. "commandment"). A religious duty. In its most limited sense, it includes the 613 mitzvot (commandments) of the Torah. In a broader sense, it also encompasses the many commandments found in the Mishnah and the subsequently enacted rabbinical ordinances. In a still broader sense, a mitzvah includes the performance of any meritorious deed.

Molech. A pagan cult whose practices included child sacrifice. The Torah prohibits Jews from engaging in any such practice (Lev. 18:21 and 20:2-4; Deut. 18:10).

Nachmonides. Rabbi Moses ben Nachman, a Spaniard who was born in Gerona in 1194 and became widely known as a great legal scholar. He wrote a commentary on the Torah which remains a classical work.

Nazirite (lit. "to dedicate"). A person who dedicates himself or herself to God for an allotted time by making a vow and remaining in a state of purity. During the period of dedication, the Nazirite was forbidden to drink wine, cut his or her hair, or approach a dead body. When the period of dedication was over, the Nazirite brought a sacrifice to the Temple (Num. 6:1-21). In the Bible, Samson (Judg. 13:3-7) and Samuel (1 Sam. 1:11) were Nazirites for their entire life. It is possible that John the Baptist was a Nazirite (cf. Luke 1:15). An entire tractate of the Talmud is devoted to the laws of the Nazirite.

New Year. See *Rosh Hashanah*.

Nisan. The first month of the year in the Jewish religious calendar (Exod. 12:2), usually falling during March or April. The Exodus from Egypt took place in the month of Nisan. The Passover celebration begins on the fifteenth day of Nisan (Exod. 12:6, 14).

Noachides. Non-Jewish ethical monotheists.

Orthodox Judaism. Often referred to as "traditional Judaism." The movement is characterized by its belief in the absolute accuracy and immutability of the written and oral law. It is the most conservative branch of Judaism.

Passover. See *Pesach*.

Passover-offering. The special sacrifice required by the Torah in commemoration of the Exodus from Egypt (Num. 28:16-26). The Gospel makes express reference to this sacrifice (Luke 22:7). As a consequence of the destruction of the Temple, the only place where sacrifices could take place, the laws regarding sacrifices are not presently operative. In Christian teaching, Jesus became the sacrificial lamb (Rev. 7:14).

Pentateuch. See *Torah*.

Pentecost. See *Shavuot*.

Pesach (lit. "pass over"). The celebration of the Exodus from Egypt and one of the three Pilgrim Festivals (the others being *Shavuot* and *Sukkot*).

The holiday, also called Passover, is so named because God stated that he would "pass over" the houses of the Israelites when he slew the firstborn in Egypt (Exod. 12:13). The holiday is also known as the Festival of Unleavened Bread since Jews are required to eat unleavened bread on the festival; nothing with leavening may be eaten (Exod. 12:15). On the first night of Passover, Jews gather with family and friends to eat a sumptuous meal and recount the redemption from slavery and the Exodus from Egypt (the meal and recounting are referred to as the Passover *seder*). According to the Synoptic Gospels (Matthew, Mark, and Luke), Jesus' Last Supper was the celebration of Passover (Matt. 26:17-19; Mark 14:12-16; Luke 22:7-13).

Pharisees (from the root of the Hebrew word *perushim*, "to separate"). Movement in Judaism which began in the fifth century B.C.E. The Pharisees were the representatives of the people, in contrast to the aristocratic Sadducees, and strove to make Jewish learning available to all. The Pharisees were also strong proponents of the oral law, which was denied by the Sadducees. They were known for their teachings on mercy, kindness, and humility. In contradistinction to the rival Sadducees, the Pharisees also believed in the immortality of the soul, the resurrection of the dead, and the coming of the Messiah. After the destruction of the Temple in 70 C.E., the Sadducees ceased to exist, but the Pharisees endured and became the ancestors of modern-day Judaism. The Pharisees play a prominent part in the Gospel, where they are commonly depicted in a negative light (Matt. 23:13-29) and as the opponents of Jesus (Matt. 12:14).

Phylacteries. See *Tefillin*.

Pilgrim Festivals. The three festivals which the Israelites were instructed to celebrate, "at the place which he [God] will choose" (Deut. 16:16). The place chosen by God would eventually become Jerusalem (cf. Exod. 23:17). The three festivals are the Feast of Unleavened Bread (*Pesach*), the Feast of Weeks (*Shavuot*), and the Feast of Tabernacles (*Sukkot*) (Deut. 16:16). The Gospel states that Jesus' parents went to Jerusalem every year at the feast of the Passover (Luke 2:41), in compliance with the Torah.

Priests/High Priest. The male descendants of Aaron, the first High Priest. In Judaism, unlike virtually all other religions, the Priesthood is hereditary (through the father). With the destruction of the Temple, the Priesthood lost most, but not all, of its functions. Consequently, the Priesthood has endured through the centuries and continues to this day. The Hebrew word for priest is *kohan*. Accordingly, those Jews whose last names are Cohen, Cohn, Kohan, and derivations thereof (such as Karlin) are members of the Priesthood. According to a recent article in the *New York Times*, a study of thousands of Jews who stated that they were *Kohanim* (Priests)—the descendants of Aaron—showed that their DNA had similar characteristics which could only be explained by having a common ancestor. This DNA link also astonishingly showed that Jewish fathers had faithfully and accurately informed their children of their hereditary status down through the centuries.

Purim (lit. "lots"). Jewish holiday recounted in the Book of Esther. Haman, an evil minister, sought to exterminate all the Jews of ancient Persia. His plans were thwarted, however, by a Jewish man named Mordecai and his niece, Queen Esther. The holiday is so named because Haman cast lots (*purim*) to decide the day that the extermination of the Jews would begin (Esther 3:7 and 9:24-26). This victory over evil is celebrated in the synagogue by reading the Book of Esther and partaking in raucous behavior: Every time "Haman" is mentioned, the congregation stomps its feet and twirls noisemakers to drown out the name of this evildoer.

Rabbi (lit. "my master"). A title given to a person of religious authority. In ancient times, a person would be called "rabbi" either because of formal ordination or out of respect, and was first and foremost a teacher and arbiter of the law. Now one becomes a rabbi only by formal ordination. Additionally, if a contemporary rabbi leads a synagogue, he or she (women may be ordained in the Conservative, Reform, and Reconstructionist movements) must be involved in day-to-day synagogue activities (pastoral duties, administration, etc.). The Gospel of John makes reference to Jesus as "rabbi" (see, for example, John 1:38 and 3:2).

Rashi. Acronym for Rabbi Shlomo Yitzchaki. Born in 1040 in northern France, he wrote a commentary to the entire Hebrew Bible and Talmud. Rashi's style is concise and exceedingly clear. Because he is the foremost of all commentators, Rashi is deemed necessary reading for all Jewish students of the Bible and Talmud.

Recanti. An Italian rabbi and legal authority who lived in the late thirteenth century and wrote a commentary on the Torah.

Reconstructionism. The most liberal movement in Judaism. The Reconstructionist movement began in the 1930s. The movement denies the Divine origin of the Torah, and emphasizes Judaism as a continuously evolving civilization. As such, it deems it proper for each generation to "reconstruct" Judaism to make it adaptable to modern times.

Reform Judaism. Next to the Reconstructionist movement, the most liberal movement in Judaism. It began in the mid-nineteenth century as an outgrowth of the Age of Enlightenment in Europe and a counter to traditional (Orthodox) Judaism. The Reform movement is distinguished by its lenient interpretation and application of the law.

Rosh Hashanah (lit. "head of the year"). The Jewish New Year. Rosh Hashanah marks the creation of the world and ushers in the Ten Days of Repentance, which culminate with *Yom Kippur* ("Day of Atonement"). A *shofar* (hollowed-out ram's horn) is blown on Rosh Hashanah, to awaken the Jewish people to repentance (Lev. 23:24; Num. 29:1). According to tradition, God writes his decree for all humankind on Rosh Hashanah and seals it on Yom Kippur. Rosh Hashanah is also known as *Yom Hazikaron* ("Day of Remembrance") because God remembers all of his creatures on this day.

Sabbatical Year. The seventh year of rest for the land. The Torah states that for six years the land may be worked, "[b]ut in the seventh year there shall be a sabbath of complete rest for the land, a sabbath for the LORD" (Lev. 25:4). No planting, sowing, or reaping was allowed during this time. Historical records show that the Sabbatical Year was enforced in ancient Israel. Indeed, benevolent conquerors such as Alexander the

Great even waived taxes for their Jewish subjects during the Sabbatical Year. After the destruction of the Temple and, later still, the Jewish State itself, the law of the Sabbatical Year went into suspense. With the beginning of the Zionist movement in the nineteenth century and the reestablishment of the State of Israel in 1948, the Sabbatical Year once again became operative.

Sadducees. A movement within Judaism that flourished from the second century B.C.E. to the first century C.E. The Sadducees were the rivals of the Pharisees. Unlike the Pharisees, who were supported by the common people, the Sadducees were wealthy aristocrats. Additionally, the Sadducees did not believe in the oral law, the coming of the Messiah, life after death, and the resurrection of the dead, all fundamental teachings of the Pharisaic movement. Moreover, because the foundation of the Sadducean movement was the Temple, the Sadducees disappeared virtually overnight when the Temple was destroyed. The Sadducees are mentioned in the Gospel as the enemies of Jesus and, quite interestingly, the allies of the Pharisees (Matt. 16:1).

Sanhedrin (from *synedrion*, Greek for "sitting in council"). The higher courts of law of ancient Israel. There existed the Lesser Sanhedrin, composed of twenty-three judges, and the Great Sanhedrin, composed of seventy-one judges. The Gospel indicates that Jesus appeared before the Sanhedrin (Matt. 26:59), but it is not clear whether it was the Great or Lesser Sanhedrin, or even an informally convened body. The New Testament states that some of the Apostles were also taken before the Sanhedrin (Acts 4:1-23 and 5:17-41, 22-24). After the destruction of the Temple in 70 C.E., the Sanhedrin moved to the city of Yavneh. By the fifth century C.E., however, the Sanhedrin had ceased to exist.

Second Passover. The observance of Passover one month after the fifteenth day of the Hebrew month of Nisan for those who were not able to participate in the "regular" Passover one month earlier. The basis for the Second Passover is found in the Torah (Num. 9). The Second Passover is currently not celebrated.

Sforno. An Italian rabbi who wrote a commentary on the Torah.

Shavuot (lit. "weeks"). One of the three Pilgrim Festivals (Deut. 16:16). It is also known as the Feast of Weeks and, in the Christian religion, as Pentecost. Although the holiday has agricultural ties (Exod. 34:22; Lev. 23:15-22; Deut. 16:9-10), Shavuot is significant because it marks the giving of the law on Mount Sinai fifty days—seven weeks—after the Exodus from Egypt. The New Testament states that the early Jewish-Christians came together in Jerusalem on Shavuot (Acts 2:1-4).

Shema (lit. "hear"). The fundamental declaration of Jewish faith, the Shema is a prayer which incorporates three passages from the Torah: Deut. 6:4-9 and 11:13-21 and Num. 15:37-41. The heart of the Shema is the opening words, "Hear, O Israel: The LORD is our God, the LORD is One" (cf. Deut. 6:4). Jewish adult men are required to recite the Shema twice a day, in order to comply with the Torah's command, "when you lie down and when you rise" (Deut. 6:7).

Shemini Atzeret ("Eighth Day of Assembly"). The eighth day of the holiday of *Sukkot*, but given a special status as a holiday all its own. See Lev. 23:36.

Shofar (lit. "ram's horn"). A trumpet-like instrument made of a carved-out ram's horn. It is first mentioned at the Revelation on Mount Sinai (Exod. 19:16). The shofar is blown on Rosh Hashanah and Yom Kippur (Num. 29:1). In ancient times, the shofar was also blown to usher in the Jubilee Year (Lev. 25:9-10). The symbolism of the shofar is to awaken sinners to repentance.

Sukkot (lit. "booths"). One of the three Pilgrim Festivals (Deut. 16:16). It is also known as the Feast of Tabernacles. The basis for the holiday is the Torah's commandment for the Jewish people to "live in booths seven days" (Lev. 23:42), to recall the forty years that God mercifully took care of the Jewish people in the desert after the Exodus from Egypt (Lev. 23:43).

Synagogue. A place for Jewish public prayer and study. The synagogue came into existence after the destruction of the First Temple by the

Babylonians in 586 B.C.E., and it has been an integral part of Jewish religious life ever since, existing in massive numbers even after completion of the Second Temple (four hundred synagogues existed in Jerusalem alone at the time of the Second Temple). The Gospel makes reference to Jesus praying and teaching in the synagogues of ancient Israel (Luke 4:16-21 and John 18:20).

Tallit. A four-cornered, fringed garment worn during certain prayer services. The basis for the tallit is to comply with the commandment to wear a fringed garment (Num. 15:38). Orthodox Jewish men wear a small version of the tallit as an undergarment during their waking hours (see *Tzitzit*).

Talmud (lit. "study"). A massive compendium of Jewish law and analysis. The Talmud consists of the Mishnah (the oral law) and the Gemara (the rabbinical debate on the law). The Talmud is two thousand seven hundred pages in length and comprises several million words. A practice among many Orthodox Jews is to study one page of the Talmud a day, thus completing the entire Talmud in approximately seven and one-half years. See appendix 3 for a summary of the organization and contents of the Talmud.

Tefillin ("phylacteries"). Two small black leather boxes containing several Biblical passages (Exod. 13:1-16; Deut. 6:4-9 and 11:13-21), attached to leather straps and worn on the arm and head in weekday morning prayers. The basis for wearing tefillin is found in the Torah: "It shall serve for you as a sign on your hand and as a reminder on your forehead, so that the teaching of the LORD may be on your lips; for with a strong hand the LORD brought you out of Egypt" (Exod. 13:9).

Teshuva ("repentance"). An integral part of Judaism. The key to repentance is three-fold: A person must regret his or her actions, must rectify the damage caused, and must resolve to never engage in such conduct again. Sins committed against God can be forgiven by God only. Sins committed against one's fellow human beings are forgiven by God only when the sinner makes peace with the victim. Thus, on *Yom Kippur* ("Day of Atonement"), fasting and prayer may gain forgiveness for sins committed against God, but not for sins committed against others. Repentance was a major theme of Jesus (see Matt. 5:17).

Tisha B'Av ("the ninth day of [the Hebrew month of] Av"). Judaism's saddest day, commemorating the destruction of the First Temple in 586 B.C.E. by the Babylonians and the Second Temple in 70 C.E. by the Romans. The day is marked by fasting and reading from the Book of Lamentations.

Torah (lit. "instruction" but often interpreted as "law"). The Five Books of Moses: Genesis, Exodus, Leviticus, Numbers, and Deuteronomy. The Torah constitutes the foundation of Jewish law and, according to the traditional (Orthodox) view, was literally dictated by God to Moses.

Tzitzit (lit. "fringes"). A four-cornered fringed undergarment worn by Orthodox Jewish men to comply with the Torah's command, "Speak to the Israelites, and tell them to make fringes on the corners of their garments throughout their generations . . ." (Num. 15:38).

Yarmulke. A skullcap worn during waking hours by Orthodox Jewish men as a sign of piousness. Among the Conservative, Reform, and Reconstructionist movements, it is worn most typically during prayer services. In lieu of a yarmulke, many Orthodox men wear a hat.

Yom Kippur (lit. "Day of Atonement"). The most solemn day in the Jewish calendar, it climaxes the Ten Days of Repentance following Rosh Hashanah. The holiday is characterized by a strict twenty-five-hour fast. The basis for this is found in the Torah, where the Jewish people are commanded to "deny yourselves" (Lev. 16:29). On Yom Kippur, the judgments which were entered on Rosh Hashanah become sealed. Nevertheless, while fasting and prayer can obtain forgiveness for sins committed against God, fasting and prayer cannot obtain forgiveness for sins committed against others. To obtain forgiveness for these sins, one must right the wrong that was committed, or beg the other's forgiveness.

Zealots. A Jewish movement which sought to accelerate the coming of the Messiah by ending Roman subjugation of ancient Israel. After the fall of Jerusalem to the Romans in the year 70 C.E., the Zealots ceased to be a significant force. In the New Testament, it is possible that Simon ("the Zealot") was a member of this group (see Luke 6:15), as was Barabbas (see Mark 15:7).

Selected Bibliography and Suggested Reading

Ausubel, Nathan. *The Book of Jewish Knowledge*. New York: Crown Publishers, 1964.

Birnbaum, Philip, ed. *Daily Prayer Book*. New York: Hebrew Publishing Company, 1977.

Catechism of the Catholic Church. Vatican City: Libreria Editrice Vaticana, 1995.

Cohen, A[braham]. *Everyman's Talmud*. New York: Schocken Books, 1975.

————, ed. *The Soncino Books of the Bible*. 14 volumes. London: Soncino Press, 1947 and following.

Cohen, Arthur A., and Paul Mendes-Flohr, eds. *Contemporary Jewish Religious Thought*. New York: Free Press, 1987.

Danby, Herbert, trans. *The Mishnah*. London: Oxford University Press, 1933.

Donin, Hayim. *To Be a Jew*. New York: Basic Books, 1972.

Dorf, Elliot N. *Conservative Judaism: Our Ancestors to Our Descendants*. New York: Youth Commission, United Synagogue of America, 1977.

Elon, Menachem. *The Principles of Jewish Law*. Jerusalem: Keter Publishing House, 1975.

Encyclopaedia Judaica. 16 volumes. Jerusalem: Keter Publishing House, 1972.

Epstein, Isidore, ed. *The Babylonian Talmud*. 30 volumes (Hebrew-English); 18 volumes (English only). London: Soncino Press, 1935-1952.

————. *Step by Step in the Jewish Religion*. London: Soncino Press, 1968.

Fast, Howard. *The Jews: Story of a People*. New York: Dell Publishing, 1968.

Freedman, H., and Maurice Simon, eds. *Midrash Rabbah.* 10 volumes. London: Soncino Press, 1983.

Ganzfried, Solomon. *Code of Jewish Law.* New York: Hebrew Publishing Company, 1961.

Hanke, Kimberly E. *Turning to Torah: The Emerging Noachide Movement.* Northvale, N.J.: Jason Aronson, Inc., 1995.

The HarperCollins Study Bible: New Revised Standard Version with the Apocryphal/ Deuterocanonical Books. New York: HarperCollins Publishers, 1993.

Hertz, Joseph H. *The Pentateuch and Haftorahs.* London: Soncino Press, 1960.

Hoenig, Samuel. *The Essence of Talmudic Law and Thought.* Northvale, N.J.: Jason Aronson, Inc., 1993.

Isaacs, Ronald H. *Mitzvot: A Sourcebook for the 613 Commandments.* Northvale, N.J.: Jason Aronson, Inc., 1996.

Johnson, Paul. *A History of the Jews.* New York: Harper & Row, 1988.

Kolatch, Alfred J. *The Jewish Book of Why.* Middle Village, N.Y.: Jonathan David, 1981.

Lichtenstein, Aaron. *The Seven Laws of Noah.* 3rd ed. New York: Rabbi Jacob Joseph School Press, 1995.

Maimonides, Moses. *The Commandments: Sefer Ha-Mitzvoth of Maimonides.* Translated by Charles B. Chavel. 2 volumes. London: Soncino Press, 1967.

———. *Code of Maimonides.* Translated by Abraham Hershman et al. 14 volumes. New Haven: Yale University Press, 1949-1972.

Mays, James L., gen. ed. *Harper's Bible Commentary.* San Francisco: Harper & Row, 1988.

Neusner, Jacob. *The Mishnah: An Introduction.* Northvale, N.J.: Jason Aronson, Inc., 1994.

New Open Bible, Study Edition, King James Version. Nashville: Thomas Nelson, 1990.

Posner, Zalman I. *Think Jewish: A Contemporary View of Judaism, A Jewish View of Today's World.* Nashville: Kesher Press, 1979.

Scherman, Nosson, ed. *The Complete ArtScroll Siddur.* Brooklyn, N.Y.: Mesorah Publications, 1984.

——— and Meir Zlotowitz, eds. *The Stone Edition, The Chumash.* Brooklyn, N.Y.: Mesorah Publications, 1993.

Shulman, Eliezer. *The Sequence of Events in the Old Testament.* Jerusalem: Investment Co. of Bank Hapoalim and Israel's Ministry of Defense, 1987.

Strong, James. *The New Strong's Exhaustive Concordance of the Bible.* Nashville: Thomas Nelson, 1990.

Wigoder, Geoffrey, ed. *The Encyclopedia of Judaism.* New York: Macmillan, 1989.

Youngblood, Ronald F., gen. ed., *Nelson's New Illustrated Bible Dictionary.* Nashville: Thomas Nelson, 1995.

Index

Index

Index

Z

Ira L. Shafiroff is a professor at Southwestern University School of Law, where he teaches Jewish law and legal ethics, among other subjects. Professor Shafiroff received his bachelor of arts degree from Brooklyn College, City University of New York (magna cum laude) and his juris doctor degree from Southwestern University School of Law (magna cum laude). Professor Shafiroff has written numerous articles on Judaism and Jewish law for both secular and religious publications, and is widely known for his classes and lectures on Judaism in the context of interfaith relations. He lives with his family in Los Angeles.

If you would like to order additional copies of this book, are interested in attending one of Professor Shafiroff's seminars, or want to schedule Professor Shafiroff as a speaker at your church or organization, please contact:

Noga Press™
P.O. Box 11129
Torrance, California 90510-1129
(310) 320-1088